the BUSINE$$ *of* TEACHING SEWING

HOW TO BE A GREAT TEACHER

HOW TO RUN A HOME-BASED TEACHING BUSINESS

HOW TO MAKE MONEY DOING WHAT YOU LOVE

by Marcy Miller
& Pati Palmer

Edited by Ann Price Gosch

Designed by Jeannette Schilling
and Linda Wisner

Illustrated by Jeannette Schilling

Acknowledgements

Thank you to Marcy's husband, Jim, for all his computer help and work and for the meals he prepared while she typed. They were wonderful, as usual. Pati thanks her husband Jack Watson for being a wonderful mother AND father to their daughter Melissa during busy teacher training sessions and for being the perfect host to workshop attendees from all over the world during graduation dinners at their home.

Thank you to Lynette Ranney Black, who coordinates the Palmer/Pletsch International School of Sewing Arts and Teacher Training program, and to all the Palmer/Pletsch teacher training graduates who took the time to review early drafts of this book, giving their input and ideas, and especially to:

Connie R. Hamilton, Alberta Hasan, Hetty A. Jones, Janice Langan, Nancy Lovett, Eileen Wonders

Thank you to current and past Palmer/Pletsch corporate educators, who have spent thousands of hours teaching, preparing classes, and traveling around the world as they pursued their "Business of Teaching Sewing." They keep enthusiasm alive and growing for all the sewers everywhere.

Marta Alto
Lynn Raasch
Kathleen Spike
Terri Burns
Marilyn Thelen
Barbara Weiland
Ann Price Gosch
Karen Dillon
Leslie Wood

ISBN 0-935278-39-7

Table of Contents

About the Authors

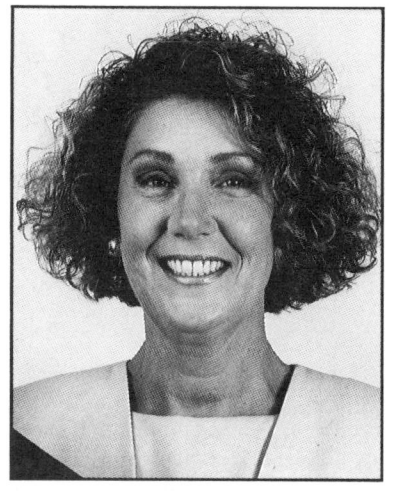

Marcy Miller met Pati Palmer right out of college and they quickly became best of friends. Since earning her degree in home economics education from Washington State University, Marcy has had a varied career, but sewing has always been a common "thread."

Marcy taught high school home economics in her hometown of Aberdeen, Washington, then became a public utility home economist in Vancouver, Washington. Her presentations to the public on electricity use, conservation and safety included machine sewing topics. Later, as a certified kitchen designer, Marcy owned a remodeling business and showroom in Portland, Oregon. Many of her remodeling jobs involved sewing rooms.

After marrying, Marcy got involved in teaching sewing as a business by attending Palmer/Pletsch sewing and teacher-training workshops. She is now a Certified Palmer/Pletsch Instructor and taught in Arlington, Texas, until her recent move to Zurich, Switzerland, where she will continue teaching sewing.

With all of her teaching experience and familiarity with Palmer/Pletsch, Marcy was an ideal person to compile 20 years of Palmer/Pletsch ideas and her own into this comprehensive manual.

Marcy, remembering a favorite teacher in her past who changed her future, says "My first two weeks in math class were a disaster. My teacher, Miss Sherman, spotted my vague, lost face and promptly changed my seat to the front of the room nearest her desk. It was amazing how incredibly clear her explanations and examples became. Her kind face and patient ways of explaining were endless as her eyes searched the room for a twinkling or a reflection of understanding. In her class I got my first 'A' and the beginning of a new interest in learning."

Pati Palmer has used her home economics degree to build a career as an international fashion-sewing authority. Today she is the owner and CEO of Palmer/Pletsch Publishing, a company renowned for making sewing "fun, fast and easy."

Having specialized in clothing, textiles and apparel merchandising at Oregon State University, Pati first became an education representative for Armo, a division of Crown Textiles, an interfacing manufacturer. In the early '70s, as a notions buyer and corporate home economist for an Oregon department store, she coordinated store-sponsored sewing fairs, produced fashion shows and taught up to 10 sewing classes a week.

In the mid '70s Pati teamed up with Susan Pletsch to write and publish sewing books and teach seminars based on the books throughout North America. Eventually they added other professionals to their teaching team. Pati and Susan also began designing for Vogue Pattern Co. in 1976 and in 1980 switched to McCall's. (Susan is no longer associated with the company.)

Today, Pati concentrates her efforts on book publishing and the company's International School of Sewing Arts and Teacher Training Institute in Portland, Oregon. The school and institute are open to the general public as well as aspiring sewing teachers.

Introduction

It seems now is an ideal time to enter the business of teaching sewing, thanks to recent changes in attitudes and public policy surrounding the teaching of sewing. Here's a little background:

Sewing in this century has been perpetuated formally through the school system in the United States and other countries. Any child wanting to learn sewing has had the opportunity. Sewing was valued as a life skill, just as important as preparing a healthful, attractive meal.

In the past, junior high and high school sewing teachers earned college degrees in home ecomomics education, which included textile science, clothing construction and clothing selection. Other home economists specializing in the sewing field majored not in education, but in clothing, textiles and related arts. This curriculum allowed time for more advanced courses: traditional custom or comparative tailoring, draping, flat-pattern design, interior design, fashion illustration, historic costume, art history and other related courses, and maybe even a minor in business. With four years of in-depth training, these home economists became trusted curators of garment construction.

Today, things have changed. High schools and colleges are feeling budget constraints and must focus on what is considered academic, not a hobby. Even some of the best home economics institutions in the United States have replaced garment construction courses with sewing labs where samples of unfamiliar techniques are made for a notebook. This is a more expedient way to teach sewing but it eliminates learning the "entire" garment construction process.

In 1994, **Family and Consumer Science** was adopted as the new name for the **Home Economics** profession. The clothing-related division includes study in **textiles, apparel design** and **apparel merchandising.** It does not mention sewing or garment construction.

Does this mean colleges no longer will offer garment construction? Generally, this seems to be the trend. Teaching family values and preventing individual and family crises seems to be the new trend.

Where will sewing teachers be trained? Will sewing be considered a craft that, like quilting, is handed down through the generations? Will it be a new opportunity for vocational schools who teach design to add construction courses? Will community colleges continue to offer clothing construction classes? Will it be a business opportunity for **YOU?**

Whether you are a college-educated home economist, a custom clothier who has learned by doing, or a home-sewer who learned from a skilled aunt or mother, consider the important values and skills sewing has taught you: coordination, patience, decision-making, manners, respect for others, self-esteem, completion, dexterity, math, geometry, confidence and creativity, to name a few. Now consider that you could pass all of these on to others in your own sewing classes. Plus, sewing occupies time productively to keep kids—and adults—off the streets. Maybe these hobbies can help solve society's ills!

This book includes more than 25 years of teaching ideas. Palmer/Pletsch as a company has taught thousands of classes in every circumstance from a full-fledged sewing school to traveling seminars and workshops. We are determined to keep sewing alive by providing the best quality teaching information possible.

If this book inspires you to start a business or build the one you have, we hope it also inspires you to improve continually. More than likely, you have attended sewing classes, read sewing books and watched videos, and decided you want to teach. Keep it up as you develop your business—and as your business grows. Try Martha Pullen for heirloom sewing, Linda McGehee for creative clothing, Stretch & Sew for sewing knits, and Margaret Islander for industrial techniques. **And come to us for fashion sewing!**

We began our hands-on workshops in 1986, teacher training in 1991, and certification in 1993. Students learn a lot and network with others interested in sewing. We also offer you the chance to see our area's wonderful and unique fabric stores! Bring an extra suitcase! Write us for our latest brochure.

Becoming a sewing teacher takes learning a topic well, ambition, enthusiasm, ingenuity, research, practice and a positive attitude. As a teacher, students will look up to you. Besides knowledge, a number of essential attributes of a teacher make learning happen: professionalism, interest, patience, helpfulness, warmth, fun, encouragement, approachability, availability, communication skills, responsibility and organization.

This book is for reference. Let it guide you, not overwhelm you. Read this manual now and later, after teaching classes. You will gain different insights after you've experienced teaching for yourself.

Happy teaching!

Pati Palmer,
President
Palmer/Pletsch

Marcy Miller
Certified Palmer/
Pletsch Instructor

CHAPTER ONE

Getting Your Business Started

"Turn on the answering machine when you need to concentrate. Each phone call interruption costs you two to three times the length of the call in time."

Know Thyself

So you want to teach sewing. **Congratulations!** It can be a fun and rewarding venture. You will find yourself very motivated to do your best because you will "be on stage." You'll never work harder while loving your work so much. You'll pinch yourself on occasion and say, "Wow, I'm doing what I love and getting paid for it." Read this book from cover to cover more than once. Each time it will nudge you to consider something different. After teaching for awhile, you will read it with new meaning.

Now is the time to take an inventory of yourself. What are your abilities? How easily are you able to share your knowledge and talent with others? You probably have done a lot of teaching in your life without realizing it and you probably possess teaching skills of which you are unaware. Even when you shared your sewing skills with others, you were teaching. Those who benefited were most likely grateful. Remembering such occasions should help you build confidence.

Because you want to teach, you will need to let others know that you are qualified. You may find talking about your talents difficult. This is because we were taught not to "brag." Some of us also received negative criticism when young, which affects our self-worth.

A way to overcome these notions is to write down your experiences and list your talents. **What do you know best and would be most skilled to teach?** For some reason, putting them on paper suddenly makes them more important. What a terrific person you are!

A subtle way to talk about yourself is simply to talk enthusiastically about what you've sewn recently or about how much fun it is to teach. ENTHUSIASM IS CONTAGIOUS!

In Chapter 18, Camera-Ready Forms, there is the following Sewing Experience checklist. Here is a sample of one that has been filled out. Now go to the back of this book and fill yours out.

Sewing Experience Checklist

1. I have _25_ years of sewing experience.

2. I am proudest of my ability to _change a pattern design a little and add creative touches_

3. My family and friends are proud of my ability to _entertain family and friends and to sew for my grandchildren_

4. My sewing specialties are _children's clothing, pants and jackets_

5. I have other sewing experience. _I've made a bridal gown and window treatments_

6. I own _2_ sewing machines and _2_ sergers.
   Other equipment: _a press, a good steam iron and pressing equipment_

7. My sewing education experience is: _high school home economics community college tailoring class 4-Day Palmer/Pletsch workshop lectures and local sewing fair_

8. I have managed myself, home and family for _20_ years.

9. I have _20_ (months or years) business experience as _a bookkeeper_

10. I have taught _15_ people. (Teaching a neighbor to sew on a button, children to tie their shoes, etc. counts.)

Networking

Networking is very important. Gradually try to meet others interested in sewing. Get names of potential sewing enthusiasts and other teachers in your area. List potential class sponsors. Use our **Industry Contacts Worksheet**. For a full-size form, see Chapter 18, Camera-Ready Forms.

Your Business Plan

Your business plan should contain the 4 W's: **Who, What, Where** and **When**. A written statement of your business objectives and goals will contribute greatly to your success. Set goals that are fun and give you a reason to work and to want to succeed. Some examples are:

The vacation you've always dreamed of
A new car
Your very own sewing room
A room addition to your home
A new home
A boat or airplane
Children's education
Improve self-esteem
Develop sense of identity
Share my expertise

A sample plan is on page 9. Do the following to help you collect your thoughts and get you organized:

1. **Write a full description of what you will be doing.** For example: "I will be teaching beginning sewing and fitting classes to adults in a space provided by a sponsor."

2. **List all the tools and equipment you own that are necessary for teaching these classes.** Give these items a legitimate monetary value for tax purposes. This will be your investment contribution to your new business. This establishes part of its monetary worth.

> sewing machine
> serger/overlock machine
> pressing equipment
> cutting/marking equipment
> notions: needles, pins, thimbles, bobbins,
>   seam ripper, bodkin, Grabbits,
>   tapes, see-through ruler

3. **List all the tools and equipment you will need to acquire.** Give each a current purchase price.

slides	slide projector/screen
posters	carrying cases for packing
portfolio	garment bags/suitcases
business stationery	hangers and drops
samples	model garments

The total amount necessary to purchase these items will be your new business investment. Here you will most likely prioritize what, when and how much. Keep good records and receipts; these are also part of your tax records.

4. **Identify sources of start-up money.** Do you have enough savings...or will you need to borrow money?

5. **List where you might find potential students.**

fabric stores	sewing machine dealers
sewing guilds	extension agents/offices
churches	businesses, such as banks
cleaners	doctors offices
grocery stores	babysitters

6. **Describe all marketing tools you will need and when you will be acquiring these aids.**

> portfolio
> business stationery
> flyers

7. **Describe in detail how, to whom and when you will distribute your marketing tools.**

8. **Describe in detail how you will monitor your marketing strategy.**

> List appointments and their results.
> List groups receiving flyers and the number
>   of flyers.
> Ask clients how they heard about your class.
> Measure income per class.
> Measure the amount of income compared
>   with time and expenses.

9. **Determine a realistic time schedule for meeting interim or long-term goals.**

Be sure to follow your plan and refer to it often. You can expand your definitions as you grow. You will probably need to alter some of your plan as you grow and discover your market.

Time Management

Purchase a datebook with a calendar and address section. A "month at a glance" calendar is best for scheduling classes. It allows you to view weeks at a time. A loose-leaf style allows you to add note pages for to-do lists.

Tip: Write what you wore to class in your datebook...so you won't wear the same garment twice in a row!

Because you do not have secretarial, bookkeeping or other help, plan time to make lists. By making a **To-Do List** each evening for the next day or first thing in the morning, you will be much more efficient and accomplish 10 times what you would without a list. It will keep you on task.

Decide what your **best** time of day is. If you're a morning or night person, perform your most complicated tasks when you are at your best.

You also might use your best time to prepare model garments, samples and other items for your classes, leaving routine bookkeeping and correspondence to other times of the day or week that are less productive.

It is very valuable to determine the number of hours you have available for your business. In your schedule, you should allow time for:

- Class preparation
- Marketing and promotion
- Correspondence
- Returning phone calls
- Record keeping
- Evaluating and creating
- Self and family

Put these tasks in the right order for you. Many people, for example, place family first. Evaluate what your family's needs are and when you need to be available.

The most important rule in time management is to **DO IT NOW.** If you procrastinate, you'll spend a lot of energy that could have been used to just get it done.

Getting Help

The U.S. Small Business Administration has many publications available for helping you develop your business. One especially for drawing up a business plan is titled **Business Plan For Retailers**. Two additional publications worth reading are "**Thinking about Going into Business**" ("MA2-025) and "**Checklist for Going into Business.**"

The SBA has a Small Business Development Center (SBDC), usually associated with community colleges and universities. The SBA also sponsors an agency called SCORE, which stands for Service Corps of Retired Executives. This is a volunteer agency organized to provide expertise to new and existing small-business owners. This is a free service provided by the U.S. government and private citizens. There is a nominal charge for some of their publications, workshops and seminars. It would be beneficial to schedule an appointment with one of the volunteers and discuss your ideas with an experienced business person.

The county extension agent in your area will also have brochures and advice available. Plan to schedule a meeting with the home economist on staff to discuss your new business. Ask to see sewing publications Extension has produced. Your county agent may refer people wanting sewing classes to you.

As you can see, getting started can be a big task. You have many jobs to do. We encourage you to set goals, plan your time and follow through.

Forms for Planning

The following forms will help you in your planning. For full-size blank forms, see Chapter 18, Camera-Ready Forms.

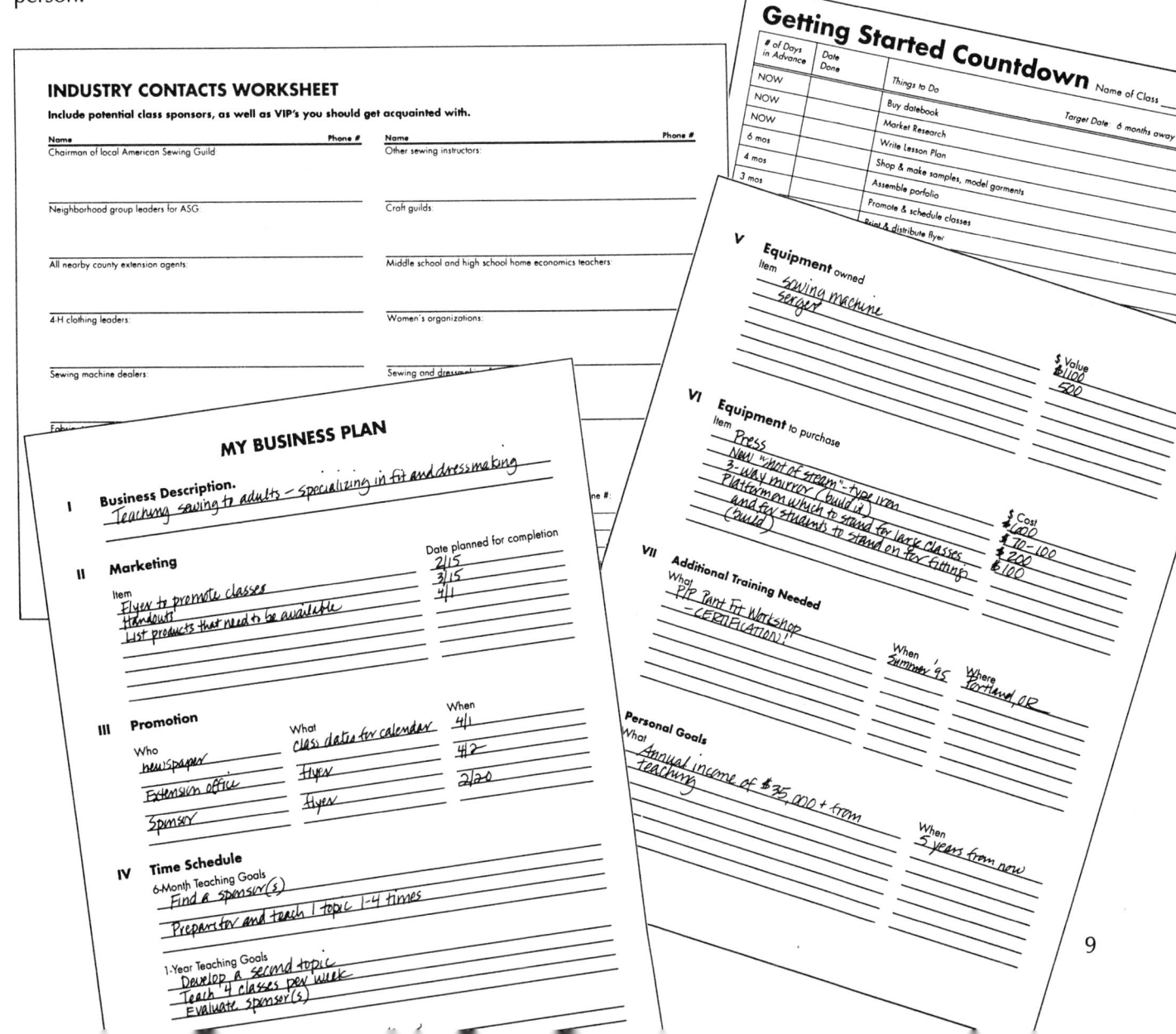

Zoning

Zoning regulation and zoning permits apply if customers will be coming to your home. When you apply for your business license, ask for all zoning regulations that apply to business in your neighborhood. These regulations are designed to control business activities in residential areas and to protect the integrity of the neighborhood.

These items may apply to home-based *sewing* or *teaching* businesses:

- Number of clients coming to your home per day
- Number of vehicles allowed to park on the street
- Type and size of signage
- Number of employees
- Type of delivery vehicles coming and going
- Whether or not you can teach classes in your home

Business License

Check with your city and county about laws and regulations governing home-based businesses in your neighborhood. They also will advise you about required permits and licenses. Most cities and counties require a business license.

Fees vary from place to place. I have found licenses from as low as $25 to as high as $250. Frame and display your license in your "business office." This adds to your credibility with clients and to your own self-confidence and image.

Insurance

A separate business policy may be required to insure your business for liability, fire and theft. Homeowners insurance policies do not cover business operations and equipment in your home. Check with your insurance agent to see what your current policy allows and if upgrading is possible.

Some insurance companies have attachments or riders that can be added to your existing policy to provide coverage. Be sure to account for all your valuable sewing equipment, samples, model garments, books, records, patterns, slides, projector and other teaching tools. And don't forget that fabric "stash" you have been collecting.

You may need to upgrade your automobile insurance to include business use. Make sure you, your teaching tools and sewing equipment are covered if an accident should occur as you drive to class or in case of theft. Delivering samples, garments or advertising materials also is considered business use of your car.

If your business requires customers to come to your home, your liability insurance must be increased. Carry additional coverage for:

- Bodily injury
- Property damage
- Hired independent contractors for whose performance you are responsible
- Libel and slander
- Legal and court costs

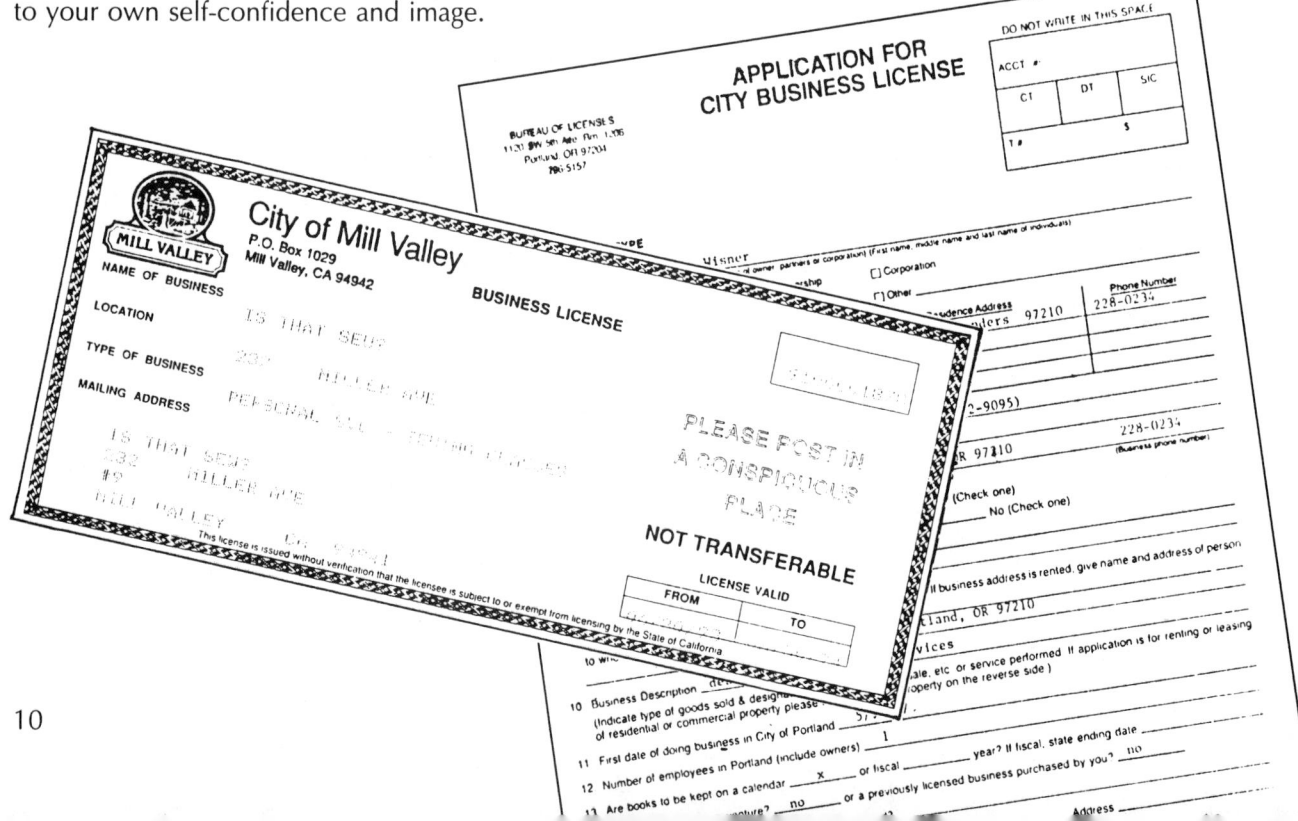

Taxes

Taxes are part of the expense of running a business. Anticipate them as you develop your budget and determine your overhead. See Chapter 7, Money, for more information on identifying expenses and establishing your pricing.

Sales Tax

All states with a sales tax, gross receipts tax, franchise tax board or whatever tax they claim on goods sold, require you to apply for a resale tax number. This entitles you to sell products and collect sales tax. You must report this tax and pay it to the state in which you reside.

Forms are provided to you when you receive your tax number. You are required to collect the tax on the products you resell or manufacture for resale, such as crafts, accessories, garments and home furnishings.

Every state that has a sales tax has a different way of defining what is a taxable item or service. Generally a service is not taxed and a class is considered a service.

Income Taxes

As soon as you receive your business license, you must file a Federal Identification number. Form SS-4 registers you with the IRS, Social Security Administration and the Department of Labor. For these forms, see your local IRS office. No fee is required.

The IRS office also has forms and information for paying federal income taxes, which self-employed people must pay quarterly. Consult a tax professional about additional taxes and record keeping that may be required for your area, such as state or local taxes.

If you are teaching out of your home, ask your tax consultant about deductible household expenses, such as heating, cleaning, garbage collection, telephone, and electrical usage—plus a portion of your mortgage or rent based on the square footage of your classroom.

Record keeping need not be complicated nor time-consuming once you have a system. You might schedule your bookkeeping to coincide with reconciling your monthly bank statement.

Property Taxes

Property taxes are usually paid through the county. Your city may also levy a tax. The tax amount is based on the value of your business equipment and supplies. Check out the situation in your area.

Other Business Taxes

Some areas have additional taxes. For example, a business may be required to pay a transit tax to help support the public transportation district your business is located within.

Employee Withholding and Social Security Taxes

At some point you may need help preparing for or teaching a class. If that person does not meet the definition of "sub-contractor," you might be liable for income tax withholding and social security.

A Telephone Tip...

When ordering a phone line for your home based business there is no need to get the more expensive "business" line. The phone company does not require it for a home-based business. You will, however, be giving up your "free" yellow pages listing.

*"Starting any business takes hard work.
There is no set formula to success. We can give you tips,
tools and ideas, but only YOU are responsible
for your own success."*

CHAPTER TWO
Business Image

"It doesn't take a lot of money to look professional today. New technology makes it easy."

Now you have a business plan and have made sure you are legal—by checking out your area's zoning and licensing requirements, by getting appropriate insurance, and by becoming aware of federal, state and regional tax situations, including sales, income and property taxes. You have started networking. You have identified how to prioritize and manage your time. Before you announce to the world that you are "in business," there are a few more steps to take. You need to develop a business "identity."

This is the fun stuff! What kind of business image do you want to project? Consider not only who you are and what your style is (see Chapter 3, Personal Image), but also whom you want as your customer and what kind of image will attract customers. This image will be communicated in several ways, especially through your printed business materials, which can include:

1. Business Cards
2. Letterhead Stationery
3. No. 10 Envelopes
4. Agreement Forms
5. Invoices

Your Business Title

Establishing your title is the first step in marketing your skills. Your personal business title needs to reflect what you do. Note the following examples:

Marcy Miller,
Professional Sewing Instructor

Lynette Ranney Black,
Sewing-for-the-Home Specialist

Janet Smith,
Certified Palmer/Pletsch Sewing Instructor

Mary Jones, Bridal and Eveningwear Sewing Consultant and Instructor

During a discussion about business titles at one of our Palmer/Pletsch teacher-training sessions, the following was everyone's favorite title because it was contemporary, classy and general:

Your Name,
Fashion Sewing Professional

OR

Your Name,
Fashion Sewing and Image Professional

Business Name

In addition to your title, you may want a business name. The business name can relate to sewing or be general. It can include part or all of your name.

Wedding Sewing Specialties
Special Touch
Suzy's Sewing Systems
Cathy's Creative Kids
Heirloom Happenings
Kinder Sewing
Cynthia Miller Sewing Classes
The Fashion Sewing Co.
Fashion Sewing Inc.
The Creative Sewing Company
Sew Easy...A Sewing School
**   for Grown Ups**

You may choose to file your business name by registering it with your county. Usually the department of licenses and permits in your county courthouse is where you will find the necessary documents. Upon filing, a search is made of existing names to guarantee there are no duplicates. Registration prevents anyone else in your county from using your business name.

You may also want to register your name statewide for the same reason. States vary in their requirements. Some states have a single fee for this registration; others may have a fee for each county.

If your business name is very clever and you see growth potential, it is wise to protect it. If you plan to teach in a larger geographic area, such as the entire country, you may wish to register your name as a trademark with the federal government. Imagine what would have happened if Ann Person hadn't registered **Stretch & Sew**®!

While this would protect your mark or name and record its ownership, you would need to provide your own legal defense in the event of trademark violation. Registering beyond your state is expensive. You need to have a good reason for doing so.

If your business name is YOUR name, it is less likely that you would have a problem. Years ago Pati Palmer and Susan Pletsch decided that it would be very unlikely that another Palmer/Pletsch would exist.

For more information and an application form to register a trademark, write to U.S. Patent and Trademark Office, Washington, DC 20231.

Your **local** Small Business Administration and the SCORE agency can be a big help advising you about what you need to do and where to do it.

Identifying Information

Your cards and other business stationery are part of your professional image. These papers also need to give information and define the type of business you are doing. Use this list as a guideline:

1. Who and where you are:
   name and business name
   address
   area code and phone number
   FAX number if you have one

2. What you do:
   (instructor/teacher/fashion
   designer/consultant)

3. What do you specialize in?
   (serger, children, bridal, fit, image)

4. Specifics regarding availability:
   days of the week
   times of day
   by appointment only

Logo

A logo, when carefully selected, will help identify your business personality and promote your skill, class or product. Be creative but keep your goal in mind. You can design your own letterhead and business cards. Pati Palmer remembers when she used rub-off letters to create surprise business cards and stationery for her husband Jack Watson for his new business. She chose black ink on beige paper.

Today, with sophisticated quick-print copy centers, you can have a great logo of your name in a special typeface. They also have many nice-looking "stock" business card designs available. Mail-order sources for cards and other stationery are available. Be creative by selecting from their wide variety of colors, sizes and print styles. Papers Direct offers great variety. (See Chapter 17, Resources.)

After you "feel you have arrived" in business and the money is rolling in, you can treat yourself to a **great ego experience** by hiring a graphic designer to create and design a special emblem or logo. Palmer/Pletsch's design director Linda Wisner says, "Think of a logo as being more than a graphic. It is a marketing tool that portrays your business style, and is usually the first business impression a potential client gets with the presentation of a business card." A graphic designer will want to know about you. What you do and the style of person you are can be professionally illustrated. Your graphic designer will ask to see samples, shapes, colors, and other logos or styles that appeal to you.

This can be an expensive investment unless you have an artistic friend who owes you a huge favor or would trade classes or custom sewing for artwork. Consider $700 to $1,500 an average range for designing a logo, business cards, stationery and envelopes. Naturally, this will vary from location to location.

We'd like to say that if you have the money, DO IT! What a great way to start out a business! But, realistically, we suggest putting a custom-designed logo low on the priority list when you begin your business. Even the printing will be a sizeable investment—up to $1,000.

You may change your mind about what you like doing after a few months or a year. For example, you decide to specialize in teaching children to sew. After six months, you realize you would much rather teach adults. You'd have to toss all your beautiful stationery and business cards if their focus was on children. At a future time, when you are well on the road to success, you can upgrade your logo.

Letterhead

Next most important need after a logo and business cards is your letterhead stationery. This letterhead can be used for your agreement form with your sponsor, for your invoice when collecting for a class, and for all of your correspondence. A No. 10 envelope is the business envelope to have printed as an all-purpose size.

Business Card and Logo Examples

Note: Business cards are usually 3½"x2". These have been reduced to let us show you more ideas.

Most of the business cards here are used by teachers who have become Certified Palmer/Pletsch Instructors. Some were created by professional graphic designers, some by the teachers themselves and some by print shops. Zondra Hart's card is printed on a preprinted color design. Similar designs are available through printers, catalogs and office supply stores.

These three cards use strong graphics that emphasize their specialties.

Holly Rae Designs

HOLLY R. BUTRYN
designer - dressmaker
716 - 665-2486

Specializing in:

CUSTOM DRESSMAKING

WEDDING APPAREL

ALTERATIONS

Janice G. Langan
Certified Instructor in Serging

For Information Call
(707) 584-1934

Connie Hamilton
(317) 362-3040

New Home • Viking
Sales • Service
Classes • Notions

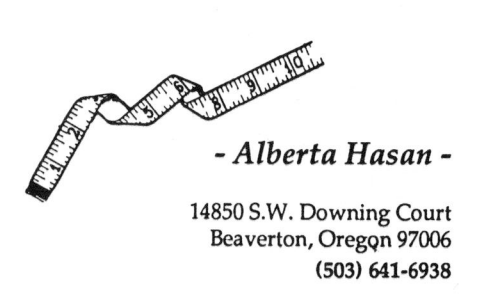
The SEWING CONNECTION

1880G US 231 South in Liberty Square
Crawfordsville, Indiana 47933

JUDITH RASBAND
- Home Economist In Business -
(Clothing and Cosmetic Specialist,
Educator, Consultant, Columnist, Author)
P.O. Box 7052 University Station
Provo, Utah 84602 (801) 224 1207

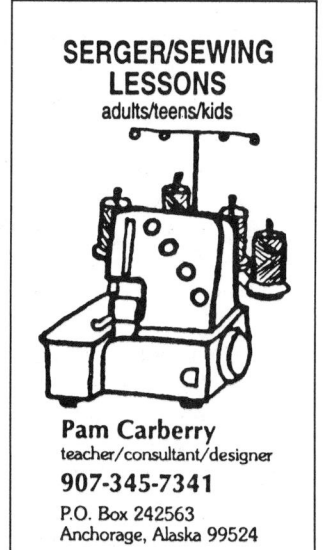

SERGER/SEWING LESSONS
adults/teens/kids

Pam Carberry
teacher/consultant/designer
907-345-7341
P.O. Box 242563
Anchorage, Alaska 99524

- Alberta Hasan -

14850 S.W. Downing Court
Beaverton, Oregon 97006
(503) 641-6938

Ecole de Couture
Céline Ross

JANOME
BERNINA

Machine a coudre
Depositaire autorise

4900 Jean-Brillant,
Montreal, Quebec
H3W 1T7

Sur rendez-vous seulement
Tel. / Fax: (514) 344-1462

Bette's Sewing Studio

Bette L. Wilson

(602) 622-1100
1974 West Romany Rd. • Tucson, AZ 85713
Certified Palmer / Pletsch Fit & Tailoring Instruction

Consider using your name or initials as a graphic element or logo.

for
KATHLEEN SPIKE

Design
Dressmaking
Instruction

1880 S.E. Heiney Road
Gresham, OR 97080

(503) 665-6505

custom tailoring & dressmaking

Marla Kazell

(503) 624-4822
13333 SW 72nd #10E
Tigard, OR 97223

Zondra L. Hart
Design-Dressmaking-Instruction
118 Main Street
Cooperstown, NY 13326
607-547-8348

See Strasse 130
8700 Kusnacht
Switzerland
41 1 810 1511

MARCY MILLER

PROFESSIONAL SEWING & FITTING INSTRUCTOR

Consider using your photo as the graphic— it will immediately introduce you!

Fabric-inspired graphics can be used as background or as an actual logo such as the one above.

touch of class creations

Martha Lynn

Box 84
Rumsey, Alberta
T0J 2Y0
Telephone: **368-3879**

• custom sewing • one-of-a-kind designs • sewing lessons •

• distinct silk and dried floral arrangements •

SEW FITTING

Linda S. Weisberg

1491 Morgan Drive
Elk Grove Village, IL 60007-3183
(708) 980-7130

Palmer/Pletsch Trained Instructor

The three cards to the right use a needle and thread theme. To the left are two variations of tape measures. Many more possibilities exist using all kinds of sewing notions as graphic elements.

Sewing Lessons & Workshops   "Country Classic" Custom Designs
Sewing Machine Sales & Service   Color & Figure Analysis

Karen's Sewing Centre

Karen Wiebe
(204) 242-2059

RR #2
Manitou, MB. R0G 1G0

15

Business Forms

As your classes grow, printed sponsor agreement forms and invoices will be a very professional addition. See Chapter 17, Resources, addresses of catalogs that offer stock or custom business forms.

The agreement form should be filled out, dated and signed when you schedule classes. Once an agreement is entered into, both parties are committed to begin the steps toward achieving mutually successful classes or workshops. For more information on agreement forms, see page 35.

Your cancellation policy may vary with the type of class. For a short lecture class that requires minimal preparation, the cancellation date could be close to the actual date. Two days might be reasonable and fair.

When the class is longer or requires more preparation, such as a workshop or series of classes, set the cancellation date further out. Encourage people to register in advance by setting the registration cut off date a week before the actual class. Keep your cancellation policy open to rescheduling, consolidating or other alternatives.

Sources of Business Cards and Stationery

For economic reasons you may want to compare discount office warehouse type with quick printers' estimates. If prices are close, do business with the person you would most enjoy working with on a regular basis and who is conveniently located to you. Remember, time is money. In a sense you are selecting your silent business partners.

Palmer/Pletsch uses a small family-owned printer who continually comes in at a lower price than the other sources we have mentioned. The two have now done business together for nearly 15 years. If there is ever a quality problem, the printer stands behind the job, an advantage of a long-term business relationship.

In comparing prices from quick printers, mail-order catalogs and discount office warehouse suppliers, we find there are significant savings when large quantities are needed. The cost is always lower when ordering 500 copies or more.

All of the sources have very inexpensive PLAIN business cards for a small investment. Many offer 1000 business cards for $6.95. This is the beginning. To have a logo printed on the card adds a few dollars.

To select a different type style, change the paper stock or color of ink, or print on both sides adds to the price of printed materials. When selecting your "papers" weigh the amount of creativity, cost, service, and convenience available from these sources. Remember creativity is part of the image. (For more information working with printers see pages 80-85.)

Large quantities of standard forms, such as invoices and preprinted checks, are the most inexpensive from the mail-order catalogs. It would be wonderful if we needed **large quantities** of invoices and checks.

In Chapter 17, Resources, you will find mail-order companies that have standard and custom forms available. They will print your business information on the forms you order.

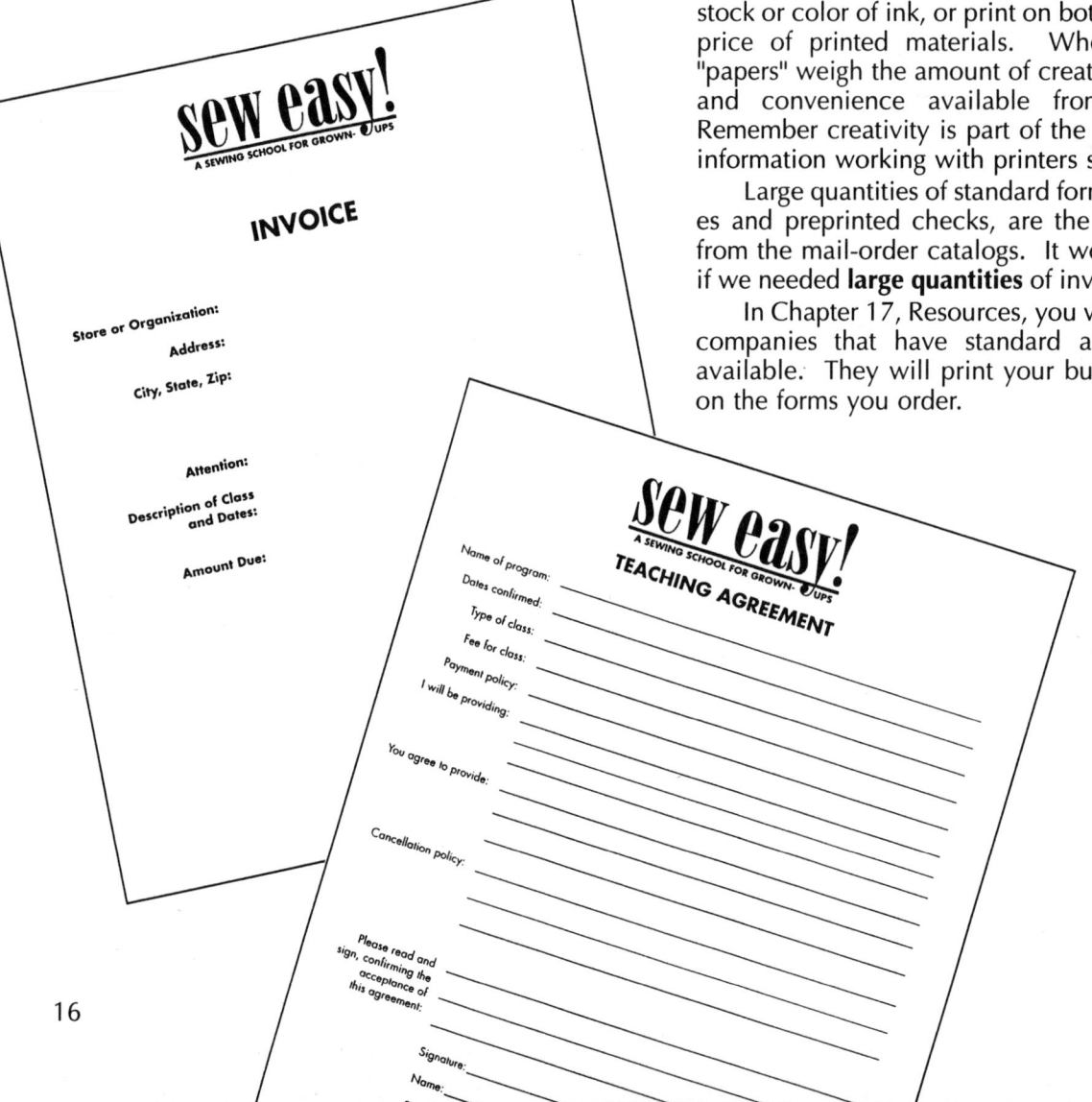

CHAPTER THREE
Personal Image

You and **only you** can decide what image you want to portray. The following words describe **positive** potential images to which you may aspire:

is poised
has class
is down-to-earth
is approachable
has achieved
is fashionable
is looked up to
makes others happy
makes others feel good about themselves
gives good advice
sews all the time

is creative
is confident
is interesting
is successful
is happy
loves people
loves teaching

Your appearance is the first message you send to others. The brain interprets this first impression and helps others form an opinion about you very quickly. A positive appearance does not necessarily require being "beautiful" or "handsome." Being clean and professionally dressed is the bottom line of appearance. People who reject being judged by their appearance and dress accordingly are being self-defeating.

If you want to study style, line and design, read the Palmer/Pletsch book on wardrobe planning. It also includes tips for sewers on selecting patterns and fabric.

Personal Style

Although your body type was determined by genetics, never to be changed (unless through plastic surgery), you CAN choose your personal style. Choose one that compliments your body type. Your clothes define not only your personal style but also your fashion savvy. The illustration to the left shows two distinctive styles—tailored and romantic.

Clothing

If you are teaching fashion sewing, you are in the "fashion" business. The more your image reflects this, the more students will want to sign up for your classes. This doesn't mean you have to dress "high" fashion. Classic fashion works for nearly everyone.

You are a ROLE MODEL to your students. Therefore, part of your job is to give them someone to look up to. You can be this "notch above" and an inspiration to your students by using quality fabrics in current styles. Also, you can add sewing details your students will admire.

When Pati Palmer started her teaching career in a department store, students would tell her they came to class just to see what she was wearing. Pati says that in those days she sewed 24 hours a day and loved the latest fashions, but never realized that **her own wardrobe** would be a selling point for her classes!

Make sure your sewing quality is the best. Trim enclosed seams well and press **during** construction. Also, present garments well, making sure they are cleaned and accessorized. See Chapter 11, Teaching

Tailored Personal Style

Romantic Personal Style

Tools, for more ideas on model garment presentation and other teaching visuals.

If you feel you can't look professional or fashionable because you are overweight, change your attitude. Try to find styles that work for your body. The art of camouflage does wonders. Read the Palmer/Pletsch wardrobe-planning book for ideas! Also, take care of yourself. You'll need all the energy you can get. Start walking. It is an easy way to begin toning your muscles and it might motivate you to trim down.

As a teacher, you can be very visible in your community. Your appearance will be noticed wherever you go. This means looking nice when you go grocery shopping. You might upgrade your casual wardrobe from "sweats" to "classy casuals." If sewing time is limited, this is where you can buy ready-to-wear, because you must sew what you wear teaching.

Classy casual ideas

Accessories

Accessories are an important part of a fashion wardrobe. Many people who sew don't spend time adding the finishing touches. Take your clothing to a store that has a good accessory selection. Find a salesperson who looks fashionable and ask for help putting your outfit together. If you like what he or she does, you've found a gold mine. As sewers we are not exposed to fashion on an ongoing basis like a person who spends everyday around new ready-to-wear trends. It's hard to be "great" at EVERYTHING we do, so get to know your new accessory specialist.

Though you may spend a lot on your personal accessories, quality accessories last forever. For accessories you hang on model garments, shop for sales. Then, if any of those accessories disappear while teaching, you won't be disappointed.

Remember that noisy accessories will detract from your teaching. Seasonal or "fun" jewelry is acceptable when it is tasteful and adds character to the costume. At Christmas, a necklace of bells might be acceptable if your lecture/demonstration does not cause the bells to jingle.

Don't forget that belts are also an accessory. They are a great addition to trousers. You can make the waistline of the pants larger and just cinch in the belt in the morning when your waist is smaller.

Earrings draw attention to your face, especially to your eyes and expressions. You want your audience to watch your face as well as your hands. This helps them learn. Wear earrings that are flattering in shape, style, color and size for your face. Large earrings are nice with short hair.

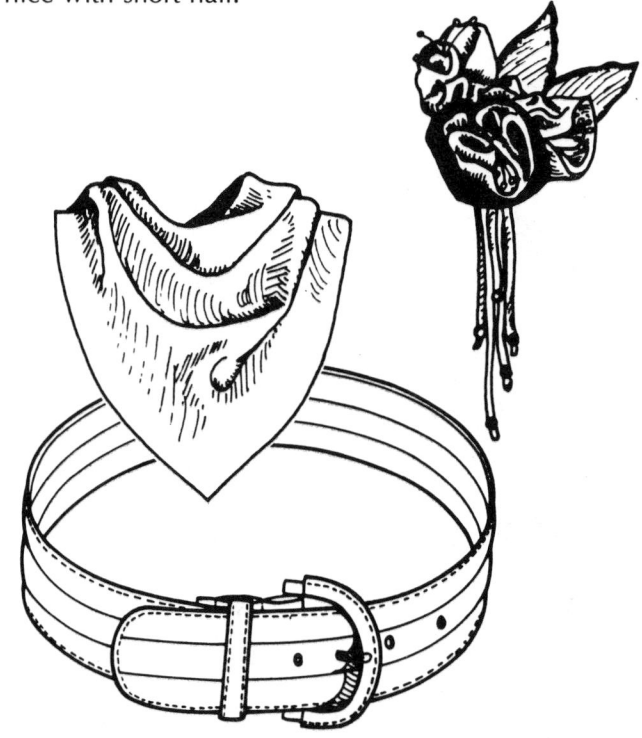

Shoes

You will be standing and walking most of the time. Choose shoes that are fashionable, complementary to your wardrobe and comfortable. Basics are the best buy. Now that low heels are fashionable, comfort is easy to find. Closed-toe shoes are considered to be the most professional-looking. A flat, closed-toe shoe may be worn with pants, suits, tailored dresses, city shorts, stirrup pants and even leggings.

Legs

Hosiery is what connects the shoes to the costume. Darker shades and opaque stockings are always safe for fall and winter. Lighter shades work for spring and summer. To extend the life of winter clothing, wear sand or off-white stockings with them in the spring. Black wardrobe pieces look summery when worn with light stockings.

One color to avoid is SUNTAN. Just because it was one of the first pantyhose colors available, many people continue to use it. You will look more fashionable in newer shades. For classic looks we recommend sheer black, sheer taupe, sheer sand (a very light taupe), and sheer off-white. If you use colors, use fashion magazines as a guide to current trends. Sometimes red hose need red shoes, and other times matching looks garish.

Cleanliness

What's most important is immaculate personal cleanliness—good grooming. At the least that means no bad breath or body odor. Ask your best friend if you pass these tests. Not only should **you** be clean, but so should your visuals and your model garments. If you use your own wardrobe to show students sewing ideas, avoid wearing perfume. Perfume stays with fabric and your display garments will smell. Also, many people are sensitive to perfume scents.

Hair

There are no "bad hair days" when you have a professional haircut in a style that is good for you and easy to take care of. If you don't have a good hairdresser, ask a friend whose hair you admire to recommend a hairstylist.

Make an appointment with the stylist to have a discussion about your hair **before** the cut. Take pictures of ideas you like and ask for opinions. Your hair texture and thickness will be a clue to the cut a good stylist will recommend. Also, if "wash 'n' wear" hair is important to you, let the stylist know.

You will grow to trust and depend on this person. The care of your hair will be the stylist's responsibility. A good stylist will eliminate the grow-out pains you've experienced in the past. He or she will be able to trim as it grows so that any length looks good. Hair that is well-styled and becoming makes you feel good about yourself. It can even **change your personality!!**

Hands

Your hands are seen the most during classes. You will be talking and working with your hands. People watch what your hands do. Your hands and nails need to be well-groomed. Chipped nails, loud polish and noisy jewelry will detract from your teaching. If you are not fortunate to have strong nails, you can "buy" nails through a salon. But, short, clean, filed, unpolished nails can look perfectly fine. Investing in an occasional manicure may help turn your hands around!

Your Voice

Nothing is as hard to listen to as an irritating voice. Listen to sewing video tapes. Are some voices easier to listen to than others? A lower-pitched voice is generally a more pleasant tone to hear. Shrill, high-pitched voices are very uncomfortable to people's ears. Analyze the qualities that make some more pleasant to listen to than others. Then record your voice and listen to it. Do you like it?

How loud you need to speak depends on the size of the room and the number of people listening. Often your students will listen more carefully if you speak softly.

The speed of your speech is another consideration. Speaking too fast or too slowly can cause you to lose an audience. As you are speaking, take spot checks of the audience:

Are they falling asleep?
Do they look confused?
Are they alert and hanging on your every word?

According to a survey done by Harvard Business School, 7% of the words you say are retained. Over 50% of your gestures, expressions, tone of voice, and body language are heard and retained. We recommend variety! Change voice levels and tempo occasionally. Be enthusiastic, and use gestures. Ask questions. This will keep your audience awake. See Chapter 10, Teaching Techniques, for more.

Grammar

It doesn't matter how rich you are, how you look or where you went to school, your social class is determined by others when you speak. One's speech is a repeated public announcement about background and social standing. Poor grammar instantly downgrades your image. Yet many people today have fallen into habits of bad grammar. Some common grammatical errors made today are:

1. Using adjectives instead of adverbs to describe verbs. For example, some say, "He works good." It should be, "He works well." Well is an adverb to describe the verb work. Adverbs answer the question, "How?"

   "His work is good" is correct because in this sentence work is a noun. What kind of work? Good work. Good is an adjective to describe the noun work. Adjectives answer the question, "What kind of?"

   Good is an adjective and well is an adverb. If you ask the question, he works (how?), use well. She is sewing good. No, it should be "she is sewing well." She is sewing nice. No, she is sewing nicely.

   Many adverbs are formed by adding -ly to an adjective. "Her sewing is perfect" (adj.) vs. "She sews perfectly" (adv.).

2. Using plural verbs with singular subjects. The most common is using don't in place of doesn't. "She don't mind quality fabrics." It should be "She doesn't mind quality fabrics."

3. Splitting the infinitive form of a verb or split infinitives. To work, to make, to be are examples of the infinitive form. "I would like to comfortably fit into a dress" should be "I would like to fit comfortably into a dress."

4. Improper verb tense. "Look what you done" should be "Look what you have done" or "Look what you did."

5. Use the objective form of a pronoun when it is the object of a preposition. For example, I is the nominative form and me is the objective form. "Come shopping with Susan and I" should be "Come shopping with Susan and me."

6. The subjunctive mood of a verb expresses doubt or a wish or condition contrary to fact. "I wish I were a doctor." "If I were you, I would buy a new car." Even though I is singular, the plural form of the verb is used. "If I was" is not correct.

The subjunctive mood also expresses future possibility such as "if I were conducting a seminar on..." If you are expressing a past experience, "was" is correct. "If I was visiting a store for the first time, I would have called the manager in advance."

7. Lie and lay cause confusion. When used in the present tense, lay takes an object; lie does not. For example:
"I am laying the book down." (Book is the object.)
"I am lying down." (There is no object.)

Confusion can come in the past tense: "Yesterday I laid the book down" vs. "Yesterday I lay down all day." The past tense of lay is laid; the past tense of lie is lay.

This review of the tenses of both verbs may help you as a quick reference:

Present:	lay (takes an object)	lie (no object)
Past tense:	laid	lay
Past participle:	(have, has, had) laid	(have, has, had) lain

If you didn't have a good grammar teacher in school, you might feel threatened by this discussion. Don't be! Many grammar mistakes have become colloquial language. For example, "It is me" should be "It is I." Yet the latter sounds very formal. "It is me" is very commonly used.

Some people are so charming they can get away with poor grammar. Others may be willing to change if someone points out their one or two common grammar mistakes. If we are not conscious of them, we can't improve.

We do not like the current trend of deteriorating grammar, so our stand is to draw your attention to it! AND guess what? That is a risk, because now you will expect all of us to have perfect grammar too!!

Lastly, **never swear!** To some, it means you have a limited vocabulary. To others, it can be very offensive. It's like smoking in class. **Don't do it!!**

Attitude, Empathy and Acting

Image goes beyond appearance. It is your whole manner of being. Be POSITIVE. No one wants to come to class to hear someone's problems. Often students come to class to leave problems.

Be ENTHUSIASTIC. The more enthusiastic you are, the more your students will learn. Teach them to want to sew as well as how to sew. A smiling, enthusiastic teacher with a sense of humor will be the inspiration your students are looking for. Enthusiasm is contagious.

Help your students learn to have a good self-image. Compliment them whenever appropriate. Your students are looking for your attention and approval. You must make yourself available to them in a friendly, personal manner. Being helpful, patient, warm and fun is easy.

Tell stories about your own successes and failures in sewing **(please stick to the subject at hand)**. Include interesting, humorous anecdotes. Students will feel more at ease and possibly more confident knowing that someone as talented as you has had a disaster or three.

To put students at ease, ask them questions about their sewing or pattern and fabric choice. Ask where they plan to wear their finished garment or display their quilt or home decorating item. Your fresh, genuine curiosity will open the door to success. You'll be popular and get many referrals. Isn't that great? Encouraging, complimenting, flattering and accepting others can lead to good personal relationships and to being a successful, popular teacher.

"The world is a stage" and teaching is your opportunity to act out your favorite role. Projecting yourself in an entertaining way calls upon the actor in you. Pizzazz and drama are major teaching tools and qualities. Some teachers have actually taken speech and drama classes. It is almost impossible to over-dramatize a specific technique. The more exaggerated you describe each step, the better the learning process.

Your personal image must be reflected in all that pertains to your sewing profession. Stationery, business cards, notes, flyers announcing your classes, phone manners, and every other way you communicate should reflect your style. Your samples, teaching area, office or studio are the tools of your trade. They must also reflect your professional image. See Chapter 2, Business Image, for more information.

CHAPTER FOUR

What to Teach

"Teach what you enjoy. When you become GOOD at ONE subject you have the confidence to sell yourself effectively to sponsors and consumers."

Deciding what to teach is EASY! Usually we have a skill or subject we know and love. That is what you should teach. It is also important to research what is needed. It would be a waste of time putting together a dynamite program no one wants.

How do you discover the needs and wants in your area? Ask your local fabric stores, sewing machine dealers, local home economics teachers, county extension offices, adult education programs, friends and others. Take a poll of what is being taught. Is something missing or is there a demand for more teaching of existing classes? Be creative. Design an unusual class. For example, you could design a class called "Teens and Outdoor Exercise Wear" or "Children and Basic Needle-and-Thread, Hand-Sewn Crafts." Here are more class topic ideas:

- Beginning Sewing for Children, ages 5-9
- Beginning Sewing
- Fitting
- Brush-Up Sewing
- Time-Saving Sewing
- Tailoring
- Pant Fitting and Sewing
- Beginning Serging
- Introduction to Serging
- Creative Serging
- Advanced Serging
- Swimsuits
- Copying Ready-to-Wear
- Sewing for the Home
- Sewing for Mother-to-Be
- Sewing for Children
- Sewing for Nurseries
- Serge a Sensational Wardrobe
- Sewing Western Wear
- Sewing Lingerie
- Men's Pants
- Men's Tailoring
- Men's Suits
- Sewing Ultrasuede® and Leather-likes
- Aerobic and Active Wear
- Quilting Fashions
- Sewing Christmas Gifts
- Sewing Seasonal Decorating Ideas
- Sewing for the Bride
- Sewing Glitz for Prom Night
- Couture Details for Tailored Suits
- Couture Evening Wear
- Perfect Bound Buttonholes

- Sew a Skirt in a Day
- Tailoring Shortcuts
- Sewing Shortcuts
- Creative Jackets
- Vests
- Embellished Vests
- Embellishing Sweatshirts
- Sewing with Velvet
- Sewing with Wool Gabardine
- Easy Coats
- Bow Ties and Cummerbunds for Men
- Sewing on the Bias
- Holiday Gift Ideas
- Christmas in July
- Heirloom Clothing
- Sew a Travel Wardrobe
- Fusible Interfacings
- Sewing with Knits
- The 2-Hour Shirt
- Sewing with Silk
- 3-Hour Silk or Silky Blouse
- Casual Couture
- Designer Details
- Sew Like a Pro
- Designer Details Made Easy
- Sewing with Sheers
- Children's Sewing Camp
- Successful Serging
- Bridal Sewing Techniques
- Perfect Machine Buttonholes for Any Fabric
- Teen Sewing
- Perfect Pressing
- Trousers
- Ultraleather™ Pants
- Private Lessons
- Supervised Sewing Lab

Whatever your class idea, it most likely appeals to a specific group of students. Advanced couture dressmaking, for example, will appeal only to experienced sewers and maybe an adventurous sewer, but hardly to a beginner.

You will be a more confident and effective teacher if you choose to become an expert in one subject. You can turn a single subject into MANY class topics, lengths and formats. For example, if you focus on fit you can also teach beginning sewing.

Here's Some Inspiration...

Up to your ears in fitting problems?

Sew Pants that Really Fit!

Learn the Palmer/Pletsch system of fitting commercial patterns:
- You don't have to draft your own pattern to get a good pant fit.
- Find out how your body varies from a commercial pattern and buy any pattern and make it fit.
- Sew the same pattern in any fabric using our *Fit-As-You-Sew* method.

Plus—You'll learn dozens of sewing tips and see an exciting collection of fashions:
- Fast, easy zippers.
- Pockets that don't gap.
- Tricks that make your tummy flatter.
- Waistbands that don't roll.

Bonus—Following this 3-hour slide/lecture program you may try on McCall's #8173 gingham pant shells to determine your correct size.

Sponsored by:

(name)

(times)

(dates)

(location & phone # for registration)

Meet Pati Palmer, sewing expert and author of *Pants for Any Body*. Pati has fitted thousands of people in pants, and she can fit you, too.

Sew Pants that Really Fit!™
To assure a seat, you must pre-register in person or by phone. Or, mail this coupon with your registration fee.
Name _____
Address _____ State _____ Zip _____
City _____
Home Phone _____ Work Phone _____
Class date and time preferred _____
Check enclosed for $ _____

Cancellation Policy: Refunds honored up to 24 hours before class. You may sen

---

The flyer at left is casual, fun, yet serious about what it has to offer. It may appeal to a different type of person than the flyer below, which has a more sophisticated look. Know your customer, or the kind of customer you want to attract.

Classic Trousers ALL-DAY SEMINAR

FITTING & SEWING

Now, finally, you can REALLY learn to fit Classic trousers. Classic trousers never go out of style, and when they fit correctly, they can flatter any figure. We'll make sure each of you has a chance to try on our gingham fitting shells and tell you what to do to fit YOUR body.

We start by teaching you how to fit. When you learn fit, you can handle any fabric, any pattern design and weight change (not that *that* happens!)

We'll demonstrate tissue fitting and *Fit-As-You-Sew*™, followed by the best techniques for getting good results in zippers, fly fronts, waistbands that don't roll, trouser details—where the crease should be, flat pleats, pockets that don't gap, and tummy control stays— and even an easy way to underline pants.

Sponsored by:

(name)

(times)

(dates)

(location & phone # for registration)

(price)

Fitting and Sewing
To assure a seat, you must pre-register in person or by phone. Or, mail this coupon with your registration fee.
Name _____
Address _____
City _____ State _____ Zip _____
Home Phone _____ Work Phone _____
Class date and time preferred _____
Check enclosed for $ _____

Cancellation Policy: Refunds honored up to 24 hours before class. You may send a substitute.

Sewing for the Bride

Every couple should have the beautiful wedding they dream of having. At a cost as much as 80% less than ready-to-wear, sewing is the answer...with the extra advantages of limitless design choices and custom fitting for the entire wedding party.

In this slide-seminar Lynn will take you from begining to end of the process...including accessories and undergarments.

Meet Lynn Raasch
Palmer/Pletsch Corporate Educator

Sponsored by:

(name)

(times)

(dates)

(location & phone #
for registration)

(price)

Heirloom Sewing

on your serger

with Marta Alto
Serger expert and
Certified Palmer/Pletsch
Instructor

Learn how to create the look of heirloom French handsewing—lace inserts, pintucks, entredeaux—all on your serger. Many laces, trims and ribbons serge beautifully.

Marta will show you, through slides and samples, inspirational ideas, and the techniques that will make your serging easy...and the results beautiful.

Sponsored by:

(name)

(times)

(dates)

(location & phone # for registration)

(price)

Sewing Silk & Silkies

Discover just how simple sewing with silk and silkies can be. The techniques aren't difficult, just different.

In this seminar you'll see slides and beautifully made sample garments to inspire you. Marta will show you easy techniques that give great results. She'll give you tips on fabric care, pattern selection, interfacings, cutting, marking and sewing on slippery fabrics, plus how to use bias to make the most of the drapability of these fine fabrics.

Meet Marta Alto
a Certified Palmer/Pletsch
instructor.

Sponsored by:

(name)

(times)

(dates)

(location & phone # for registration)

(price)

Sewing Silk & Silkies

To assure a seat, you must pre-register in person or by phone.
Or, mail this coupon with your registration fee.

Name

Address _____ State ___ Zip ___

City _____ Work Phone ___

Home Phone _____

Class date and time preferred ___

Check enclosed for $ ___

Cancellation Policy: Refunds honored up to 24 hours before class. You may send a substitute.

Fusible Interfacing

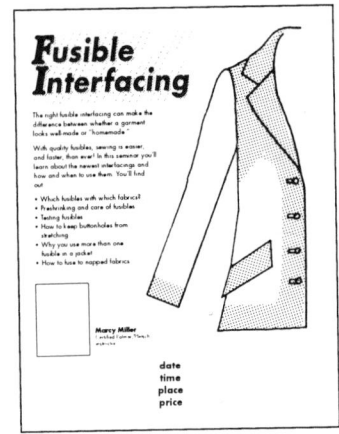

The right fusible interfacing can make the difference between whether a garment looks well made or "homemade."

With quality fusibles, sewing is easier and faster, than ever! In this seminar you'll learn about the newest interfacing and how and when to use them. You'll find out:

- Which fusibles with which fabrics!
- Preshrinking and care of fusibles
- Testing fusibles
- How to keep buttonholes from stretching
- Why you use more than one fusible in a jacket
- How to fuse to napped fabrics

Marcy Miller
Certified Palmer Pletsch
Instructor

date
time
place
price

24

Do you know the new tailoring shortcuts?

Learn to sew a jacket in only 8 hours! Attend the Palmer/Pletsch **Easiest Tailoring** seminar for today's jackets and coats.

Tailoring can be fun, fast and easy. Learn timesaving tricks in our 3-hour class.
• Choose "no-fail" tailoring fabrics
• Easy Measure-Free™ fitting ideas
• The newest fusible interfacings and how to use them
• Pucker-free sleeves
• Quick machine lining
• Coats—quick to sew and the greatest money saver!
• Tips on tailoring luxury suedes like Ultrasuede®

Plus! Professional details:
• Tailored pockets   • Shoulder pads
• Buttonholes   • Topstitching

Learn more in just 3 hours than you have in years of "hit and miss" tailoring!

Meet Lynn Raasch
Home economist and Palmer/Pletsch sewing professional. Lynn's seminars are a combination of teaching, inspiration and entertainment.

Sponsored by:

(name)

(times)

(dates)

(location & phone # for registration)

(price)

Easiest Tailoring
To assure a seat, you must pre-register in person or by phone. Or, mail this coupon with your registration fee.

Name _____
Address _____ State ___ Zip ___
City _____
Home Phone _____ Work Phone _____
Class date and time preferred _____
Check enclosed for $ _____

Cancellation Policy: Refunds honored up to 24 hours before class. You may send a substitute.

Marcy Miller will introduce you to the **5 Basic Pieces** that make up a travel wardrobe. With a three-piece suit of jacket, skirt and pant, plus a two-piece dress, you'll be set for any business week on the road. Add a few extra tops, including one for evening, to have a travel wardrobe for business or pleasure. Learn how to select colors and fabrics that work best for you. Marcy will also demonstrate the added versatility of a few carefully selected accessories. Then learn the fitting and sewing tips that will make creating your travel wardrobe fun and easy.

date

time

place

price

SEW A TRAVEL WARDROBE

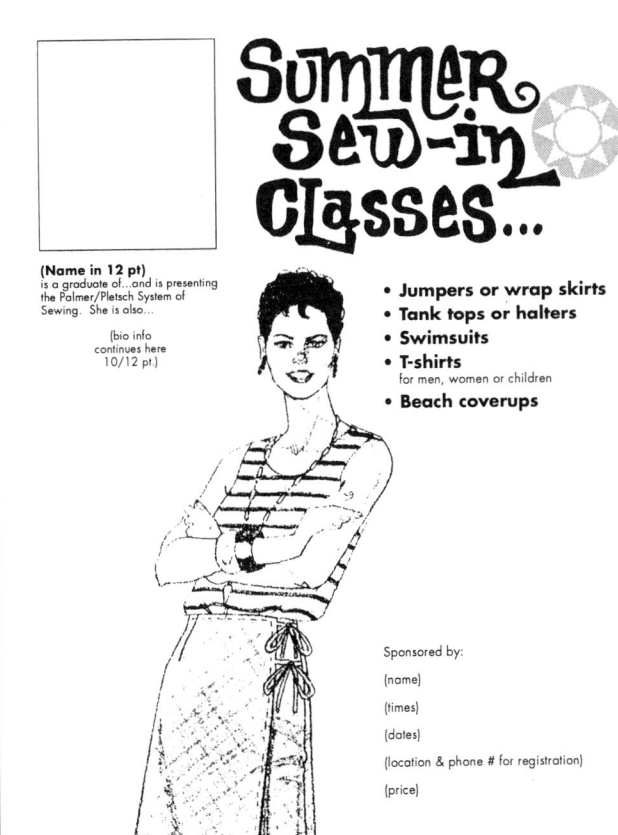

Summer Sew-in Classes...

(Name in 12 pt)
is a graduate of...and is presenting the Palmer/Pletsch System of Sewing. She is also...

(bio info continues here 10/12 pt.)

• **Jumpers or wrap skirts**
• **Tank tops or halters**
• **Swimsuits**
• **T-shirts**
  for men, women or children
• **Beach coverups**

Sponsored by:

(name)

(times)

(dates)

(location & phone # for registration)

(price)

✿ Jumpers or Wrap Skirts
Make a quick summer skirt or jumper. Use your imagination on fabrics from denim to soft knits and print jerseys.

✿ Tank Tops or Halters
Make a tank top or halter for sunny summer days. Choose from single or doubleknit fabrics for sporty or evening wear.

✿ Swimsuits
Try making a swimsuit this summer. A great way for teenagers to learn to sew and save lots of money. We suggest a two piece swimsuit in jersey, cotton knit, cotton woven prints, Qiana doubleknit or single knits (they don't sun-fade).

✿ T-Shirts for Men, Women or Children
Make your choice and sew for your family. Use knit fabrics and learn the quick professional methods. Taught by Bev Smith. Try a turtle, crew or V-neck pattern.

✿ Beach Coverups
A popular class for something fast and simple for day, patio, beach, or evening. May coordinate with a swimsuit. Great for the busy teenager. Try our wonderful stretch terry or cool gauze. Anything goes. We suggest simple patterns and we'll teach you the finishing touches.

Two-sided mailers allow more room for information, but cost more to print.

25

Whom Do You Want to Teach?

What you teach affects the age group that will be interested, the size of your class, the amount of space you'll need, and the amount of preparation.

What age group do you want to teach?

1. Adults

2. Teenagers:
   Girls
   Boys
   Mixed (in classes without fitting)

3. Children

Teaching Children

Teaching children to sew is very rewarding and valuable to you and the student. Young children get so excited with their own success and achievements. You will see them learning and growing before your very eyes. Children 4 years and older can begin to master sewing skills. The skill level and the amount of time to achieve the learning experience is the most important part of this class. Also the number of students per teacher must be limited to a maximum of 10. Use your own judgment on how many 4-, 5-, and 6-year-olds you can control in a group situation. Remember their attention span is very short. Also they are too young to know the etiquette of group learning. You must set the rules and begin to teach them group participation, listening, and sharing.

*"When I began teaching, a teacher told me that a good rule of thumb is to figure it will take an adult **three times longer** than it took me to make something, and a child **five to six times longer**. That tip has helped me tremendously."*

Nancy Lovett
Palmer/Pletsch teacher training graduate
October 1992

There are many good sewing programs available designed specifically for teaching children, such as Kids Can Sew, Kid Sew (Primary Patterns), and, for children as young as 5, The Winky Cherry System of Teaching Young Children to Sew.

If you love children, Winky's program is one of the easiest to teach. It is an ideal course to offer after school. You could teach two one-hour classes a day and charge by the month. At 5 and 6, both boys and girls are interested. Preparation is minimal compared to sewing model garments for adult classes. Also, you don't need to deal with sewing machines at these young ages. You'll just need to take a supply basket to a school or other location in which you are teaching.

Also, the program is wonderful in that it helps mold responsible young children. Parents will be behind you 100% because you are reinforcing many desirable qualities through sewing.

The program begins with hand sewing and continues on to introduce basic machine skills. Each level is part of a building block of skills. It is best to start at level one even if the child is 8. This child will quickly get through this level of hand sewing stuffed shapes, whereas a 5-year-old will hold an interest in hand sewing for a year or more.

Read Winky Cherry's teaching manual for **The Winky Cherry System of Teaching Young Children to Sew**. Watch her video containing all the information you need from equipment to rules for the classroom.

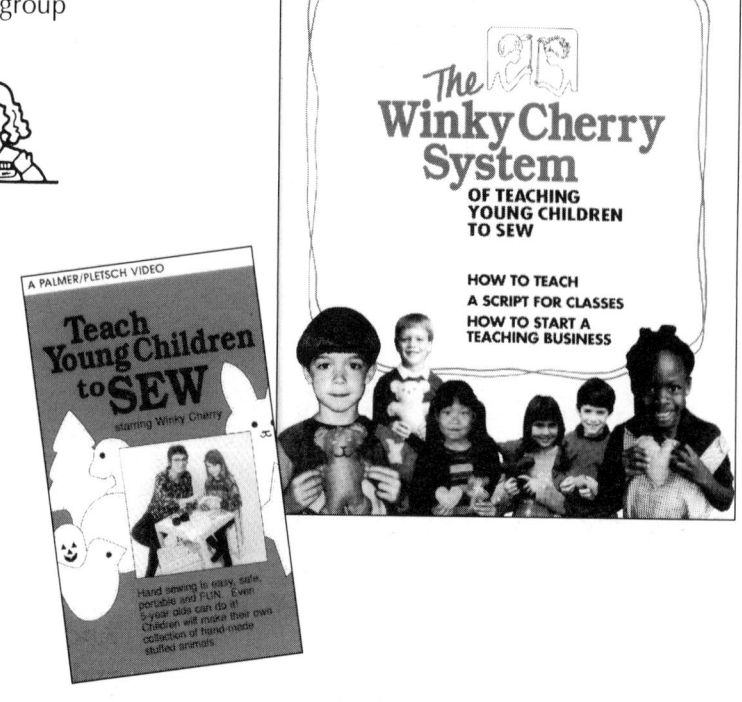

Also available from Palmer/Pletsch is a "Teacher Supply Kit," assembled with all the quality items needed to get you on your way in this process designed for 5- to 9-year-olds.

If you purchase the first kit with book, supply box, teaching manual and video, your total investment in your business is under $100. There is no franchise fee. This is a real bargain today. PLUS, you may qualify to purchase kits wholesale to include in classes or to sell for a profit if you are not teaching in a store.

Teaching Teenagers

Teaching teenagers has another set of challenges. Again attention span is the most important consideration. Most teenagers want to sew for the purpose of having something they want or need. Therefore, the class needs to be structured around these items. They usually are fashionable articles of clothing, carrying packs or satchels, or decorating items for their rooms.

Teaching teenagers is fun because of their enthusiasm and exuberance. It is the enthusiasm that needs to be channeled toward their project and controlled so that everyone has a good experience. The best way to manage this type of class is to have every moment filled with your showing and their doing. You, the teacher, need to help and supervise **ALL** of the time these students are working on their projects. Teenagers desire and require a lot of personal attention. If there are problem students, refund their money and politely ask them to leave.

These classes of children and teenagers are tomorrow's sewers. They will be students of yours again someday. It is your responsibility to inspire and motivate them to acquire this wonderful creative talent of sewing. Encourage them to be adventurous with their sewing and be proud of their accomplishments. It is self-esteem and confidence we are teaching our students as well as sewing skills.

Flyer for children

Flyers for teens

CHAPTER FIVE

When to Teach

"Your weekend may need to be Sunday and Monday. To be successful, you have to be available when your students are available."

Collect class schedules of local sewing machine dealers, fabric stores and craft shops. Note types, times and lengths of classes. Ask the store owners or managers what days and hours are best for classes. They will know this if they plan advertising. The first of the month is usually better timing for sales than the end of the month—that's when the paycheck arrives.

Fashion, of course, has seasons. Planning classes around wardrobe seasons is very effective. Spring/summer and fall/winter are logical ways to divide the year. Jackets, coats, suits and pants may do better in the fall. For summer or fall, consider Halloween costumes, holiday decorating and entertaining. Christmas and Hanukkah gifts make ideal mini classes or free lectures in the fall. Blouses, dresses, pants and shirts do well in the spring. Get ready for summer with sportswear, shorts and swimsuits.

Some topics are good throughout the year. Of those listed below, would you feel any are seasonal?

Wearable Art	Home Decorating
Exercise and Swimwear	Children's Wear
Sweats and Sweatsuits	Skiwear
Teen classes	Polar Fleece®

See the class-time reference chart on the next page for specific suggested topics and preferred times of year.

Time of Day

In some areas people are more available during the day, and in others, evenings are preferred. People available during the day usually prefer weekdays. The rest of the people often prefer Tuesday and Thursday evening or Saturdays.

Those who work outside the home usually have a more structured schedule. They will attend mostly on Saturdays and probably prefer the one-time lecture or workshop. They also will attend a series on a week night as long as the series is not too long. Probably one evening a week for three weeks would be the longest. A fourth week, if necessary, might work, but it could deter them from committing their time so far in advance.

Classes that range from four to eight weeks will usually have student absences. When students miss a class or two, they get behind or lost, so plan how they can make up what they miss. Most teachers do not hold a separate class for absentees.

The best solution might be to have the students come early or stay later at the next session. At that time you can discuss quickly what was covered in the session they missed. On a one-to-one basis, the student will hear better, see better and be able to move on in the class more easily. If the class missed was a particularly complicated subject, a second demonstration at the beginning of the next session probably would benefit everyone.

Blocks of time that are good for classes will depend on the location of the class. If you are in a retail store, store hours or shopping center hours will help determine the times. You will need to know opening and closing times. Also consider the parking facilities and whether they have a closing time when determining evening classes.

Best Times Weekday or Weekend

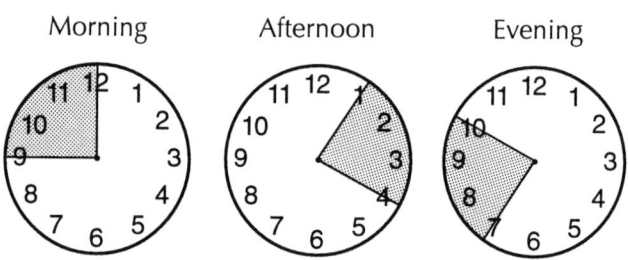

	Morning	Afternoon	Evening

Mornings: 9 am to Noon OR 10 am-12:30 pm
Afternoons: 1-4 pm OR 1:30-4 pm OR 12:30-3 (depends when school is out in some areas)
Evenings: 6:30-9:30 pm OR 7-10 pm for three-hour sessions; 7-9:30 pm for 2½-hour sessions (In large cities, it may be impossible to get to class until 7.)
All-day workshops: 9 am to 4 pm (allow a 45-minute lunch break)

Class Time Reference Chart:
Suggested Topics and Preferred Time of Year

February-March-April

Making a Spring Suit
tips on tailoring

Easter Parade Dresses
personal fit techniques

Dresses for Daughters
special feminine frills

Easy and Fashionable

April-May-June-July

Sew Fast & Easy Knits
knit techniques

**Beginners or Advanced New Casual
& Street Wear**
new fabric and designs

Hot Summer Wear
teens and beginners

Swimsuits with Splash
sewing Lycra® and swimsuit fabrics

Aug-Sept-Oct-Nov

The Four-Hour Jacket—Fit and Fast

Ultrasuede® & Ultraleather™
sew with confidence

Halloween Costumes
scary stuff for beginners and others

Holiday Gifts or Decorations

Serger Mania

January-February-March

Pillows of Perfection
types, styles and fabrics

Redecorate for the New Year
draperies, table covers, slipcovers

Outdoor Wear
ski clothes and fabrics;
tents and sleeping bags;
backpacks; sweat suits

Year 'Round

Hot, Active Aerobicwear

**Easy Fashion For Beginners,
Teen and Advanced Sewers**

Fit for Fashion

Pattern Fitting
fit a basic shell, then fashion garments

Pants for Anybody
fit a basic, sew a trouser

How to Choose Pattern and Fabric

Save Time and Sew Fast
shortcuts to cutting, fitting and sewing

Sewing with Sergers
various serger projects

Basic Fit

Pant Fit

CHAPTER SIX

Where to Teach

"Consider the 5 C's: Comfort, Cost, Convenience, Competition and Cooperation. All are part of your decision."

When planning a class and deciding where to hold it, think about your options. You may have many choices.

Your Home

If you want to teach in your home or if your home is your only option, consider the available space. Do you have a bedroom or family room that easily could be converted to a sewing classroom for a day—or forever? Would it hold 10 to 15 students for a lecture/demonstration or five to 10 for sit-and-sew? How many could attend a workshop at one time in your home? How would this affect your family and their routines?

Do you have a space with an outside entrance? What about parking and the neighbors? Have you checked zoning laws to see if you can teach in your home?

The most common room used for teaching is a spare bedroom or the corner of a family room or dining room. But the "ideal" place is a room with its own outside entrance and a bathroom nearby. It would be the least disrupting to your family. Also, you wouldn't have to have a spotlessly clean house.

You might have a basement, a garage or an auxiliary apartment attached to your house. These are ideal spaces to convert to a sewing and teaching studio.

Below is a simple layout from the Palmer/Pletsch book **Dream Sewing Spaces** by Lynette Ranney Black. The sketch below is of a dining room area converted to a teaching area by Palmer/Pletsch teacher training graduate, Bette Wilson from Tucson, Arizona.

If you teach in your home, you can keep interfacings and a few convenience notions available for sale. In a city where there are many fabric stores, however, this may not be worth the investment.

Can you turn a garage or bonus room into a teaching/sewing studio?

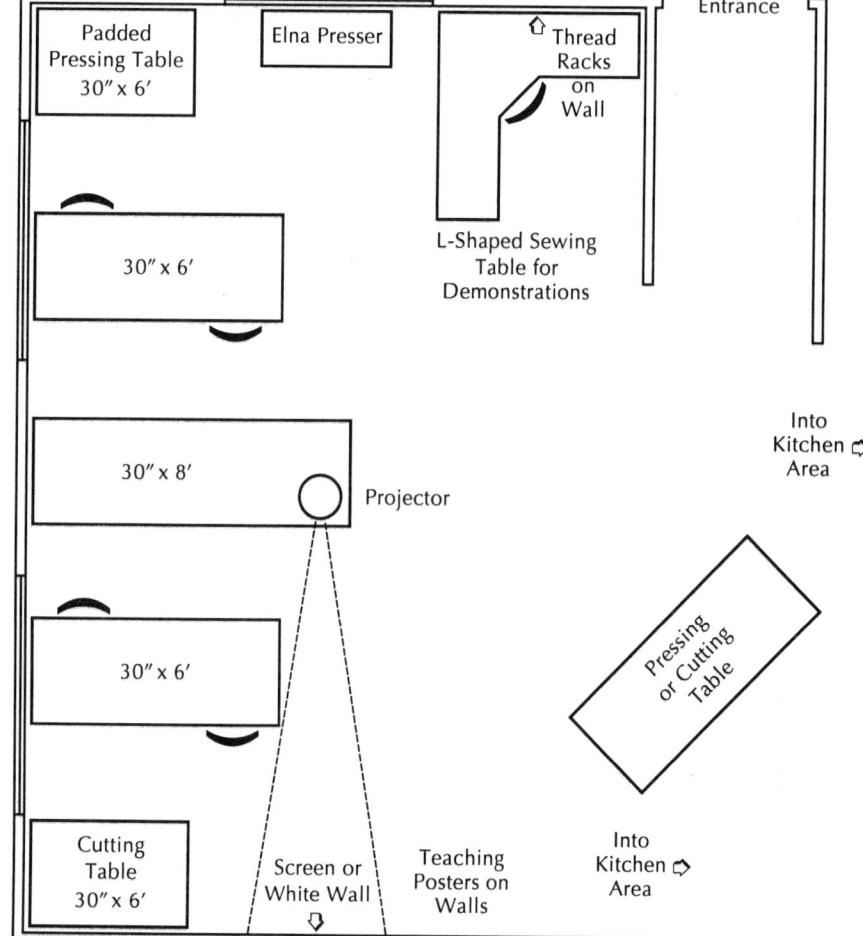

Padded Pressing Table 30" x 6'

Elna Presser

⇧ Thread Racks on Wall

Entrance

L-Shaped Sewing Table for Demonstrations

30" x 6'

30" x 8'

Projector

Into Kitchen ⇨ Area

30" x 6'

Pressing or Cutting Table

Into Kitchen ⇨ Area

Cutting Table 30" x 6'

Screen or White Wall ⇩

Teaching Posters on Walls

If you are in a town with NO FABRIC STORES, you can buy from a wholesaler and set up your own mini store to help your students and to make extra money. NOTE: Some wholesalers may require that you have a resale licence before they sell to you.

The main advantage of teaching in your home is convenience and comfort. You will have no commute or lugging of equipment or samples. You can have refreshments available for students in your kitchen. You may also have some tax advantages.

The main disadvantage is that you'll have to work harder to get started. You'll need to get your word-of-mouth machine going. You'll need helpful friends and community resources. Enlist local fabric stores to help spread the word for you, too. After all, you are developing sewing customers for them.

Fabric Stores

You might hold your class in a favorite fabric store. Being in a store gives you very good exposure for attracting new students and provides the store with more business. Many stores have ongoing classes and mailing lists of students who enjoy taking classes.

A problem for many stores today, especially the chains, is that they do not have a private room in which to teach. While researching local fabric stores, speak with the manager about your plans for classes. He or she may be willing to create a semi-private, *screened* space for you. Such a space should be out of a major traffic area. Place chairs around you and your demonstration to help reduce noise. You can screen off an area using sound-absorbing dividers, but you will lack some privacy. If you are teaching a serging class, this may not be a problem, but for a fit class it would.

If you use a stockroom, it can be dusty, rustic, and unprofessional. Decide if it can be easily upgraded for use as an occasional classroom.

An employee lunchroom makes a nice classroom space. You could even have hot or cold drinks available. But it would inconvenience the employees, your best promoters.

The fabric store owner's motivation for holding your classes is to increase business by building traffic, selling more product and enhancing goodwill. In exchange, you could ask the management to promote your classes in their store or include them in their advertising. You also might ask if they would be willing to promote your classes to their mailing list. If they don't want the cost, are you willing to pay for it yourself? Then you might ask if you could have a set of labels. Be careful in asking for this because these names are a valuable part of the store's assets. Owners many not be willing to give them out.

Some stores will want a small percentage of the class fee (10-20% is fair) to cover their extra overhead expenses, especially if they handle registration. Add that amount to your fees and see if the price of the class is still saleable. If YOU handle EVERYTHING including registration, chairs, tables, and equipment, stores may be willing to donate the use of the space at no charge. See Chapter 7 for more on money.

If you are lecturing in a retail outlet, **you cannot sell products** directly. The retailer will be responsible for this. Mini-demos or classes that promote the store's products make you more beneficial to the store.

Survey the store's inventory and include their fabric, patterns, equipment, notions and books in your classes. **You can sell ANYTHING YOU BELIEVE IN!** If the store doesn't carry a favorite notion, ask if they would. **NEVER sell your own products direct to the customer when in a store unless the store doesn't want to buy the product and has pre-agreed to let you sell it.**

The more profit the classes generate for the store, the more classes you will teach for that sponsor. You need to be and feel as valuable to the sponsor as they are to you. See Chapter 10, Teaching Techniques, for more specifics. Also, see Chapter 14 for ways to sell yourself to stores.

Sewing Machine Dealers

Sewing machine dealers sell one or more brands and generally offer service on all brands. Most dealers have a following of customers who continue to upgrade their machines and techniques. And sewing machine manufacturers encourage their dealers to hold classes to help customers make better use of their machines and to promote accessories and new machine models. This practice provides an enthusiastic group of potential students for classes.

Sewing machine dealers will love your classes that use their machines to the fullest, show what the latest equipment can do and sell accessories. **It takes a special owner to appreciate the goodwill created by classes that are not machine-based.** For example, fit and pant fit may not include sewing. Ask, "Are you willing to provide a wide range of classes that will make your customers better sewers, including classes that may not always focus on a machine?"

Much of what we have said about fabric stores applies here. However, sewing machine stores have a few special considerations.

You will need to use a store's brands of sewing machines, sergers, knitting machines, presses, etc. for your classes. **Become very familiar with the equipment you will be using.** Fumbling with unfamiliar machines causes you to appear unqualified and incompetent. It also makes the machine look difficult to understand or use—which does not help you, the store owner or the student. Possibly the owner will loan you a machine until you become familiar with it. After all, if you like the machine, you will be the best salesperson. You may also be offered a special purchase price for the store's equipment because it is always best for you to own what they sell. If you can't stand their brand, you'd better not teach for them!

Avoid discussing other brands of machines. Be sure to ask the store owners their opinion about discussing other brands. Your students may have questions regarding other machines. Generally, you are safe if you answer questions positively and without bias toward any machine manufacturer. Being negative about brands not carried by the dealer doesn't create goodwill either. If you can't be positive or at least neutral, say nothing! **The best way to promote a dealer's products is to say you own them!** That speaks for itself!

Other Public Places

A class, seminar or workshop can be held in many other places, such as churches, community rooms and libraries. Survey the area and locate what will work for you. Consider working through sewing and craft guilds, parks and recreation departments, county extension agents and community colleges.

If you are having a one-day workshop and you are responsible for all the physical requirements, think about the extra effort that may be required for setup, cleanup, move-in, and move-out. For example, you might not want to select a second-floor location.

If possible, find a room at no charge or with a minimum cleanup fee. This will help keep your expenses down and keep the class fee more reasonable so you can attract more students. These places may not have tables, chairs, stages, microphones, screens or other physical requirements, so you would need to find an outside source, preferably one that delivers and picks up. Here again, what is the cost? Do you have time, a vehicle or someone to help you with this?

Money questions are important to resolve when securing a public place. Some organizations have regulations on charging and collecting money on the premises. Do they allow you to charge a fee to your students? Can you collect on the premises? Can you sell items at the class? If a not-for-profit group rents or loans part of their property and you teach for a profit, you may be in violation of their tax status. This can be resolved by requiring all registrants to pay you or your sponsor ahead of time.

Community colleges and recreational districts publish a catalog or calendar of events with dates and times, and handle registration and collection of fees. For most of their classes, they pay an hourly fee for the number of hours of teaching time. It is often less than if you taught independently and handled your own promotions, but it saves you time. And they usually take care of class needs for space, tables, chairs, projectors, screen, and microphones. Most allow for cancellation if a class doesn't reach a minimum size.

If you have a unique program, you might be able to set your own fee. Set a minimum class size so the college doesn't lose money. The minimum would cover your fees and their expenses.

Hotels

Meeting rooms in many hotels are convenient and easy-to-use for your classes. The hotel supplies chairs, tables, screens and microphones, and the staff helps you move in and set up. Check for adequate electrical outlets if you are planning a sit-and-sew class. Because the rooms are private, with draperies that can be closed, hotels are ideal for fit classes and slide programs.

Hotel policies vary, so get rates and options in writing when you make reservations. Some hotels will provide the room at no charge or for a small fee if lunch is included. Then figure that lunch charge into your class fee.

The Perfect Classroom

See Chapter 10 for how-tos on setting up a classroom in a variety of locations and for different purposes. There are different challenges between lecture and hands-on classes. There are definitely challenges if you must teach on the selling floor of a store and need quiet and privacy.

See Chapter 8 for a variety of class formats, from short, free demonstrations that are best held on a store's sales floor to paid classes that require more privacy.

CHAPTER SEVEN
Money

A MESSAGE TO TEACHERS:
"Don't make money your goal. Do what you love and do it WELL. The money will follow."

A MESSAGE TO RETAILERS:
"Allow teachers to make money teaching. Only then will more strive to be teachers and help your business grow."

Set an income goal for a year. Then your challenge will be to decide how many classes you can teach and whether you can charge enough to meet that goal. Teaching is ideal as a "part-time" job, yet many have made it their full-time income.

The difficulty in relying on teaching as steady full-time income is that there are times of the year it is difficult to fill classes. For example, you may have to switch to teaching teens in the summer. December is another challenging month. Maybe it just becomes your vacation time. Also, the smaller the market, the more versatile you may need to be in the number of subjects you can teach. Offer a variety of topics to keep enticing the same people to return.

If you need to teach the same topic five times a week to earn the money you want to earn, it may not be possible to fill all classes in a sparsely populated area. You may have to travel around to fill this many classes. Consider the extra expenses you'll incur. Still, sparsely populated areas usually have good attendance because there is little competition from other activities.

Specialization

In a large market, it may be easy for you to specialize—allowing you to become faster and better. You become known for your specialty.

For example, a Certified Palmer/Pletsch Pant Fitting Instructor specializes in pants, but does more than teach. She also does the following:

1. Custom sews pants.
2. Custom fits pant patterns for others to sew.
3. Gives pant-fitting slide/lectures for large audiences as a way of promoting small hands-on classes.
4. Teaches hands-on trouser fitting and sewing.

Other related teaching options are:
1. Teen summer classes where boys and girls sew pull-on shorts.
2. Plus-size pant classes.
3. Pull-on pant classes.
4. Skirt classes (easy to teach once you've mastered pants). Make a pull-on skirt in "Learn To Sew in a Day."

Research the Market

It is important to know what is already being taught in your area, where, and how much is being charged. If you want to offer a competing class, you may need to be better or less expensive than the competition, or far enough away, to generate students.

Research the market by picking up flyers, schedules or calendars of classes being offered by local fabric and craft stores. Note the descriptions and fees being charged. Keep these in a file for your reference. Get to know other teachers. You just may be able to promote each other!

An Easy Income Formula

Define what you want or need to earn, then see if it is practical. "I want to earn $2,000 every month. I can teach two topics each month in a series of four sessions. Therefore, I will need to sign up 25 people per topic for a total of 50 students at $40 each (50 X $40 = $2,000)."

If these sessions are 2 hours each, that is $5 per instructor hour for your students to pay ($40 ÷ 8 hours = $5/hr). Is that a realistic amount to charge? Ask yourself, "Can I do this? Is this enough?" **Remember, all of your costs will have to come out of this amount of money.**

Start by setting a realistic goal. Accomplish that, then set a higher one. You can always charge less in the beginning to get started, then raise your prices as you become more experienced and in demand.

Time & Expenses

Although a person in an 8-to-5 job may feel good about making $10 an hour, you need to make $25 to $50 an hour for **actual teaching time** to cover your nonpaid time and nonpaid benefits (those which an employer pays). You need to cover your time for preparation, organization, setup, marketing and promotion for each class. You also will have an investment in equipment, samples, posters, slides, model garments, printing, forms, gas, etc. In addition, you may have decided to invest in your own education. All of these need to have a value placed on them as part of your business.

What is Involved in Nonpaid Time?
- Writing the lesson plan
- Shopping for products for samples and model garments
- Making samples and model garments
- Organizing and/or producing slides
- Creating and writing the outline
- Assembling kits unless a kit fee is charged
- Preparing and printing handouts
- Locating the space
- Setup time, class time and pack-up time
- Travel time
- Marketing and promotion
- Communication with sponsor

How to Get More Out of Your Preparation Time
- Teach the same class more than once.
- Promote all the times you are offering the same class in one season on the same flyer.
- Make technique samples with great care so they can be used for many years.
- Build many techniques into each model garment so you can make less and show more.

What Expenses Will You Have to Cover?
- Equipment purchases
- Sewing supplies for demonstration, samples or model garments
- Products you plan to demonstrate, books, kits
- Printing and duplicating handouts (such as lists of suggested fabrics, interfacings, pattern numbers or techniques), flyers and posters
- Advertising postage
- Cost of space (unless free)
- Cost of slide program, whether purchasing slides or making your own
- Gas for car

Calculating Expenses
The FEE per student per class depends on many variables: **the costs involved, the number of times taught and the number of students attending.** The class has to be worth the fee! A $20 fee may be too high for a 2-hour lecture. Make the class more valuable...with good-quality handouts and samples.

To lower the FEE PER STUDENT, increase the number of students taught or consider charging a separate fee for supplies, often called a kit fee.

If you repeat the same class more than once, preparation time and expense can be amortized over all the classes. Most classes can be taught an unlimited number of times if you continue to update information and visuals. Some classes are seasonal and cannot be reused until next year.

The example below and on the next page gives you an idea of how much time and money could be invested in a project or class.

Pricing

Pricing has no hard and fast rules. We just want to make sure you are "valuing" your time and considering your expenses.

A Simple Pricing Calculation
Use the guidelines Palmer/Pletsch offers during teacher training: A very simple way of calculating an **average** fee is to charge $6 per hour of instruction per student. Here is an example:

A series of 4 classes, each 3 hours long
equals 12 hours of class time.
12 hours X $6/hour = $72 series fee
(fee you could charge per student for the class series)

This is only a guide. If you take 20 students and they sew at home, you might need to drop the fee. If you take only 10 students and it is a hands-on class with personal attention, you might be able to charge a lot more.

To find out how much could you make, calculate a variety of fees and numbers of students just to get an idea. Then offer what you think will sell.

Some Examples:

A hands-on class:

$80 fee X 10 students = $800
(your income for the series)
If the series contains 12 teaching hours, divide
$800 by 12. You are making $66 per hour
of actual teaching time. The student is paying
$6.66 per hour of class time.

Would you do a better job teaching five students in a hands-on class and be happy making $33 per teaching hour? **Often it is better to start smaller and grow as you gain experience!**

A lecture class:

$30 fee X 20 students = $600 (your income for the series)

If your actual teaching time is 12 hours, divide $600 by 12 and you are making $50 per hour of teaching time. The student is paying $2.50 per hour of class. Can you get more or less than $30 for this class in your market?

Again, even though the rate per hour of teaching time sounds high, remember it needs to cover your actual expenses as well as your preparation and promotion time and your unpaid benefits.

More Pricing Examples

Three 2½-hour sessions (7½ hours total) for $45/student X 10 students = $450

Four 2-hour sessions (8 hours total) for $48/student X 10 students = $480

Six 2-hour sessions (12 hours total) for $72/student X 10 students = $720

Six 2½-hour sessions (15 hours total) for $90/student X 10 students = $900

One 7-hour session (7 hours total) for $65/student X 5 students = $325

Remember, your experience, size of class (perceived individual attention), and geographical area will determine the price.

Another Way to Calculate Pricing

For the purpose of calculating labor, we'll use the cost of preparation time at $15 per hour and the cost of actual teaching time at $50 per hour. You may want to adjust these according to your experience and geographic area.

Just to give you perspective, $10 per hour is equal to about $20,000 per year if working 40 hours per week with no vacation time. $15 per hour is equivalent to about $30,000 per year without benefits.

Amortizing Class Costs

When you teach a class many times, you can spread out the costs.

Preparation and expenses:

30 hours @ $15 per hour =	$450
Expenses =	$350
COST OF CLASS	**$800**

Divide the total of $800 by the number of times you have scheduled the class. For example, you have scheduled the same class eight times:

$800 divided by 8 = $100
(expense cost per class)

ACTUAL COSTS OF EACH CLASS

Example:

2 hours @ $50 =	$100
(class length X teaching rate)	
Car costs =	$40
Portion of Prep Costs =	$100
TOTAL	$240

Now determine the FEE per student:
Divide the total of $240 (your costs per class) by the number of students you can teach per class. If it is 20, divide the cost per class by this number:

$240 divided by 20 = $12.00/class/student

If this is a series of four classes, the total class fee for the series would be 4 X $12.00 or $48 for eight hours of instruction. Ideally, this would be the minimum you could charge to cover your time and the preparation costs. Some may be able to charge more and others may have to settle for less.

Interestingly, this comes very close to the Palmer/Pletsch formula of $6/hr. of instruction per student. Use it as an easy guide.

Agreement Forms

A teaching professional needs a **simple but proper** agreement form. Do not call it a "contract" because strong legal terms often intimidate sponsors. This form should include:

- Name of class
- Type of class (lecture, demo, workshop, etc.)
- Specified dates of class
- Teaching fee—per student or per class
- Description of your responsibilities
- Description of sponsor responsibilities
- Cancellation policy
- Signature of responsible parties

Examples of Palmer/Pletsch Agreement forms are on the next page. A camera-ready form for your use can be found in Chapter 18. Use a separate form for each class. Include different dates for the same class on the same form. Use your letterhead, keep it simple and fill in the appropriate information about your classes.

Collecting Fees

Some people find it difficult to ask for money. Lawyers bill for their services, so why shouldn't you? Your time and talent have value, so don't be embarrassed to charge for them just because you love what you do. Remember, your customers choose to spend money on flowers, restaurant meals, ballet for the children and myriad other things. They have options when it comes to spending their money, and you might as well be one of them. People can justify anything they feel will make them a better person. Think of what all of your students will gain in inspiration, information and personal development under your guidance!

Generally, requiring full payment when students register for a class will encourage them to show up. Collect payment from your sponsor either at the beginning or when you have finished the class, depending on what you and your students or sponsor have agreed on. If the class is just one session and you're charging your sponsor based on the attendance, prepare your invoice in advance, leaving a space for the fee-per-student calculation. At the end of the class, present your invoice to the sponsor and collect.

If the class is a series, you may ask your sponsor for half of the tuition before the class begins and the remainder midway through or at the end of the series.

If you have specified a registration cutoff date, you could mail your invoice to the sponsor at that time. Either way, be sure you and the sponsor agree when you will collect payment.

If you are teaching a distance from home, never leave without being paid or you may never see the money! Unfortunately, this has happened occasionally. Sometimes the store is not doing well financially and the fees collected go to pay bills. Then the sponsor finds he or she can't pay you even though that was the intention. Depending on the sponsor's size and sophistication, you might suggest a separate account for class tuition be set up to ensure the money is available to pay you when the class is completed.

To simplify record keeping, prepare your invoice (see sample below), and agreement form, in duplicate—one for your records and one for your sponsor. When you receive the signed agreement from the sponsor, file it under "Pending Classes." Upon completion of the class, prepare the invoice, attach your copy to the agreement form and collect your payment. Mark the invoice paid when you receive payment. Then file the two forms under "Income—Classes," and you'll be ready for tax time.

More Ways to Enhance Your Income

If you are teaching fashion sewing, why not consider becoming an image consultant? With many of the image companies, you can earn income from color consulting, makeup and body analysis. Two companies with which we are most familiar are in Chapter 17, Resources. If this interests you, research the companies and see if you have what it takes.

Other sidelines you might consider include home-based jewelry selling, custom bra fitting and, of course, custom sewing.

Volunteering is another way to enhance your income. Yes, be a speaker for a woman's group, lead a 4-H club or offer makeovers for battered women. Or get involved in a variety of professional groups or fund-raising activities. All of these opportunities enable you to meet people who might take your classes or use your other services.

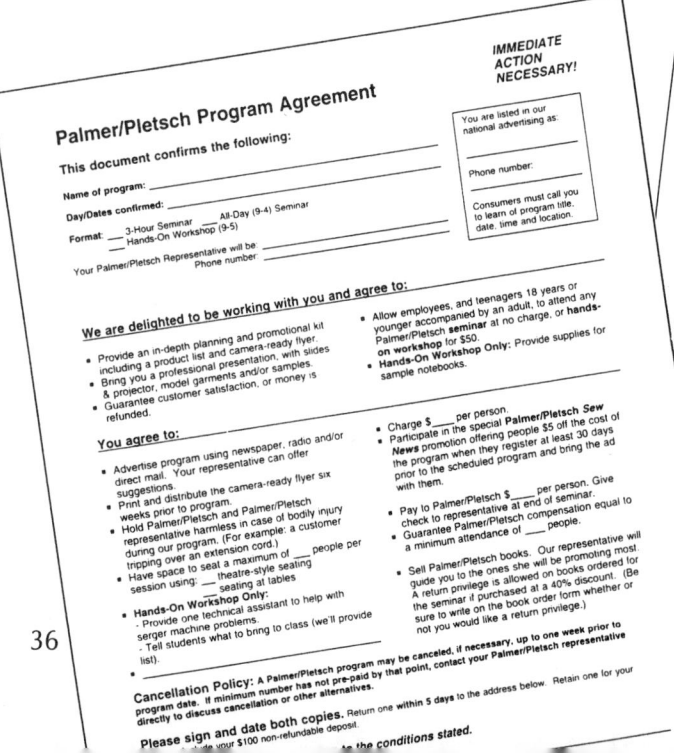

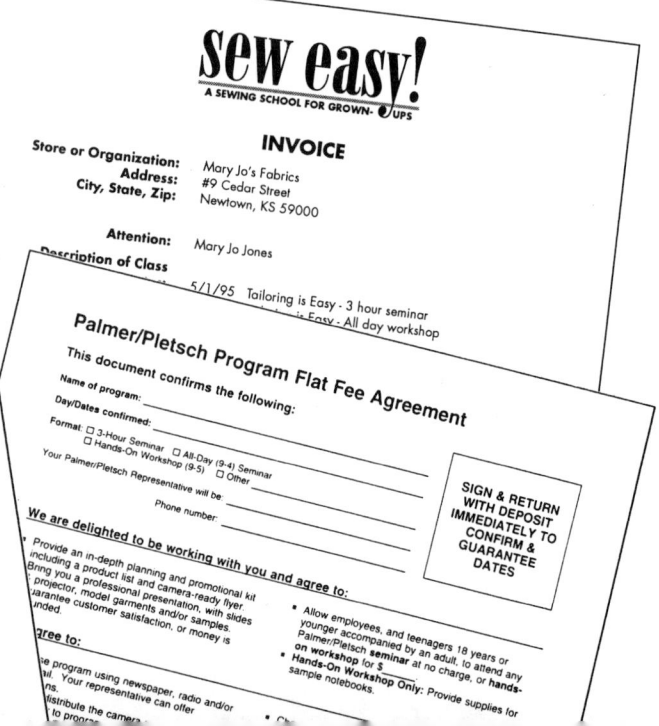

CHAPTER EIGHT

Class Formats

"If you can teach all formats comfortably, you are on the road to success."

Will your programs be lecture or lecture/demonstration seminars or hands-on workshops? Will they be one-time classes or a series? How long will each session be? Will they be free or paid sessions? These are a few of the decisions to make.

Free Formats

For promotional purposes, offer a 20-minute free lecture or demonstration to store employees. A 30-minute or one-hour free lecture is ideal for a guild, club, or consumer show. Give a great lecture and you'll fill classes that follow. Since this lecture is to promote you and your other classes, it must be perfect in every way. Show a technique you plan to teach in an upcoming class. Be sure to tell observers what else they will learn in your class. Remember, however, that your audience did not come to hear an "advertisement," so plan your message carefully and keep the program educational.

Make your visuals high-quality, clear and easy-to-see. Have several oversized samples in many fabrics and colors for the audience to examine. The attendees will determine the quality of your teaching by the quality of this free lecture. For information on physical setup, see Chapter 13, Classroom Setup.

Ideas for Free Demos

New and Not-So-New Nifty Notions
Sew Easy Tips
Mini or Maxi Ruffles
Perfect Points and Corners
Custom Serger Piping
Sew Up Some Scraps
Getting Ready to Sew
Buttons, Buttons Everywhere
No-Hassle Zippers
No-Show Fly Zipper
Fusing without Frustration
Perfect Pressing: How to Use Equipment
Buttonholes by Machine
Tailored/Designer Buttonholes
Pockets (a specific type—welt,
     double-welt, patch)
Handstitching and Hemming
Placemats and Napkins
Designer Looks from EASY Patterns
Accessories
Speed or Time-Saving Tips
What's New in Fitting
Teaching Young Children to Sew

Be prepared to sign people up for your future classes. Have registration forms handy as well as sign-up sheets for mailing lists. The following forms are found full-size in Chapter 18, Camera-Ready Forms.

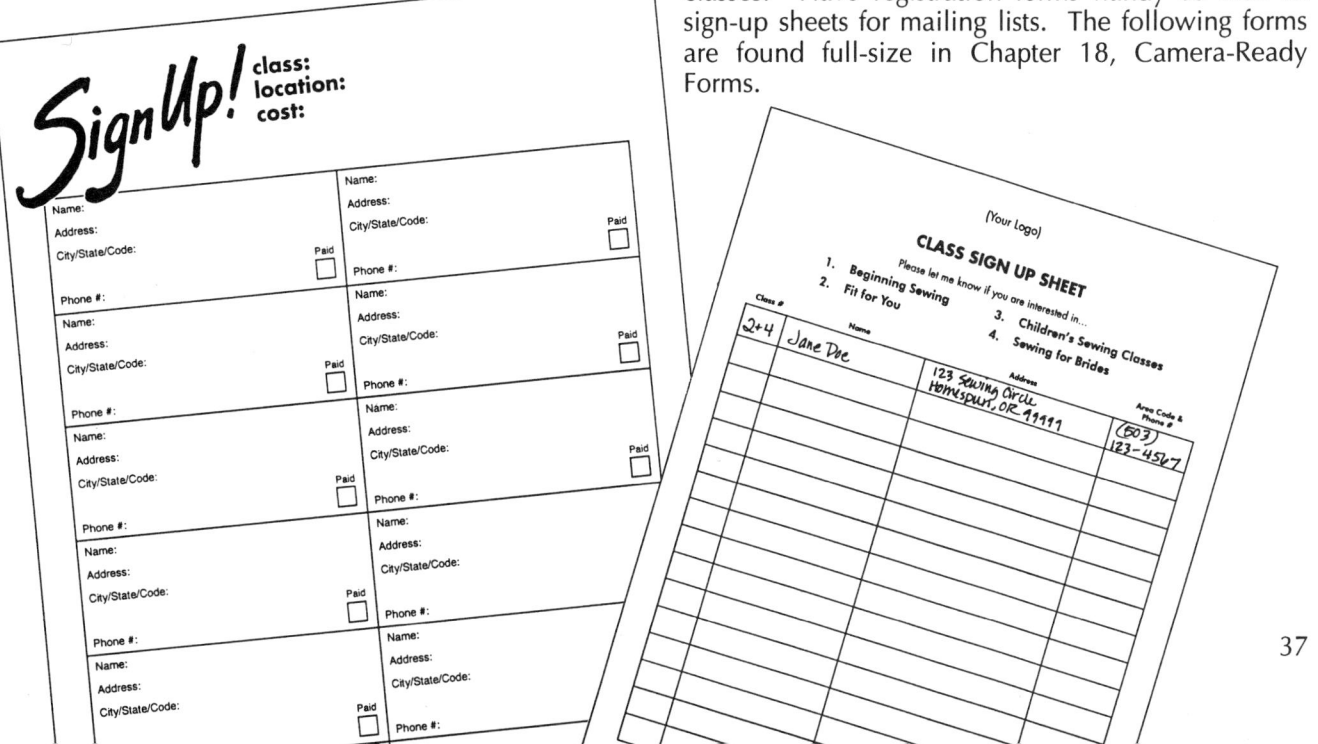

Besides promoting specific classes, solicit information from your audience. Provide a list of potential class topics and let them write down their interests. When you call them later, you can steer them into the classes that are filling or the ones closest to their requests. The time spent will be worth it. Use our Classes by Request form, shown full-size in Chapter 18, Camera-Ready Forms.

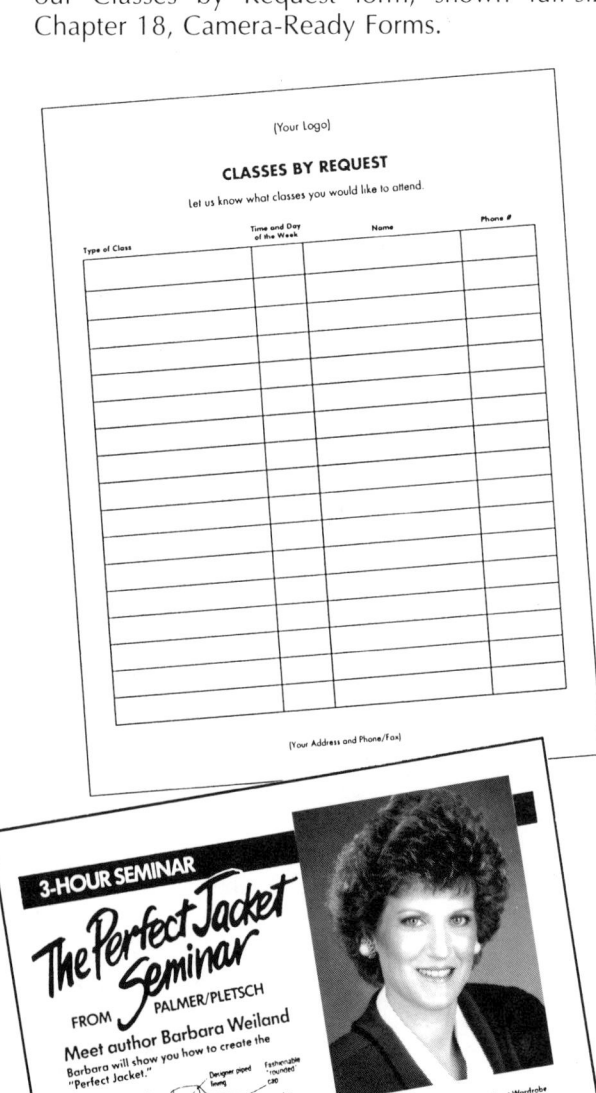

Paid Formats

Seminar—Lecture

"Seminar" implies one session. Lecture implies no sewing in class. A seminar can accommodate many more students than a demonstration or a hands-on sit-and-sew. Therefore, it is usually priced less expensively than other formats. It can be one to three hours in length or all day. You may have posters, model garments and samples to display or pass around. If you use slides, you can accommodate an even larger audience. Limit the size of the group, though, to what the audience is able to see and hear. Set your fee based on the class length, content and the size of the group you want. To draw a large audience, choose a general topic and make the fee reasonable. If you charge $7.50 per person for a two-hour seminar and 100 people come, you make $750. **If a class is too inexpensive, though, people can become suspicious. Don't undervalue a class.**

Seminar—Lecture/Demonstration

This is a one-session class where YOU lecture and demonstrate sewing techniques. Such a class is usually three to six hours in length. Limit the audience size so they can clearly see your demonstrations. For physical requirements, see Chapter 13, Classroom Setup.

Make samples "larger than life" to exaggerate the technique for easy viewing—that is, unless your samples are home decorating projects. Window coverings, bed skirts and the like, obviously, must be made in mini form to conserve space. The same is true for many outdoor projects, such as tents and sleeping bags.

Series—Lecture/Demonstration

"Series" indicates that classes are held over a several-week period. A workable series today is four weeks of 2½-hour classes. In the early '70s, people would sign up for eight weeks, but today, people seem reluctant to commit that far out. The advantage of a series is that students have more one-on-one time with you. In exchange, you can develop a loyal clientele that will sign up for other classes.

A series can consist of lecture only, but a lecture/demonstration is more effective. Your students take notes as they listen to you and watch you sew and/or fit. They sew their own projects at home. If they are sewing garments, you assist with fitting, too. Plan ahead to be prepared for each session. The larger the class, the more step-by-step, pass-around visuals you will need to prepare. Small groups (fewer than 10) can simply stand around a machine and watch you. **In any series, keep a complete calendar record of your activities and what you wear to each class.**

Series—Hands-On

"Hands-on" series implies STUDENTS sew in class. Sessions are two to three hours in length and the series is two to six weeks long.

Students need room to cut, press and sew. Decide if students will bring their own machines or if you (or your sponsor) will provide them. Pressing equipment is needed, as is space with a mirror if fitting is involved.

The first time you teach a hands-on class, you may want to limit the attendance to as few as three to five students. **You want "word of mouth" to work FOR you, not against you.** With experience, though, most teachers can handle a maximum of 10 students effectively. We know one expert who limits all her hands-on classes to three people, but charges a premium. She sells the quality of her instruction and the individual attention she is able to provide in such a small group.

Regardless of size, you are giving much more personal attention in a hands-on class, so you can charge more per student. Use the top of our "average" price range guidelines in Chapter 7, Money.

Hands-On Workshop

"Workshop" implies one all-day session or several consecutive all-day sessions. Since it is hands-on, students sew in class under your supervision. Allow six or seven hours each day with breaks for snacks and meals.

For the hands-on series, limit attendance to as few as three to five students the first time you teach this format and increase to 10 students as you gain experience and confidence. Set the class fee to reflect the time involved and the results to be achieved.

Because you and your students are in the room together all day, space organization plays a big part in the workshop's success. Plan work stations according to the needs of the activities that will take place. A quilting workshop, for example, has different requirements from a garment-sewing workshop. For more information, see Chapter 13, Classroom Setup.

Open Sewing Lab

If you're a very seasoned sewing teacher, one of the best ideas is to invite people to sew the projects of their choice under your supervision. Usually such a class meets once a week, and can go on indefinitely. A good time for people with families is 10 a.m. to 3 p.m., but shorter evening sessions are another option.

Because students are sewing on any project they want, you must be skilled enough to tackle most sewing and fitting challenges. When you're just starting out, limit the sewing lab to six students. If you demonstrate a technique, all students may want to watch even though the technique is being used by only one person.

Sit-and-sew labs are usually paid by the month, with fees collected at the beginning of each month. Set your fee according to your skill level and your clientele's ability to pay for your service. A reasonable fee is $15 to $20 per student per session.

CHAPTER NINE

The Lesson Plan

"A lesson plan can come from the table of contents of a good sewing book."

Outline Each Class

Create an outline for each class, describing in detail the order of your class and what and when slides, samples or model garments will be used. At the end of this chapter, we are including an **ACTION-BASED** outline for one class. This will give you a format to use.

When you actually teach the class, keep your outline handy, but try not to read it. Instead, place your visuals in the order they will be shown. These become your "notes," leading you to lecture in the proper order.

A book's table of contents is often a lesson plan. The following are some examples:

Beginning or Brush-up Sewing:

Tailoring:

Table of Contents

Basic Serging:

Table of Contents

TABLE OF CONTENTS

TABLE OF CONTENTS

Wardrobe Planning:

Clothes Sense
by Barbara Weiland
and Leslie Wood

STRAIGHT TALK ABOUT
WARDROBE PLANNING

Pant:

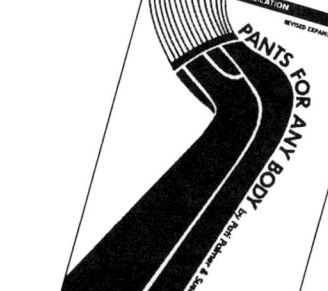

PANTS FOR ANY BODY
REVISED EXPANDED EDITION
A PALMER/PLETSCH PUBLICATION

Table of Contents

Couture:

Palmer/Pletsch
COUTURE
THE ART OF FINE SEWING

BY
ROBERTA
C. CARR

Table of Contents

41

In addition to using a book's table of contents as a guide, use a pattern's guidesheet. It is often a ready-made lesson plan. Palmer/Pletsch guidesheets for their McCall Pattern Co. designs also include many tips.

The guidesheet itself can help you determine where to start and stop each class. Add to the guidesheet extra techniques you will demonstrate. You might want to cut it up and paste it onto 8½" X 11" paper for easier photocopying. Make the guidesheet a roadmap for your class.

Making costumes for Halloween would be an excellent place to use a guidesheet as a lesson plan. Another might be a class on pillows or other home decorating items.

A good technique for testing or evaluating your lesson plan is to have potential students review it. And if you know other sewing professionals, seek their advice. It is very important to listen to what they tell you—the novice *and* the professional. Correcting a small or large flaw in your plan, in the beginning, will result in a smoother, more successful class.

If you are not an experienced teacher, schedule a limited-size class the first time you teach it. With a smaller class size, you will be more at ease and able to solve any minor problems that might arise.

One of the hard things in teaching is knowing how long to make a class. Some teachers have found it will take an adult student three times longer than it would take the teacher to make something and a child five to six times longer.

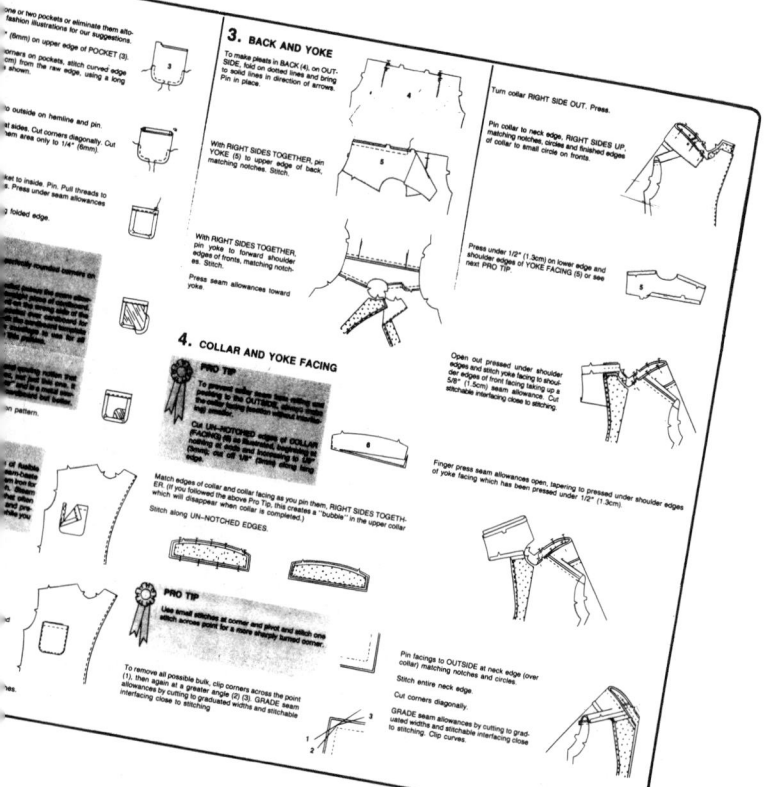

Outline for Creating a Lesson Plan

1. **Determine objective: "What am I teaching?"**
2. **Write detailed, step-by-step description for meeting the objective.**
3. **At each step, note use of technique: visuals, demo, slides, samples.**
4. **When technique is difficult, or difficult to demonstrate, plan to repeat two or three times.**
5. **Plan for questions and/or allow for personal one-on-one help.**
6. **Provide tips and references regarding objective.**
7. **Ask for student evaluations. Use a general form and collect them at the end of class or series.**
8. **Evaluate yourself. Compile student evaluations. Analyze your plan. Revise as necessary.**

Use a pattern guidesheet as an outline for a class. The top example is McCall's 3-Hour Shirt #5781 and at the bottom is their 1-Hour Skirt #7244.

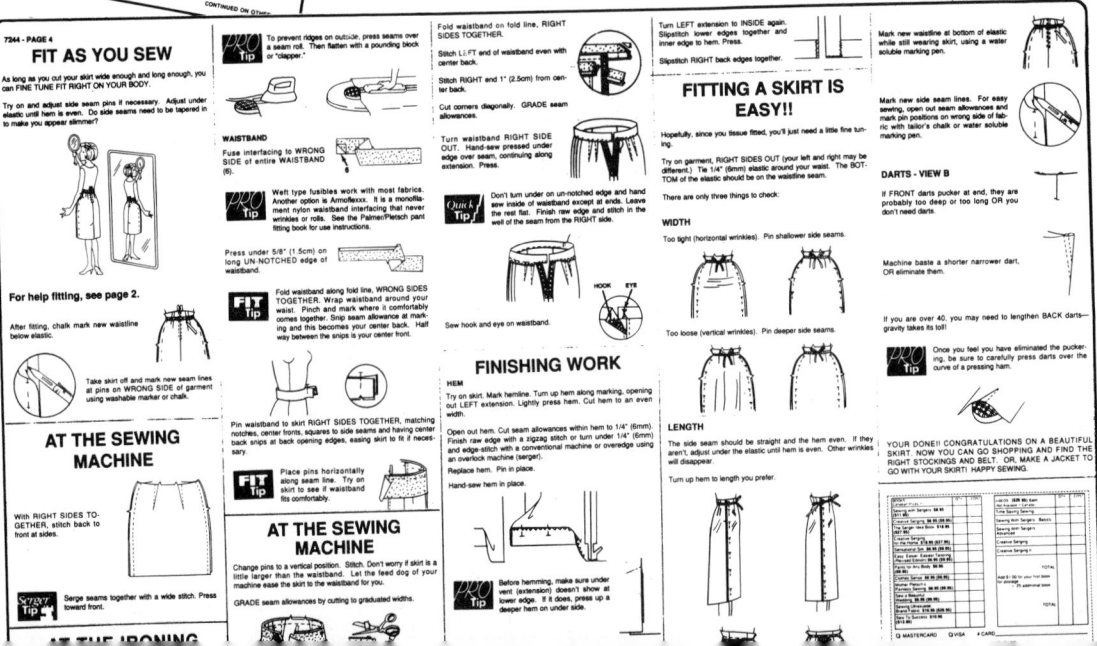

SAMPLE ACTION-BASED LESSON PLAN:
Successful Beginnings Workshop

On the next page is a lesson plan for a one-day beginners' workshop. It is designed for one teacher to instruct six to eight students, depending on space available. Marcy can do this workshop in her home easily with four. It becomes more difficult to move about and to hold their attention with six.

This workshop is designed for the student who has never been exposed to sewing or a sewing machine. They can "try out" sewing to see if they enjoy it before they invest in equipment. They need not own a sewing machine. It is an ideal class for sewing machine dealers to offer.

This class was planned for adults, who usually know how to participate in a group activity. Teenagers need more supervision.

The fabric and pattern for a pull-on skirt are provided by the instructor. Let students select a rayon or poly-rayon gaberdine (usually under $10/yd and 60" wide) in the color of their choice. Some students will need one length, others will need two. You may arrange with the store for a discount and pay the bill after the class.

The student does not bring anything to class. A kit of sewing supplies is at each machine with all the necessary tools and sewing aides for the beginner. This kit is assembled and provided by the instructor or the sponsor and remains their property to be used again and again.

After measuring, the students select their size pattern, and you show them how to tissue fit and straighten fabric if it is a woven. Cut using scissors or a rotary cutter.

For the fee charged, the student receives a skirt, use of the equipment, a **Painless Sewing** book (you may buy from Palmer/Pletsch at wholesale price), instruction and personal supervision to make the skirt. Hopefully, the student also will become motivated to attend another class and continue sewing.

LESSON PLAN: Successful Beginnings Workshop

OBJECTIVE: The student will learn to select, measure, cut and sew, by machine, a pull-on skirt. Instructor will provide everything. Text is **Painless Sewing** by Palmer/Pletsch.

LECTURE: Lecture on how sewing fashions is easy and successful. Show simple, easily constructed fashions that are from current fashion magazines or catalogs. Fashion slides, posters and/or a notebook of pictures should reflect current fashion and fabrics for various figure types. Show fitted and dirndl skirts in several lengths.

DEMONSTRATION: Demonstrate difference in fabrics: fibers and weaves.
Discuss what each is best used for:

- Fibers: Pass samples of wool, cotton, silk, rayon, acrylic, acetate, and polyester
- Weaves: Pass samples of plain, twill, crepe, and satin weaves
- Knits: Pass samples of single and double knits
- Blends: Pass samples of 100% cotton and wool as well as poly/rayon, poly/cotton, and poly/wool blends.

Note: Read the "Fiber to Fabric" chapter in **Painless Sewing**.

LECTURE: Slide/poster lecture showing drape and weight of fabrics. Using same samples, discuss what fabrics are best for four figure types.

DEMONSTRATION: Demonstrate why fabric was chosen for garment and discuss care of garment and how fabric should be prepared. Display model garments:

Skirts in different fabrics
Top or tunic to wear with skirt
A vest to wear with skirt (short or long, button or no-button)

LECTURE: Slide/poster lecture on selecting your size pattern. Talk about ease.

DEMONSTRATION: Demonstrate on students how and where to measure.
Show skirts of different lengths.

ACTION: Teacher measures students and records waist, high hip and hip measurements in the **Painless Sewing** book.
Students decide on hem length.

LECTURE: Talk about how to measure pattern.

DEMONSTRATION: Show skirt pattern: front, back, and waistband.

Demonstrate flat-pattern measuring and discuss ease.

Discuss markings on tissue (pg. 9 **Painless Sewing**).

ACTION: Students trim around and press pattern pieces, then flat pattern measure.

LECTURE: Discuss fabric preparation and preshrinking (pg. 22-24 **Painless Sewing**). If you've preshrunk fabric in advance, tell them. If not, show a skirt you made without preshrinking, after it has been washed. (If it looks good it will be alright to let them select fabric without preshrinking.)

DEMONSTRATION: Demonstrate how to lay out fabric and the use of "in-case" seam allowances (pg. 67 **Painless Sewing**). Pull a thread in wovens to show how to cut on straight grain (pg. 79 **Painless Sewing**).

Demonstrate how to hold and use scissors and how to cut and mark fabric.

ACTION: Students lay out fabric and pattern.
Teachers check layout.
Students cut and mark fabric.

LECTURE: Using the sewing machine

DEMONSTRATION: Demonstrate threading the machine, filling and threading the bobbin, and changing stitch length.

Demonstrate how the sewing machine sews, good and bad tension, and how to adjust tension.

Demonstrate sewing on fabric and how to make a seam. Sew samples of 5/8" seams, 1" seams and 1/4" seams. Show students where the different sizes are used.

Demonstrate sewing on mediumweight woven cotton, single knit and a polyester silky. Demonstrate sewing fast and puckering. Show how to control fabric and puckering. Demonstrate "taut sewing" (pg. 11 **Painless Sewing**). Sew slowly, showing how to feed the fabric and to control the width of the seam.

(continued next page)

ACTION: Students fill bobbins and thread machines. Teachers check. Students sew on fabric pieces that are striped or checked following the lines on the fabric. Students sew different seam allowance samples on medium-weight woven cotton, single knit and polyester silky. Teachers check samples. Students sew center back seam of skirt. If it has a vent, demonstrate pressing and sewing. Pin side seams with wrong sides together for fitting.

LECTURE: Quickly discuss how to and why you fit-as-you-sew.

DEMONSTRATION: Student tries on skirt with elastic around waist and teacher pin fits and adjusts under elastic until hem is even. (See the McCall's Palmer/Pletsch 1-Hour Skirt #7244.)

ACTION: Teacher fits each student. Student marks side and waist seams, re-pins right sides together and sews side seams.

LECTURE: Discuss and demonstrate the use of a serger.

Display poster of serger parts and how sergers sew (pg. 13 **Sewing With Sergers** by Palmer/Pletsch).

DEMONSTRATION: Demonstrate how to press seams open, how to use a pressing cloth and seam roll, and how to finish the seams with a serger.

Demonstrate a straight-skirt hem that doesn't show (pg. 107-108 **Painless Sewing**).

Demonstrate the various types of elastics used for waistbands. Show how to sew a casing for a waistband and methods of inserting elastic into casing and securing the ends to finish. Demonstrate topstitching the elastic. You may use Stitch 'n Stretch Elastic.

ACTION: Students press side seams open, serge seam allowances and press up hems. Prepare and sew casing. Insert elastic and finish. Hem skirt. Teacher hands out evaluation forms. Students who finish early can practice guiding fabric and serging samples of different thicknesses and types of fabric with the serger.

WRAP-UP: Provide list of other Palmer/Pletsch books and other sewing publications. If your class is not sponsored by a retail store, pass out a list of mail-order sources. Notions catalogs are very helpful for beginners. (See Chapter 17, Resources.)
Promote your future classes. Show model garments or samples and pass sign-up sheet.
Collect evaluation forms.

TEACHER'S PREPARATION LIST:
Successful Beginnings

☐ **Design and construct posters:**
(14"x17" minimum):
10-12 fashion pictures of skirts
pattern size chart (enlarge and mount)
(pg. 58 **Painless Sewing**)
diagram of where to measure on body
outline of three skirt pattern pieces for marking
and in-case seam allowances
basic sewing machine describing important parts
serger describing important parts (Use pg. 13 from
Sewing with Sergers.)
three hem finishes
samples of elastics

☐ **Assemble fashion notebook**

☐ **Prepare handout sheets:**
measurements record or use **Painless Sewing** book
evaluation
sign-up sheets for other classes

☐ **Prepare samples:**
model garments with machine and
serger techniques (at least one skirt)
samples of equal-size fabrics before and
after preshrinking (optional)
samples of notions
select and mark sample fabrics for fabric lecture
(8"x10" minimum) (optional)
students' practice-fabric samples (or they can use
scraps of their fabrics)

☐ **To do for each class:**
Prepare pattern for demo.
Preshrink and prepare students' fabric (optional).
Prepare practice fabric samples (optional).
Copy handouts.
Make yourself a "bring list."
Check classroom setup.

☐ **Supplies available for student use:**
paper scissors
press cloths, seam rolls and pounding
blocks (clappers)
roll of masking tape and paper lunch bags for
fabric scraps
gridded rulers
sewing machine and serger needles
hand sewing needles
patterns mounted to tag board
hem gauges

assortment of thread colors
chalk and washable inks
tape measures

☐ **Student sewing kit:**
Use a zip-top 1 gallon bag to hold the
following:
Grabbit with plastic or glass head pins
paper and cloth scissors
thread (if fabric is cut ahead)
fabric (if cut ahead)
book (**Painless Sewing**)
handouts

☐ **Setup list for sponsor (or instructor):**
A cutting and sewing station for each student:
2'x6' table
sewing machine
electric power and extension cords
good lighting
student sewing kit

2-3 pressing stations:
padded board top
steam iron
pressing cloth
seam roll
pounding block (clapper)

garment rack
full-length mirror
hand-held mirror
1-2 sergers threaded with a light and a dark thread

optional for slide presentations:
slide projector and extra bulb
screen or good viewing surface
shades for window

other books, notions and items for sale

CHAPTER TEN

Teaching Techniques

"Speak from the heart and from experience and you will speak with conviction."

Introduce Yourself

Each time you begin a group presentation, introduce yourself. Tell students who you are, how you are qualified and why you are there. For example:

"Hi, I see everyone is very eager for this afternoon's presentation. I'm Marcy Miller and I'm going to demonstrate just how easy sewing can be. I am a home economist and have taught high school. I have always loved to sew. Little by little, over the years, many of my friends and I discovered shortcuts. Also, sewing machines, fabrics and notions have changed to make sewing quick and easy today."

If you do not have a college degree or formal training in sewing or teaching, refer to Chapter 1 and read your "personal assessment" again. You will find other things that will be interesting to your students such as how long you have sewn, who you've sewn for, and your favorite items to sew. Do you collect fabric like others collect antiques?

We had a lady in a class who believed there was nothing worth mentioning about her background. Then we found out her husband had been with the state department and she'd shopped all over the world for fabric while being a supportive government wife.

Your Ego

You will develop a great ego as a good teacher, but remember the other end of the spectrum. Don't **let a great ego hurt you. Always be humble and you'll be appreciated more. Show a genuine caring about your students.** Before class ask them how their weekend was or ask about their family. Compliment your students if they are wearing an interesting outfit or if their hair looks great.

Further Introductions

If there is time, have the students introduce themselves. Ask them to stand, say their name and give a few comments about themselves, such as where they live or if they work outside the home or a little about their family and sewing interests. You might ask them to address why they are taking your class.

There are also some housekeeping things to get out of the way before you begin to teach. They are items that will make your class more comfortable. The following is a checklist to which you can refer:

☐ Say something nice about your sponsor.

☐ Explain the order of the class, what you will teach and when.

☐ The restrooms are...

☐ Lunch or break will be at...

☐ No smoking in the room please.

☐ Get out a pencil and paper for note taking.

☐ Control rules (see later in this chapter).

☐ If you have a fit or "I need help" sign-up sheet, explain how to use it.

Get to Know Your Class

Each group of students has a personality. There are some that are fun and some that are very serious. There are humorless classes that will NEVER laugh at your jokes. Getting to know your students takes time. You will be better equipped to teach if you find out a little about each person. Start a card file on each student during introductions. Make notes about interesting things you want to remember.

If you are teaching a series of classes, hand out a questionnaire at the first class. Ask them to leave it with you at the end of class. You can use our questionnaire or develop your own. (A full-size questionnaire you may copy is in Chapter 18.)

Sample Questionnaire

Be a Student

Teachers are often the worst students. Some tend to NEED to talk a lot, often to be recognized for their abilities. Some expect to learn a LOT when really they won't, because they are so experienced. However, the **one** new thing they do learn will probably be as valuable as the 20 new things others learn. If they are already experts, ask for their quiet cooperation and suggest they look for teaching ideas.

Taking classes will help you observe teaching techniques. When you are in a class as a student, watch how others teach. Pretend you are at a beginning level and play the part of a new sewer. What do you see and hear as a person unfamiliar to sewing terms? You will have to concentrate on this one to see how important concentration is.

Class Control

Setting rules for the classroom makes it possible for everyone to achieve his or her goals. You are in charge. If you lose control, everyone will blame it on **YOU**. Start with control, but in a friendly, cheerful manner.

The major problem you want to prevent BEFORE it happens is an interrupting student. Some questions may not be relevant to the subject. Some discussions may ramble on without any benefit. Often the questions are personal. Before you begin a class, ask students to save their questions until the demonstration is over. As the teacher, the leader, you will need to keep the class on track. Here is a nice way to state the rule.

"This is a big class and we need to accomplish a lot. Tell me if you don't understand something, but to save time, write down other questions. I'll allow time at the end of the lecture to answer them. If you have questions that relate only to you or your own personal experiences, please save them for private consultation time after class. Before asking a question, ask yourself, "Is it relevant to EVERYONE?"

During hands-on sew-in classes, concentration is especially important. Don't allow talking above a whisper. You don't want your students to ruin an expensive piece of fabric by losing concentration while cutting. Lack of concentration while sewing a major project can be a disaster. Mention this at the beginning and repeat it as often as necessary.

For example, nicely ask that everyone concentrate, and if they have questions, come to you and ask you in a low tone of voice. EVERYONE in the class will respect you for this and be appreciative. In a class that requires less concentration, remind the class that some students need quiet time. Even YOU will appreciate this as YOU need to concentrate while helping to make decisions for students.

If you lose control in the middle of a class and you have someone who insists on interrupting with her own comments, not even questions, simply say, "That's interesting, now let's get on with the subject."

Do not be afraid to take control of your class. No one minds being asked nicely to hold questions or to keep talking to a whisper or to be courteously quiet for the person sitting next to them. You will be MORE SUCCESSFUL when you are in charge! NICELY!

Organizing Your Demonstrations

If you simply place your visuals on a table in the order in which you will talk about them, you will have an "outline" to follow. Also, hang your model garments in order of use.

Organization by Zip-Loc®

Zip-Loc® bags are our favorite organizational tool. Available in many sizes, they enable you to organize your demo step-by-step with each step contained in a different bag.

Some bags have write-on strips so you can number the bags or make other notations. Besides the makings for each step, the bag could contain a completed sample of that step or refer to another bag holding the sample.

Marcy keeps all her cutting equipment for pattern layout and cutout in one Zip-Loc bag. Scissors, tape, French curve, ruler, marking pens, weights and pins are kept together in another, portable and visible. This organization helps you prepare many classes efficiently, especially if your "cutting room" is not in your sewing room. Use a two-gallon Zip-Loc bag to assemble all your pressing equipment, including press cloths.

Organizing by Zip-Loc is also a strategy you can teach your students. After purchasing a new pattern and fabric, put them together in a Zip-Loc bag with all the other findings needed to complete the garment. When you're ready to begin the project, everything is at your fingertips.

Note: Zip-Loc bags are made in two-gallon size, but you might have to search to find them. Or, ask your grocer to order them for you!

Once you have cut out the garment, place separate parts in separate bags. This is helpful if your teaching spans several weeks. For example, all pieces that will be interfaced could be together; all of the lining pieces could go into another bag. All pieces to be sewn together and edge-finished go in another bag. As you begin your project, each bag will be used. The best part is you will have all the things together where you need them and will not waste time looking for lost pieces. When you are finished, the bags are empty and ready for the next project. Remember to **RECYCLE**. We learned what is called "management by objective" in business school. Now it's called "management by Zip-Loc!"

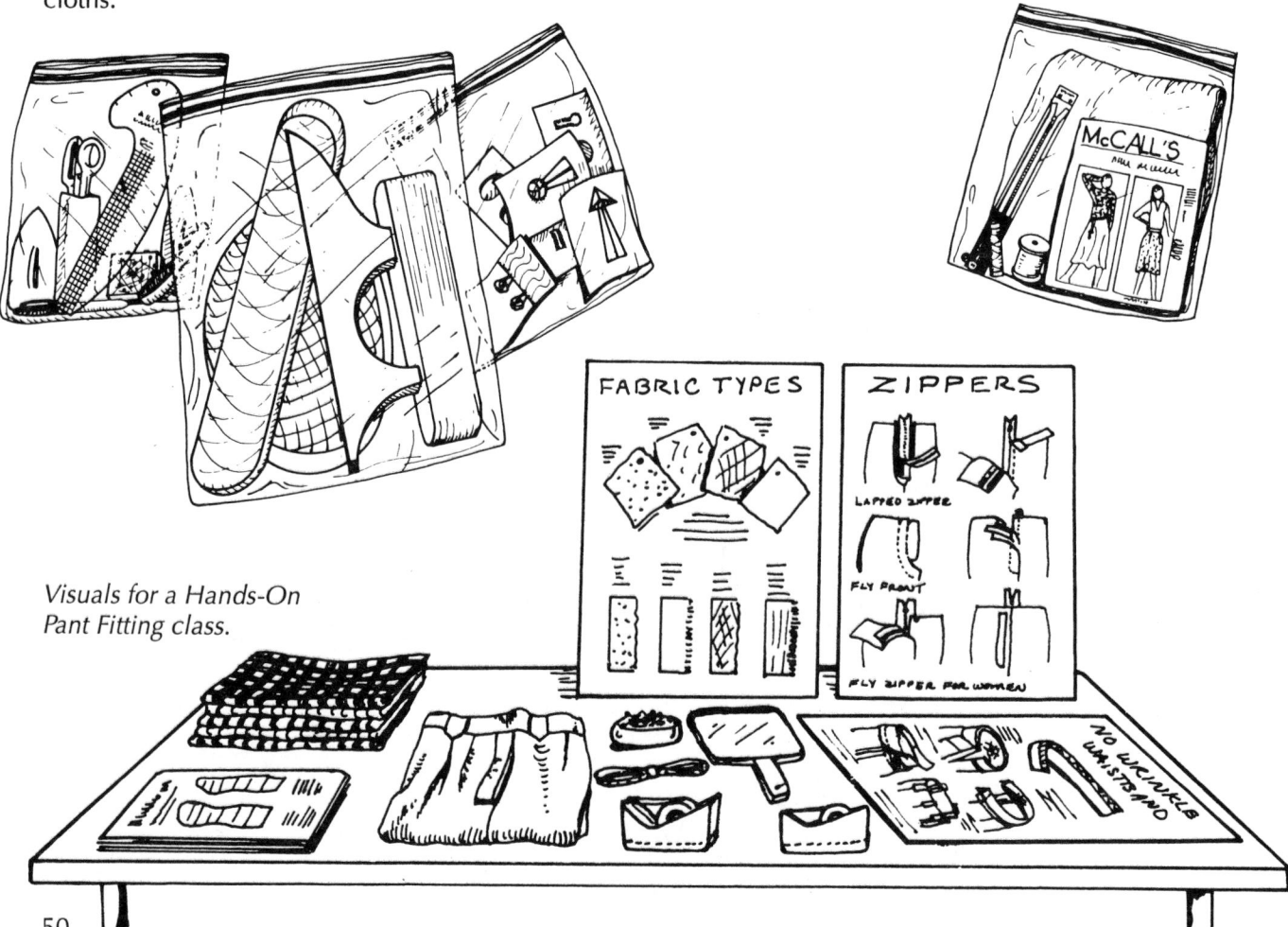

Visuals for a Hands-On Pant Fitting class.

Make a Checklist

Getting ready for the demonstration will be much easier if you make a checklist. Assemble all the items you will be using to teach and pack them in a convenient container. Pack in a logical manner because you will need to unpack and reorganize your materials at the class location.

Check off the items as you pack. If anything is missing, list it on another sheet of things to make or buy. Make sure all samples and model garments are clean and pressed.

Assembling and packing your demonstration in advance of the class will give you time to gather what you don't have and allow for last-minute distractions.

Taking time to pack in an organized way will also give you more confidence. When you are "ready to go" at least 24 hours ahead, you will be on time; and being on time **means** being all set up at least 20 minutes before the class. That way you'll be free to answer any questions and help solve problems.

Below is a checklist used by Palmer/Pletsch to set up a workshop. Use it as a guide to making your own checklists. One for another class is on page 73 in Chapter 13, Classroom Setup.

Practice, Practice, Practice

Go slowly and clearly, practicing out loud. Listen to yourself speak. Speak distinctly, using the correct terminology. Rehearse in front of a mirror. The key is **to rehearse**.

Analyze what you see. Be sure to compliment yourself when it is good. Try your demonstration on a friend or two, and watch their faces for responses. Ask them for an honest critique. Another good idea is to audio- or videotape yourself. This is very helpful for beginners. You can tape an actual class or practice as if you were performing in front of a group. When reviewing your demonstration, make notes on what needs improvement—better samples, gestures or explanation.

As a teacher, you should have someone you know listen and critique your presentation at least once every year. If you accept criticism well, ask students for suggestions. They will critique you, giving you valuable feedback if they feel you are open to being the best teacher you can be.

Speaking to Be Understood

Say what you mean as succinctly as possible. Don't fill your sentences with irrelevant material. This example may be silly, but it will get our point across.

"I, most of the time when I don't have the laundry, shopping, cleaning to do or when I don't need to go to the park with my daughter Jane and her friend Emmy, love to sew, except when my husband Henry had his gall-stone operation, but I do best when my cat is asleep."

Wouldn't simply, "I love to sew" be better??

Limit your comments to what is important at the moment. If you do not, you are wasting your students' time. This will deter your success. Try to listen to yourself consciously when talking to friends, business associates and your students, to hear if you speak succinctly.

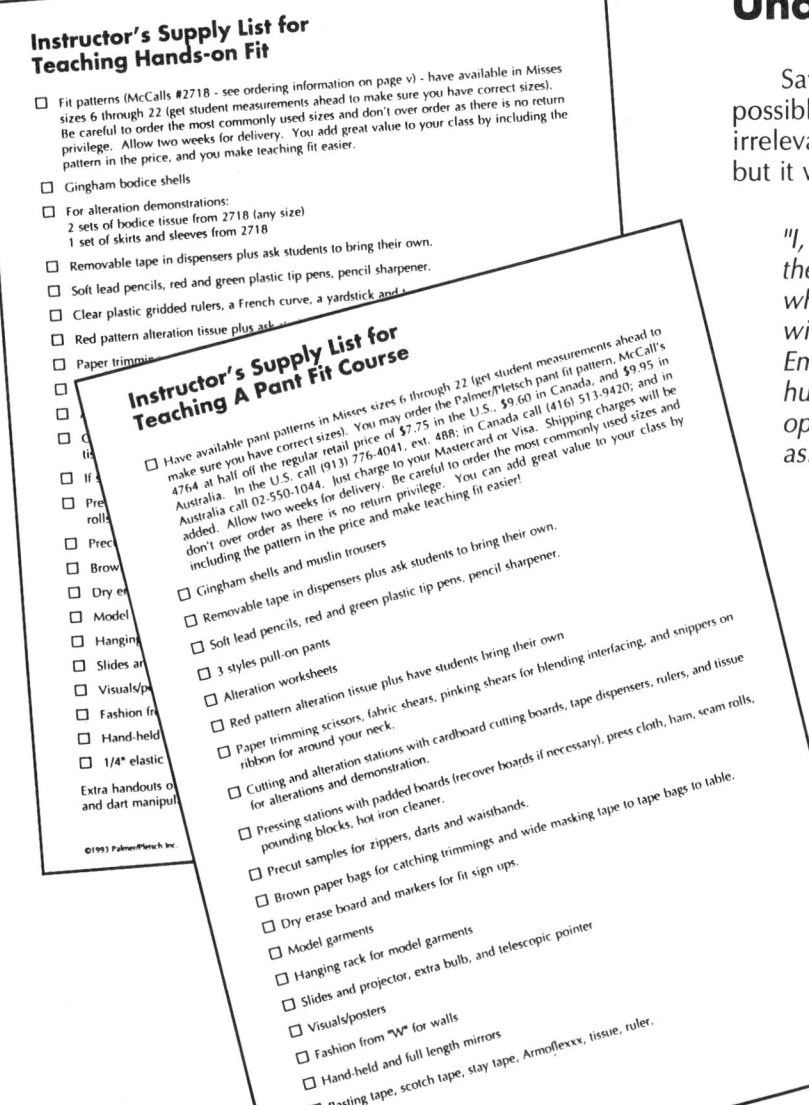

Instructor's Supply List for Teaching Hands-on Fit

Instructor's Supply List for Teaching A Pant Fit Course

51

How to Be a *Great* TEACHER

To be a good TEACHER you must be an EFFECTIVE teacher. Remember to be natural, be yourself, and to express your own ideas in your own manner. In addition, you can teach yourself the skills and techniques to be great. Palmer/Pletsch has spent over 25 years constantly improving the ART of teaching. Here is a capsule of what is most important.

Know Your Subject VERY WELL. You will speak more confidently and enthusiastically.

If this is your first lecture on a subject, PRACTICE in front of a mirror and/or video tape yourself. Practice until you feel you are comfortable and happy with your lecture.

When lecturing, stand.
You'll talk with more energy.

Put the audience at ease. If you are on a stage, mingle with the audience before class. After confidently introducing yourself, have the audience introduce themselves. See page 48 for introduction ideas.

Control class interruptions by stating the rules in the introduction.

Ask questions of the audience. This not only involves them, but keeps them awake. It's a way to make sure they are understanding what you say, makes them think about a possible answer before you give it to them, and it can just plain make the class more FUN!

Get to know your class! Each time you begin a new class, it is up to you to set the mood for that class. Everyone in the class will have different levels of experience. A good teacher acknowledges these levels. A way to avoid *"talking down"* to those more advanced is to tell students that even though some of them are very experienced, *you will start at the beginning*, as if they knew nothing. Even the more advanced will usually be happy about that and will know you recognize their level.

You can't teach until you motivate students to WANT to learn. By showing garments or samples that are exciting, students will WANT to go to the effort of sewing them. Use pictures or slides as well. Even words like, "This is how to get a professional-looking garment" can motivate students to listen to you.

Say what you are going to do. *(introduction)*
Do it. *(lecture content)*
Say what you've done. *(summary)*
These are the three parts of any speech or lecture. Make a sample outline using this format.

Place visual aids and model garments in order of use. They act as your "outline."

Demonstrations are a good time to let your audience know you are human. Tell the story about the time you did this technique differently and what the results were. Laugh with yourself and the group. Ask real-life questions like, "How many times have you set the sleeve in the wrong armhole?" Let them know they aren't alone. "Have you ever cut the top of a zipper off before sewing on the waistband? That's something you'll only do once. You'll unzip it next time!" Let them know you yourself have also learned through such creative sewing experiments.

If you are NEW to teaching, admit it right away. Usually, students will **want** you to succeed. Be confident in your teaching, yet *when you don't have an answer*, tell your class in a confident manner that you don't know. You will find the answer and let them know at the next class. They are depending on you. After class refer to your library of sewing books. Or, call other sewing professionals and bounce the question off them. If you have taken the Palmer/Pletsch Teacher Training, you can call us if necessary.

Eye contact is important. Look at everyone. Try to establish eye contact with each person at least once during the lecture. This will help you read your students' faces to see if they are under-standing your instructions. You'll know if they look perplexed.

Make sure everyone can see. Your new "eye" will quickly evaluate what students are learning. You will also be able to determine if they can see you easily or have to strain their necks. If they cannot see or are uncomfortable, it will be harder for them to learn. Try to change the seating arrangement, if necessary.

Draw visual pictures. Compare sewing techniques to things that are familiar. For example, say, "Sewing or serging across seams is like driving a car through an intersection—SLOW DOWN." Or, "Has your machine ever eaten your fabric?"

Gestures are important. Gestures add emphasis to what you are saying. Use hand motions to demonstrate how scissors cut a bevel edge when trimming a seam. Two fingers moving can demonstrate how serger needles stitch here and blades cut here. If you want students to *gently* use a pounding block versus beating the fabric, imagine the hand motions that would help make your point.

Speak slowly and clearly. This is especially important when the technique is new and difficult. Tape yourself.

Repetition is a wonderful teacher! Repeat difficult techniques two or three times. Be sure to plan time for these repetitions as well as questions and problem solving.

Ask for an action by your students.
"Make one pair of pants using your new altered pattern right away while the information is fresh." "After you sew a garment, go accessorize it." "Read the first three chapters of *Painless Sewing* before class next week."

Encourage students to go home and practice what they have learned from your demonstration right away. You might say "Go home and sew THREE pair of pants this month." They may gasp, but you'll get the point across. Also encourage them to make a reference library of their samples, so when the time comes to use that technique, they can refer to them.

Make a test sample of techniques before actually using them on a demonstration garment. You will see how it performs in your fabric.

Clearly label each sample you and your students make. For example, if making interfacing test samples, the label should describe the fashion fabric, interfacing and care instructions. Samples can be mounted on notebook paper and put in a binder to store for future reference. Or you may prefer to mount yours on poster board.

Avoid expressing your position as simply your personal opinion. When there are two ways to do something and you have a personal preference, state WHY! A GREAT TEACHER thinks through the reasons and consequences for decisions made in sewing.

Use active, not passive, voice.
"I prefer" is a more straightforward statement than "It is preferred."

Motivate your class to sew more and sew confidently. This is your ultimate goal. You will be teaching them "always-always" rules of sewing as Palmer/Pletsch Corporate Instructor Marta Alto says. It gives them parameters. But teach your rules with a RELAXED attitude. You don't want to scare your students. Let them know many rules have been broken by you and other instructors and sewers. If there is a valid reason to do something, then it's OK!

Expecting students to do their best is better than expecting perfection. Don't apologize for your sewing and tell students not to apologize for theirs. Use the 4-foot rule. If you stand back 4 feet and can't see your mistake, such as "slightly" crooked topstitching that you just KNOW is there, don't worry. If anyone is standing closer, they are not looking at your mistake!

Use ACCURATE terminology and pronunciation. Finger pressing is different from pressing. Be careful not to say "measure the garment" when you mean to measure the tissue pattern. Don't use designer names unless you know their correct pronunciation. We've all heard *Chanel* many times, but if she were a new designer, can you imagine the pronunciations?

Add value. If you are including a book or handouts in the class, USE THEM or they have no value. Referring to page numbers gives value to the time and expense you've incurred. Make a separate list of page numbers for a handy reference for techniques you'll be discussing. Another example is to say, "I've saved you time by making up the fit shells for you to try on, so try mine on to find your correct pattern size."

Invite the audience to ask questions. But read the section on CONTROL on page 49 first.

Create confidence. Admit that anything new will take more time in the beginning. Tell students that once they understand a concept, they'll be empowered. Compliment the class for each success. Encourage each student by admiring her work; for example, say, "You must like making casings." Or, "You are nearly ready for the next step."

Put yourself in your student's place. If ever you are in doubt about how to treat someone, *reverse the roles*. This gives you great insight.

Be happy. Remember, people might come to your class because it is the highlight of their day. They may be leaving a bad situation and the last thing they want to face is an unhappy, moody, or complaining person.

Make people feel good. There are many simple ways. Greet people. Smile. Call people by name. Be friendly and helpful. Act and speak as if you really like what you do. Be genuinely interested in people. Be thoughtful, concerned and considerate of others' feelings. Let others have an opinion.

Use humor. "A fabric stash is a legitimate collection." In reference to bodies that have drooped a bit with age, "Everything's gone south."

Be a role model in your appearance. Pati taught ten classes a week at Meier & Frank department store in the early '70s. She was surprised to learn that one reason her students couldn't wait to come to class was to see what she would be wearing next. Students do notice. You are their role model. Give them something to aspire to. Be a little more high fashion or creative or use better fabrics than the average person. Find a way to stand out a little.

Be enthusiastic. You can say you LOVE a method...and why!!

Move right along. Keep the pace of the class going. If demonstrating on the machine is taking too long, maybe you should have pre-sewn steps. Or, teach as you sew by mentioning other things students can think about.

Promote the Products Your Sponsor Sells

Do not forget that one of the purposes, or maybe the most important purpose, of your class or demonstration is to promote your sponsor's products. Have samples of these products to show. You want the sponsor to be successful and to help promote your classes and YOU!

Naturally, you should promote only the products you like. Plan ahead and ask your sponsor to order these items. Provide a list. Below are sample lists Palmer/Pletsch representatives have given out over the years. Create your own based on current products you like.

We've found you'll sell more when you put the items you talk about on one table. It helps students quickly find your recommendations.

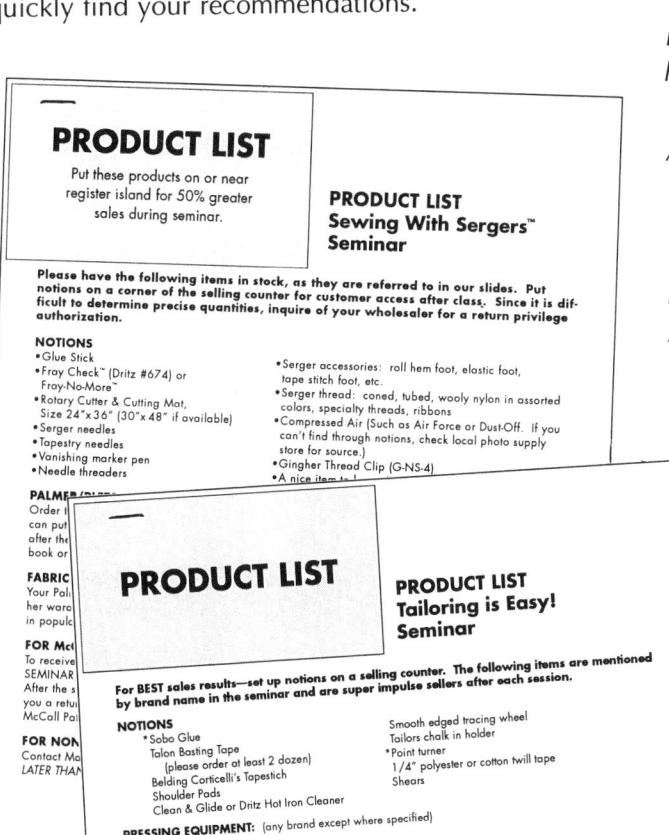

PRODUCT LIST
Put these products on or near register island for 50% greater sales during seminar.

PRODUCT LIST
Sewing With Sergers™ Seminar

Please have the following items in stock, as they are referred to in our slides. Put notions on a corner of the selling counter for customer access after class. Since it is difficult to determine precise quantities, inquire of your wholesaler for a return privilege authorization.

NOTIONS
- Glue Stick
- Fray Check™ (Dritz #674) or Fray-No-More™
- Rotary Cutter & Cutting Mat, Size 24"x36" (30"x48" if available)
- Serger needles
- Tapestry needles
- Vanishing marker pen
- Needle threaders
- Serger accessories: roll hem foot, elastic foot, tape stitch foot, etc.
- Serger thread: coned, tubed, wooly nylon in assorted colors, specialty threads, ribbons
- Compressed Air (Such as Air Force or Dust-Off. If you can't find through notions, check local photo supply store for source.)
- Gingher Thread Clip (G-NS-4)
- A nice item...

PRODUCT LIST
PRODUCT LIST
Tailoring is Easy! Seminar

For BEST sales results—set up notions on a selling counter. The following items are mentioned by brand name in the seminar and are super impulse sellers after each session.

NOTIONS
- Sobo Glue
- Talon Basting Tape (please order at least 2 dozen)
- Belding Corticelli's Tapestich
- Shoulder Pads
- Clean & Glide or Dritz Hot Iron Cleaner
- Smooth edged tracing wheel
- Tailors chalk in holder
- Point turner
- 1/4" polyester or cotton twill tape
- Shears

PRESSING EQUIPMENT: (any brand except where specified)
- Seam roll
- Pressing ham
- Point-presser/clapper combination
- See-through press cloths
- Tailor board (by June Tailor)
- Velva-board (by June Tailor)

FABRICS: I will be using a model garment wardrobe made up in the following fabrics. You should have these or comparable items:
- Wool gabardine - Anglo
- Aristoc wool flannel - Anglo
- Wool plaid or tweed - Pendleton
- Mazerak wool coating - Anglo
- Ultrasuede® - Skinner
- Matinee washable velvet - Martin
- Corduroy
- Silk suiting - American Silk Mills/Logantex
- Moyamacrae rayon linen - Moygashel
- Stretch-woven polyester
- Linen
- Voila! wool voile - Anglo
- Lana Suede wool flannel - Anglo

SHAPING FABRICS: Very important—even in the new "unconstructed" looks.
- Poly-SiBonne—at least white
- Light and Suit weight Easy Shaper
- Tri-rite or Tri-shape for sleeve technique
- Fusible Acro
- Pel-Aire
- Midweight Fusible Pellon
- One traditional stitchable hair canvas interfacing
- Jacket Package (Mid Century Textiles). Attn: Larry Rosen, 202 W. 40th St., NY, NY 10018)

PATTERNS: Current listing of patterns being used in seminar will be sent 1 month prior.

BOOKS: Be sure to order 1 dozen minimum of each of our other books to sell after seminar. Order forms are enclosed.

*Essential items to have in stock for tailoring seminar – Don't miss a sale!

Humor and Words of Wisdom

Making a class fun will relax everyone, and students will want to return to have even more fun! Over the years, Palmer/Pletsch and other instructors have shared humor and good lines. Here are some examples:

I stand up and my brain sits down.

40 isn't fatal.

Surround yourself with enthusiastic people.

Three gripes and you're out.

Enjoy life's tiny delights—flowers, sewing.

How do you get to Carnegie Hall?—practice, practice, practice.

You'll look 20 pounds thinner in garments that fit. And it sure beats exercise!

The pattern is only a manuscript, you are the editor.

What size you buy in ready-to-wear is determined by how much you pay. The more you pay, the smaller you can be!

Ripping is "reverse stitching."

We are chronologically gifted, not aging.

We are vertically challenged, not short or tall.

We are horizontally challenged, not heavy.

When Everyone is Tired, Do Something Fun

When fatigue or plain old sleepiness sets in, bodies and minds need a jump start. Getting people to move and think about something new can do wonders.

- Have everyone stand up, turn to the right, massage the person in front, then turn left and repeat.

- The princess wave is fun—wave hands high above head for 30 seconds and the veins on the back of your hands disappear.

- Exercise eyes—look at a close object (your finger 6" in front of your nose), then at a distant object.

CHAPTER ELEVEN

Teaching Tools— Your Visuals

"Spend the time needed to be the best you can be."

The Three C's

The three C's for visuals should be memorized—Clean, Clear, Current. Visuals directly impact the quality of your presentation. They take time to create, but if done well, you have not wasted your time. Yes, your time is important, so we will pass on years of tips for making them look great and hopefully SAVE you time!

Clean

Never show or pass around a dirty, smelly visual. Sounds gross? Well, we've seen it! After a sample or poster has been passed around many times, oil and dirt from hands accumulate. Since you can't ask every audience to come with clean hands, try one of the following:

- Put visuals under clear plastic to keep them clean.

- Pass visuals around and replace when soiled.

- Don't pass visuals around; instead place them on a table for viewing.

Clear

Visuals need to be as large as required for the size of class you want to teach. For a class of five, you may need no premade visuals. You can simply demonstrate a technique at a machine.

If your visuals can't be seen from a distance, you shouldn't have bothered making them. If you want to reach 100, you'll need oversized samples and posters. If you want to reach 500, you'll need slides. The best test is to sit in the back row of the room in which you will be teaching and see how clear your samples are.

Current

Use fabrics that people are sewing today for samples and model garments. Use current patterns people can buy. And, most of all, stay current yourself. Subscribe to trade journals, take classes, test new notions, and keep on top of the latest fibers and fabrics by talking to savvy buyers or your state extension clothing specialist. Buy notions and 1/8-yard samples of fabric trends. Mount them on posters. **Be the leader in informing your students of the latest, newest and best!**

Samples

Samples show techniques or ideas. Make them "larger-than-life," so your students can see the details. Bound buttonhole samples, for example, would be more educational if you made each buttonhole 3" long. Samples will perform better and look better when they are constructed of quality, easy-to-press fabrics, threads, interfacing and linings. Label each one with the materials used to construct it.

Samples should be clean, pressed and in good condition to make a good impression. When you are sewing your own clothes, make a sample before using a technique in your garment. This will not only save you time, but you'll get practice and not make a mistake in your garment. What a great way to add to your sample collection.

Make more than one sample of each technique. This gives you a replacement for soiled or worn samples. Each time you demonstrate an idea or technique, you'll end up with another sample.

Purchase remnants to save money and give you a wide variety of current fabrics. Be creative and use a lot of different colored and textured fabrics for your demos to lend a creative and interesting flair to your samples. This helps students visualize garments made from more than one fabric. Printed fabrics hide detail and generally are not good for samples. Warm colors, especially red, keep your audience awake. Blue has a calming, sedative effect.

Hint: Stand 20' away to see how your garment looks from the back of a room.

Prints hide details

Store your samples in Zip-Loc® bags, boxes or drawers labeled for easy retrieval. Over time, you might collect a box full of pockets or buttonholes or hems.

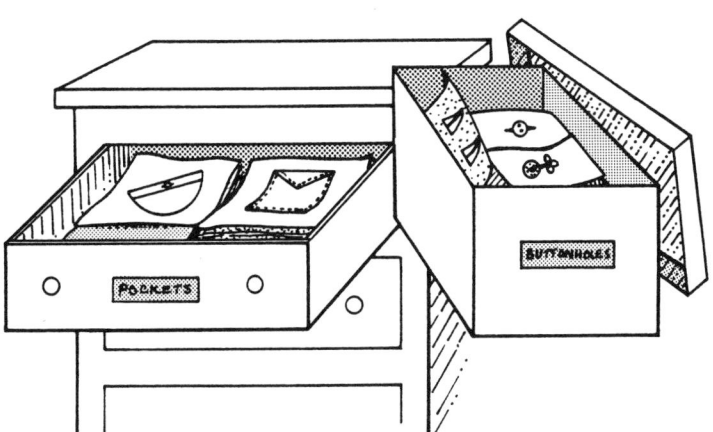

For mounting sewn samples of techniques to poster board, we've found using a stapler most effective. Staple the top edges or one side only if you want people to be able to feel the sample or look at both sides of the technique.

If you want a stand up poster, tape two posters together so they can be folded flat or opened to stand up. Put the two boards right sides together to tape. If you tape them flat, they won't fold up.

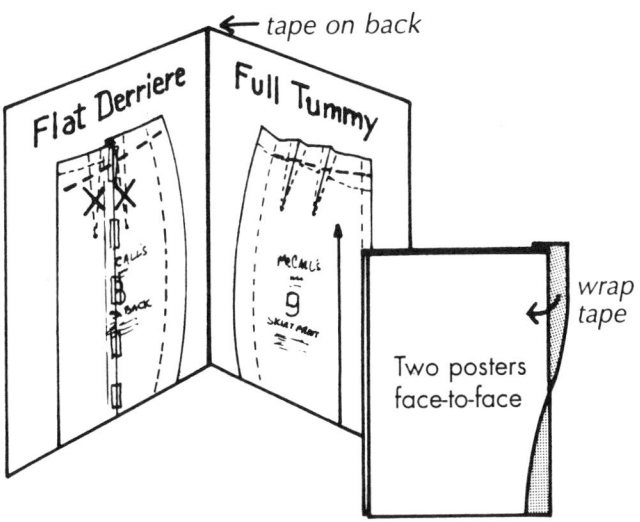

You may also attach samples to poster board with double-stick tape. The size of the poster board and sample will vary depending on whether you have made them to pass around or to stand on an easel in the front of the room.

Foam-core board covered with felt works well for a single large poster on which you can display many samples. Simply "stick" them to the board. You could use Velcro® on the back of the samples that won't stick to the felt.

Posters

Your posters need to be clean, clear and of good quality. Posters are used to teach:

- Techniques
- Fashion trends
- New products

Posters can include:

- Very precise line drawings
- Pattern pieces mounted to show alterations or design-change ideas
- Technique samples in fabric (discussed on previous page)
- Technique art from a book
- Fashion ideas from magazines or pattern catalogs

Color

Yellow is our favorite posterboard color for mounting technique samples. It is a warm color that is friendly and keeps students awake. Using **red** fabric for the samples really keeps them awake!

Cool colors are so soothing, you can become tired and relaxed looking at them. However, blue and green often work best for mounting pattern tissue. You can see the tissue better.

If you are presenting designer looks to a designer-oriented group, select a more elegant background for your pictures. A gold or silver color may be more appropriate.

Poster How-tos

For pictures taken from fashion magazines and catalogs, use 3M Spray Mount® adhesive and mount on railroad board, which is easy to cut to the size you want.

Decide posterboard size and layout by loosely placing the pictures. Lightly pencil the corners of each picture OR draw a rough sketch OR take a Polaroid® photo! Place pictures upside down on newspaper to protect other surfaces. Hold spray can 18" or more from picture. Spray lightly and evenly. Carefully place picture in place. If you don't put it in exactly the right place, this glue allows you to lift the picture and reposition it. Smooth picture from the center to the outside edge with your hand.

Mounting tissue patterns is a little trickier. Try a small piece of tissue first for practice. Prepare your tissue for mounting by trimming to cutting lines and pressing with a warm DRY iron. On the posterboard, arrange the tissue, lettering and any other item to be mounted. Mark the placement with small pencil marks that can be erased later.

Turn tissue upside down and spray the BACK side with the spray adhesive. Spray **very evenly** and **lightly** 18"-24" from tissue. Be sure to protect your work surface with newspaper or other disposable material. The spray drifts over quite a large area.

Lift and carefully place the tissue piece where you marked on the posterboard. To adjust its position, lightly lift and move to where you want it.

After placing tissue on poster board, beginning at center, smooth with your hand to all outside edges. The nice thing about tissue is that if you get a wrinkle, you can usually "smoosh" it out. (That's Palmer/Pletsch instructor Marta Alto's word!) It's still there, but doesn't show.

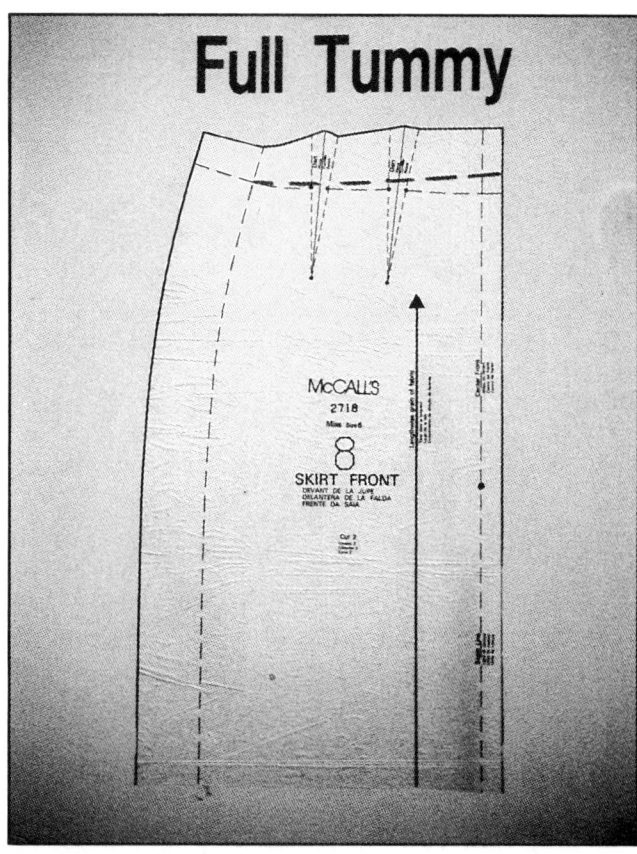

During her teacher training course, Pati Palmer shows some of the visual "mistakes" she made early in her career. One of her favorites is her red sample mounted on bright green poster board. Wow! You can hardly look at it. This is because in color theory, complementary colors on the color wheel (those opposite each other) enhance each other. But they can also fight each other when they are of equal brightness or intensity. Pati finds it hard to believe she made that visual mistake after having studied color theory in school.

She also shows an example of a sample poster showing different seam finishes. She used a small print on which the finishes were hardly detectable. This unfortunate use of time, however, improved her teaching. She shows a poster of a very detailed Vogue pattern from the early '70s that is a garment made in a fabulous printed cotton and you can't see any detail. The time spent on all the details was lost. A simple-to-sew pattern with fewer details would have given similar results! See fashions on page 57.

This is a good educational poster.

Bound Buttonholes

CENTER FRONT

LINING PATCH

This is a better poster because it is more interesting. In addition to step-by-step how-tos on an actual sewn sample, we have added photos of fashion examples and a computer was used to create the title.

Bound Buttonholes

A class in art, sign lettering or illustrating will help guide you in designing these visuals. You will learn about the materials available to make these products and the skills to use them. Art-supply stores sometimes offer free demonstrations.

The computer is the ultimate tool today, as were rub-off letters yesterday. Both are expensive. Pati solved this problem early in her career when funds were limited by buying cardboard letters from a toy store and tracing around them on black construction paper. She cut and mounted the letters to make headlines for her posters. It was tedious but professional. Hand lettering can be the most wonderful if you are skilled at this art.

You may be required to provide your own easel(s) to display your posters if they are larger than pass-around size. These can be purchased at art-supply stores. Take your posters with you when shopping for easels. Try them on for size, just like a garment. Try collapsing the easel. Try setting it up. Try carrying it.

You can laminate posters with matte acetate. This lamination will allow you to write on the visual and erase or wash it off later. It also makes it easier to keep clean. Laminate both sides for maximum protection. Visuals with fabric samples are generally not laminated because your students will want to feel and examine them.

If the poster is seasonal or fashion-oriented, you can spend less time and money to produce it because its lifetime will be shorter.

Portfolios

It is easier to manage posters if they are all the same size. But this may not be practical. Purchase a portfolio carrying case to fit the largest size you have. Check art-supply stores for gusseted cardboard or zippered vinyl portfolios. They come in 1" to 3" thicknesses. We prefer the deeper ones because you can carry more in them. When we teach a fit seminar, we even put all our fitting shells in the portfolio with the posters and samples.

Fashion Album

Often students can't relate to patterns because of the way they are illustrated, or the color or fabric used in a photo. Also, photographs against a white background may not have the same feel as a model photographed in a setting. Help students by first showing ready-to-wear fashion and then find patterns with similar lines that can be used to duplicate the look. This is especially effective with teenagers.

To help your students create a relationship between current fashion and what is available in the pattern books, create a **dream book of ideas**. Tear pages from fashion magazines or get on the catalog mailing lists of the major fashion stores.

(Pati Palmer and Susan Pletsch, while traveling North America teaching sewing, applied for credit cards from major department stores in every city. They had cards from Nieman Marcus, Meier & Frank, Famous Barr, Saks, Frederick & Nelson, G. Fox, Burdines, Bloomingdale's, Macy's, May Co., Hecht Co., Weinstock's, May D. & F. Robinson's, The Bon Marche, Dayton's, Hudson's, and you can name the nostalgic rest! Susan and Pati said "plastic fantastic" as they traveled through their youth...all to get department store catalogs in the mail.)

Another great source for fashion ideas is mail-order catalogs. Order from one and you'll be on the list for many. These catalogs are current and trendy. When reading these, note hairstyles, accessories, shoes, hosiery and the "way" clothes are put together. Knowing the latest in fashion trends keeps you in the forefront with your students.

A loose-leaf photo album with pages that have plastic pockets or overlays works great for assembling fashion ideas and pictures. Cut fashions that pertain to your class from all of your magazines, catalogs, newspapers and pattern books.

This is a very economical way to display current ideas, trends and accessories to your classes. If a look or trend goes out of style, throw that page away or remove the picture from the pocket or sticky page and replace it with a new idea. Buy additional loose-leaf pages as necessary.

The pictures can be matched up with current pattern numbers. The album can also be used as a tool to help students determine which looks are good for their figure types. If you label the particular look or page with what figure types are best, a reader can begin to relate to the current fashion that most flatters her own figure type. These fashion pictures can also be used to show appropriate fabrics for that look.

This album is a good way to "store" your own looks and likes. It can be a journal of a year's plan for your wardrobe and/or model garments.

If you are teaching teens, making an album using photos of ready-to-wear is a particularly good way to inspire them. They often relate **much better to a teen magazine than to a pattern catalog.**

Prom dress idea from a teen magazine.

60

Model Garments

When teaching clothing construction classes, inspire students by displaying garments showing the techniques you'll be presenting. Make fashionable garments from current patterns as much as possible. If a pattern has been discontinued, try to find a similar design and change the number.

There are a couple of exceptions to **only showing current patterns**. One is wearable art. The design won't be as important as the technique. You'd never have enough time to recreate these works of art every time a pattern is discontinued.

The other exception is history. Pati Palmer uses model garments from discontinued patterns to show the evolution of fashion. She has kept garments made from the early '70s. It's fun to look at how a Calvin Klein blazer used to fit. She also shows every 8-hour blazer designed for McCall's by Palmer/Pletsch. There is definitely fit history to be seen. This can be fun. Save your most distinguished relics!

Show complete ensembles and matching or interchangeable pieces to demonstrate how to build a wardrobe. This is your opportunity to shine as a professional sewing teacher. Display them with the accessories you have chosen. Give the students someone to look up to.

Be creative in your choice of textures, colors, designs and fabric types for model garments and your own wardrobe. Use a variety of fabrics. Remember that details cannot be seen from a distance on very dark colors (especially black).

Be adventurous in trying new ideas as well as techniques. Encourage your students to be adventurous. Construct your garments using quality techniques. Be proud of what you make to wear yourself. Model garments with special detail touches like those in the Palmer/Pletsch **Serger Idea Book** or **Couture** books help communicate to your students the pride and creativity of your sewing skills.

A Reminder: Garments always should be clean and pressed, not worn-looking. If you want **double mileage from model garments**, when you wear them don't wear perfume. Perfume odors linger in fabric. Look at and smell model garments occasionally to see if they need drycleaning or washing. You don't want that tell-tale "worn" smell. Even if you NEVER wear a garment, check it occasionally for freshness.

Custom label your garments by sewing tags into them. A good source is listed on page 109.

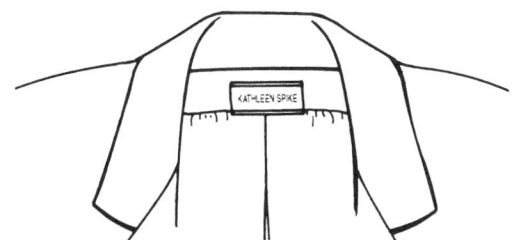

Attach tags describing what pattern, fabrics and findings were used, or put the pattern envelope in a Zip-Loc bag. Punch a hole in the top and tie 1/8" ribbon to the bag so it can loop over the hanger. Use the same color ribbon on all garments or match the ribbon to the garment.

All hangers should be the same. Use clear plastic hangers for uniformity. If you plan to hang your garments from a folding screen or over a door, hangars with swivel tops make displaying easier.

Turn a blouse, jacket and skirt into an "outfit" on a hanger using **hanger drops**. Slip them over hangers and clip a skirt or pant to them.

Use the 9" drop for pants or long skirts.

Use the 16" drops for hanging short skirts with long jackets.

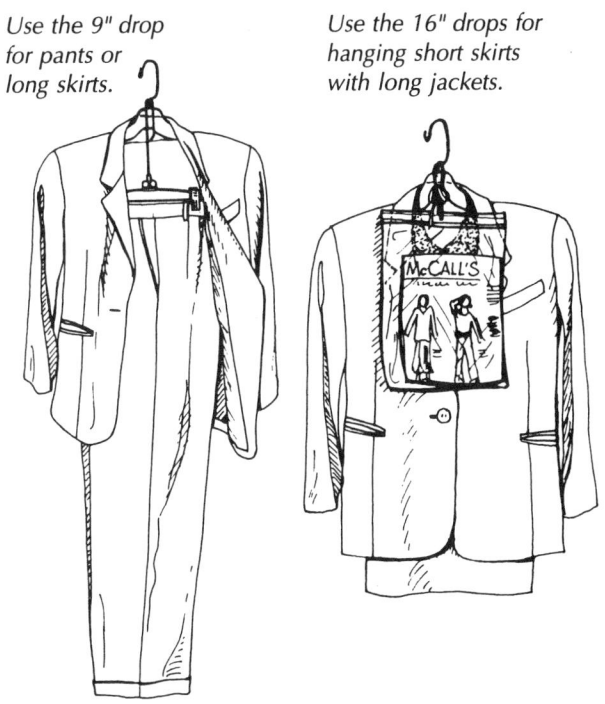

Note: See page 128 for ordering information.

Padded hangers certainly have their place as well. A lingerie class calls for garments displayed on padded hangers. **For a very impressive COUTURE look, make your own.** Easy instructions for making gorgeous padded hangers are found in the Palmer/Pletsch book, **Couture, The Art of Fine Sewing,** by Roberta Carr. (See page 126.)

Slides

A slide presentation is very effective for lecture classes. It allows more people to see close-ups of techniques more quickly. You can even create a "spotlight" to show model garments by inserting blank slides. Insert the blank slide vertically or horizontally. Some projectors are spotlights without a blank slide. Just leave a space empty. That's even better, because it lights an even larger area.

Taking your own slide photos requires not only a good 35mm camera, but also special lights, space, time and skill to take close-ups. Good close-ups are essential and a separate close-up lens can cost about $500.

Terri Burns, a knitting expert, wanted to add to her Palmer/Pletsch slides, which did not include knitting techniques. She took her camera and samples outside on a sunny day and was able to get good slides without special lights.

Never use your original slides. Have duplicates made for presentations. You have the choice of plastic or paper mounts. Paper bends easily, so we recommend plastic for its durability.

Palmer/Pletsch offers slides as part of its teacher training. Pati Palmer says that her company has thousands of slides to draw from, so she doesn't have to charge what an agency would charge to create a slide program. We've been quoted $1,000 per finished minute for sample making, scripting and photography.

Palmer/Pletsch includes up to 300 slides per topic in their teacher training—a real bargain. The slides come numbered with a script. Though it may not fit your purpose exactly, the script is a guide that can help you write your own narrative. Add your personality and put the slides in an order that suits your needs. Your narrative should be descriptive, pertinent to the subject and reflective of your style. Be sure to use the terminology and trade or brand names that apply to each slide.

Some Palmer/Pletsch teachers have stood by their projector and actually read the script during their first classes. Their students didn't mind. Pati Palmer at first discouraged this, but now feels it is better than fumbling because of unfamiliarity with the script.

Palmer/Pletsch breaks the rules. Their slides include both vertical and horizontal shots to get the largest image possible for what is being photographed. A horizontal photo of a person standing doesn't allow a close-up view of a garment.

Note: If you are asked to be interviewed on television, and want to show a few slides, they must be horizontal shots.

Initially, to save money, you can view slides on white paper and see them fairly well as you organize them. Later, you can purchase a light board for sorting slides.

If you are skilled, make your own light board. Pati Palmer's uncle Bob Palmer from Hood River, Oregon, made her first light table—a wood frame with a translucent glass top and two white fluorescent tubes under the glass.

Keep your light table clean and free from coffee cups, drink glasses and other foodstuffs. Your table and your slides need to be protected from any possible damage. A magnifying glass or *loupe*, also available at camera stores, will help you see the slide details. Select a good loupe and you will see every detail! It's like seeing the slides on a screen.

Number your slides. You can also **color-code slides** for different seminar arrangements by putting them in a slide tray for one program and running green felt tip pen over the top edges. Then arrange slides for the next program, say a longer one, and run a red pen along the top edges next to the green marks.

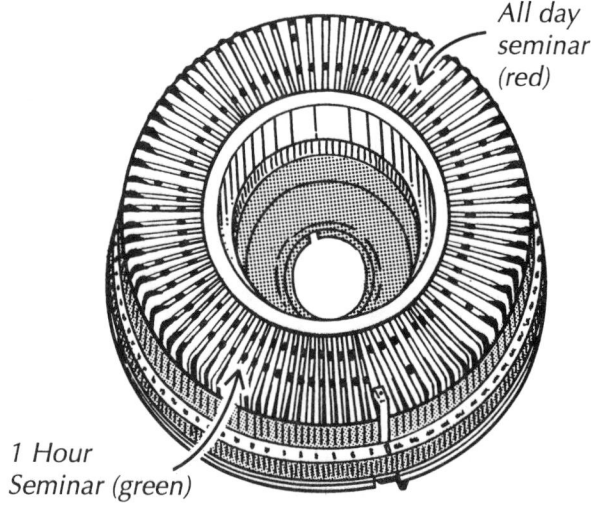

All day seminar (red)

1 Hour Seminar (green)

Store your slides in plastic "sleeves" from a camera store—each sleeve holds 20 slides. You can hold the slides up to a window and pull the ones you need. File the sleeves in a loose-leaf notebook. Handle your slides by holding the mounting in your fingers. Never touch the slide film itself. Use alcohol-free canned air to blow the dust particles from slides when they need cleaning.

Slide trays can be expensive, so shop at mass merchant or warehouse-club stores. You may choose a 140-slide tray, but we recommend the 80-slide tray. The larger tray sits on the projector longer, heating up as the projector heats up. When plastic-mounted slides overheat, they bend or warp in the projector and do not drop into place. Then you have to stop and fix the problem. A slight bend in a cardboard slide mount also prevents it from dropping through the narrower slots of the 140-slide tray.

Tip: Using an 80-slide tray forces you to control length in a short presentation.

Slide Projector

Slide projectors are expensive today. At the end of this chapter we have given you some mail-order sources that have good prices. The auto-focus feature is very important to the quality of your presentation, so make that one of your requirements.

Try to find a used projector if possible. Used projectors may be available from media centers of public or private schools or large corporations that have switched to videos for training. Look in camera stores or pawn shops. Ask your sponsors or guild members if they know of one for sale.

Also, check with friends or place a want ad in the newspaper, church bulletin board, or sewing guild newsletter. Kodak Carousel Auto Focus 760H would be a good find in a used projector. This model acts as a spotlight when there is no slide in a slot.

Using a Slide Projector

Arrive at class before your students. First, check the lights. Where are the switches? How many lights can you leave on and still see the slides clearly? A totally dark room is hard on the eyes and students can't see you or take notes.

Arriving early allows you to rearrange the room if there is a problem seeing slides. For example, your sponsor set up the screen facing a window with no window treatment and the sun is shining. You have a PROBLEM! Imagine trying to rearrange a room full of people. **ARRIVE EARLY!**

Tip: As students enter the classroom, talk to those sitting around the projector. If you are teaching a large seminar, this will break the ice. You are close and human, not a star on the stage.

We often set the projector on top of the projector case to get it higher and yet keep it fairly level. You can prop up the front of the projector, but too much propping may keep slides from dropping down. Too great a projector angle can also cause slides to have a funny angle on the screen.

Check **BOTH vertical** and **horizontal** slides. You'll want the largest possible image for both directions. If you check only one direction, the image may go off the screen in the other direction.

Learn how to remove your slide tray when it jams. Usually a little metal or plastic lever in the "hole" section of the slide tray can be released with a fingernail or file. Practice this because it is tricky.

Your projector will last longer if you carry it on the airplane, rather than checking it as baggage. Projector cases usually allow room for one slide tray, enough for a one-hour presentation.

Projector Bulbs

Always carry a spare bulb! And practice in advance—now—how to insert it quickly so you won't delay your class when the bulb burns out. Also, the manufacturer may recommend extending bulb life by letting the fan cool the projector for several minutes after turning the bulb off. Follow the instructions that come with your projector.

The bulb will last longer if you do not touch the glass portion with your fingers. Fingers can touch the casing (except when it is too hot), but NEVER the bulb. The oil from fingers will ruin the bulb. See page 64 for mail-order sources for the least expensive bulbs. Otherwise they can cost over $30 each!

Remote Control

The cord on the remote control is generally not long enough for you to stand by the screen and show slides. Buy a 25' remote-control extension cord.

When you rent a projector or use hotel equipment, you might get a battery-operated remote control. That means you won't have cords to trip over, but the batteries don't last long. Make sure you have arranged for backup batteries for the remote control.

Lenses

Projectors come with a standard lens. A zoom lens gives you the flexibility of placing the projector wherever you want. But it is expensive.

Learn how to remove the lens for cleaning. For speed, you can use a release knob or lever rather than just turning the dial. Learn also how to take apart the lens compartment inside the projector for cleaning. Use lens cleaning tissue and lens cleaner from a camera store. Dust slides occasionally with environmentally-safe canned air or use a lens-cleaning agent. Read the projector's manual for details.

Projection Screen

If you must provide your own screen, buy one that is larger than a typical small home screen. A glass-beaded finish is best in all light conditions. A gray daylight screen is the worst. When standing next to it, you can't see what is on the gray finish. A white wall can work very well because you can often get your largest image.

If you are teaching a large audience (200 people), your screen should be as **large** and **high** as possible. Learn how to raise a screen to its maximum height. The trick is to raise the lower handle first, *then* the screen can go higher. A large group will be able to see *you* better, too, if you and the screen are on a platform or stage.

Pointers

To point out details on the screen, Palmer/Pletsch has discovered a telescopic pointer that is also a magnet that picks up pins. See teaching aids from Palmer/Pletsch on page 128. New laser pointers can be awkward, distracting and unreliable, and can cost more than $300.

Microphone

You need a microphone only if you are conducting a seminar to hundreds or if you can't project well. Avoid walking in front of the loud speakers or they will "scream."

Cordless microphones are best. In the United States, you can get a decent portable system at Radio Shack. Most sponsors will not have microphones, but you or they can rent them. Be sure the remote part has a new battery and that someone knows how to replace it. For example, if you are in a hotel meeting room, and using their equipment, someone in the hotel will be familiar with microphones.

Mail-Order Sources

Owning your own projector enables you to learn how to operate it and to know it is in good working order. Read about "used" projectors on page 63 before making this major purchase. For the best prices, we recommend:

J.E. Foss
P.O. Box 357
Bethel Park, PA 15102-0357
(800) 245-6240

Prices quoted are summer catalog 1995.

Projectors:
Kodak Carousel Model 4600, auto focus, remote control, Ektanar C 102 mm f 2.8 lens. One-year warranty, FHS lamp, B 140 T slide tray (ask them to substitute 80-slide trays).
$392.00— projector
  $54.25— lens
$446.25— total

Bulbs:
FHS $19.56 each (for use with Model 4600)
EXR $17.12 each
ELH $17.86 each

Remote control extension cord:
25' cord for Ektagraphic and Carousel projectors.
EC58, $36.20

Projector Case:
Mobile plastic case for the series 4000, 5000 and Ektographic 3 projectors.
ECCASE, $69.95

CHAPTER TWELVE

Evaluations

"No matter how much you know, always be open to learning more."

Evaluations are important even if you have successfully taught a class many times. It shows others you care and are always open to improving. It gives students an incognito way of telling you how they **honestly** felt about the class. Don't stop with students. If you have a sponsor, let them know you are part of a **team** and always willing to listen to their comments. You should also evaluate yourself, summarizing your feelings about how you did at the end of each class. And finally, your students may want to be evaluated.

Student Evaluations of Teacher

You will want to know how much your students are learning, what they think about the content of the class and how they feel about your teaching style.

Provide a printed evaluation form with boxes to check or questions or statements to rate by number. It is much easier to fill out an evaluation form when the student doesn't have to think about judgmental words. However, space for a few comments will allow students to express their feelings if they so desire.

Knowing what your students think will help you know where you can improve. We have included a full-size sample form in Chapter 18; however, it is best for you to design one to meet your own needs.

Form created by Linda Weisberg, a Certified Palmer/Pletsch Instructor.

(Your Logo)

STUDENT'S EVALUATION OF CLASS & TEACHER

Class Title: _____

Location: _____ Date: _____

Rating Scale
5 = excellent
4 = very good
3 = average
2 = fair
1 = needs improvement

Please rate the following:
___ Quality of instruction
___ Overall class content
___ Amount of information
Comments: _____

___ Value for your dollar
___ Physical classroom arrangements
___ Other _____

What was the most useful thing you learned in this class? _____

What was the least important thing you learned? _____

Would you attend another of my classes? _____
If yes, what would you like to learn more about? _____

Please rate me on the following:

	Poor	Good	Average	Excellent
Level of knowledge				
Appearance				
Cleanliness				
Patience				
Clarity of presentation				
Quality of model garments				
Quality of visuals				
Enthusiasm				
Interaction with students				
Professionalism				

 and Phone/Fax)

Sample form

Palmer/Pletsch

Workshop Evaluation

Date: _____
Workshop: _____

Your evaluation of this workshop is very important so I can continue to improve the program and serve you better. Please consider each question carefully.

1. Why did you take this workshop? _____

2. Did the workshop meet your expectations? _____

3. What aspects of the workshop did you find most valuable? _____

4. What suggestions can you offer for improvement? _____

5. What other topics would you recommend for future workshops? _____

6. How did you find out about the workshop? _____

7. What is your involvement with sewing? Circle all appropriate responses.
   b. Sewing student
   Store manager
   c. Professional sewing guild
   f. Home Ec teacher
   se list your name and

Sponsor Evaluations of Class

If you are teaching in a store or space rented by a sponsor, it is important to let the sponsor know you **want** feedback and that you **want** to make sure you are doing what they expect.

A sponsor evaluation form will provide an easy way for your sponsor to communicate on your performance and your class. You will want to know what to improve or change for the benefit of the sponsor's business.

Self-Evaluations

It is very important to evaluate how you feel you did in each class. This evaluation provides a history of what was taught to whom. Use it as your "contact" sheet for future reference when scheduling new classes with the same sponsor. Record any changes in class format or room arrangement you'd like to make next time. Maybe you need additional tools or samples.

After reading student evaluations, note any problems you want to solve before the next class. Also, make note of what students liked so you can repeat these successes.

File this information with the lesson plan and other materials used for this class. Before the next class, review this evaluation and make suggested changes. Each time a class is presented, it is improved upon and you become a better instructor.

(Your Logo)

SPONSOR EVALUATION OF CLASS
I am very interested in your opinion and comments regarding the following class:

Date: _____ Time: _____

Class Title: _____

Instructor: _____

Please take a few minutes to answer questions that will help me improve the quality of the class and be of maximum benefit to you.

Did the class meet your expectations? _____

Was the attendance what you expected? _____
If no, how could we improve attendance? _____

Was the preparation and promotion what you expected? _____

What should be changed or added? _____

Did you sell product? _____

Are you interested in more classes? If so, when? _____

What topics are you interested in? _____

Please rate me on the following:	Poor	Good	Average	Excellent
Level of knowledge				
Appearance				
Cleanliness				
Patience				
Clarity of presentation				
Quality of model garments				
Quality of visuals				
Enthusiasm				
Interaction with students				
Professionalism				

Phone: _____

SELF-EVALUATION

Class Title: _____

Date: _____ and Time: _____ # Attending: _____

Name of store or other class location: _____ Average age: _____

Contact person: _____

Phone number: _____

Address: _____

Directions: _____

The successes: _____

The difficulties: _____

Physical set up comments: _____

Student names to remember: _____

Notes: _____

Evaluation of Each Student by the Teacher

You may want to evaluate each student's progress after a class has been completed. You could give them a form describing their strengths and where they could improve. Some sewers like this very much and others find it unnecessary.

(Your Logo)

TEACHER'S EVALUATION OF STUDENT

Student name: _____

Address: _____

Phone: _____ Class: _____

Date: _____

Rating Scale
5 = excellent
4 = very good
3 = average
2 = fair
1 = needs improvement

Rating the following:

___Pressing
___Fitting
___Neatness
___Sleeves
___Other

___Collars
___Facings
___Topstitching
___Hems
___Waistbands
___Buttons

___Buttonholes
___Lining
___Interfacing
___Pockets
___Special details
___Completing work

Comments: _____
_____
_____
_____
_____
_____
_____
_____
_____
_____
_____
_____
_____
_____

Teacher: _____

(Your Address and Phone/Fax)

Diplomas

Some teachers have a certificate of completion or a "diploma" they hand out to each of their students. The following is an example of a diploma for a Palmer/Pletsch workshop.

Palmer Pletsch

SYSTEM OF SEWING

CERTIFICATE OF RECOGNITION AWARDED TO

Marcy Miller

FOR SUCCESSFUL COMPLETION OF THE

Tailoring WORKSHOP

DATE *November 20, 1992*

Pati Palmer, President

INSTRUCTORS

CHAPTER THIRTEEN

Classroom Setup

"A space needs to be cozy, comfortable and inspirational."

The class format, topic to be taught, class size and location all play a part in determining classroom setup. There are different challenges between lecture and hands-on classes. There are definitely challenges if you must teach on the selling floor of a store and need quiet and privacy.

Hands-On Classes

A private room offers privacy for fittings, walls on which to mount samples and posters, and the least distractions. Later in this chapter we tell you how to conduct classes on the selling floor. Below is a diagram of a good setup for hands-on classes. This is similar to how Palmer/Pletsch 4-Day Workshops and Teacher Training courses are arranged. Photos on next page show more details. This "ideal" setup requires a lot of space, so you may have to vary from this if space is limited.

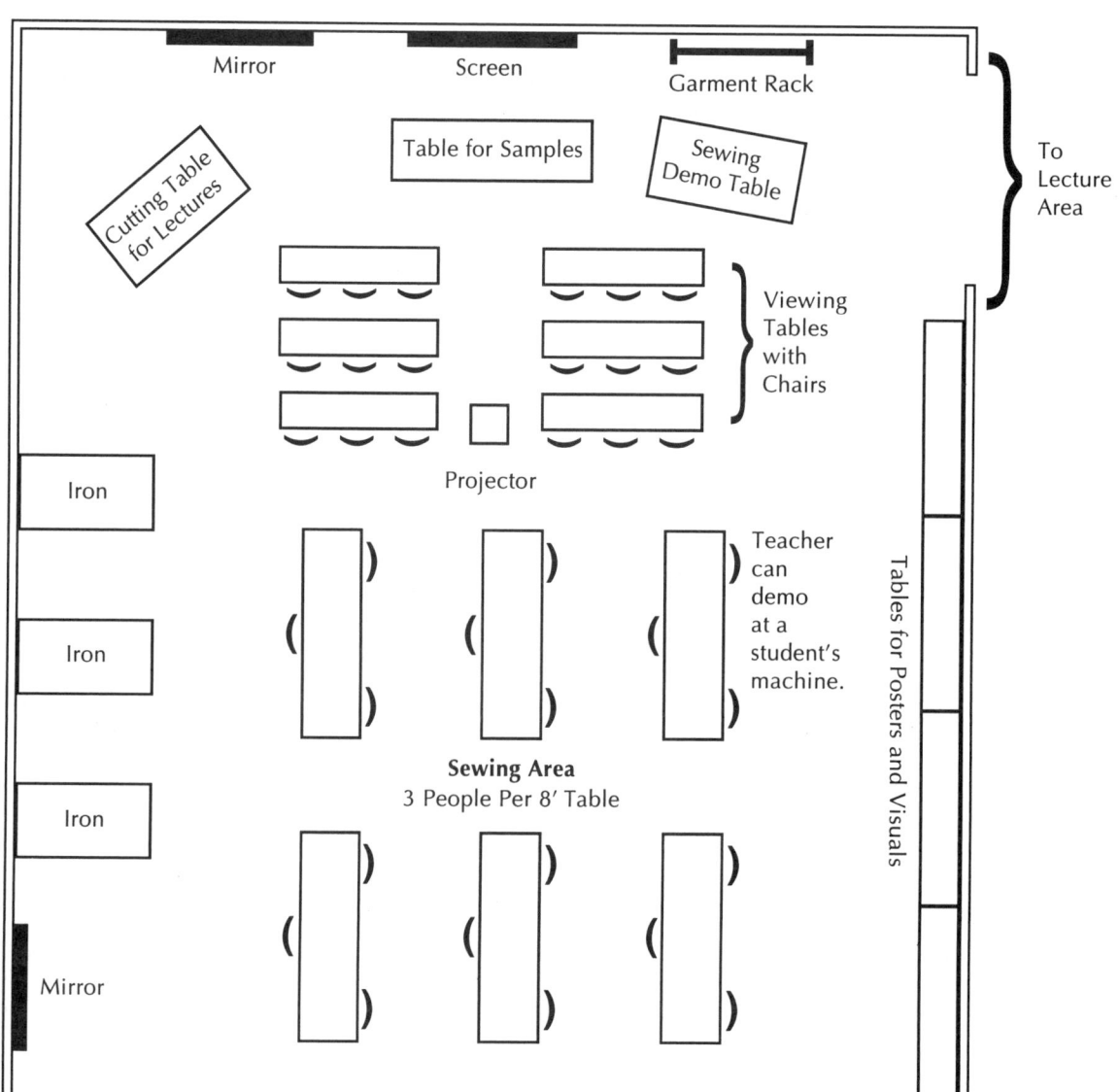

Above, an overall view of the class- room.

At left, a happy student at her serger.

Above, Pati Palmer and Marta Alto lec- ture in the slide viewing area. At right Pati demonstrates to a small group.

These photos were taken during workshops in the state-of-the-art classroom at the Palmer/Pletsch International School of Sewing Arts.

Below, a student in front of fit technique posters.

Marla Kazell and Marta Alto tis- sue-fit a jacket on a student. In the background is a bulletin board filled with pattern ideas.

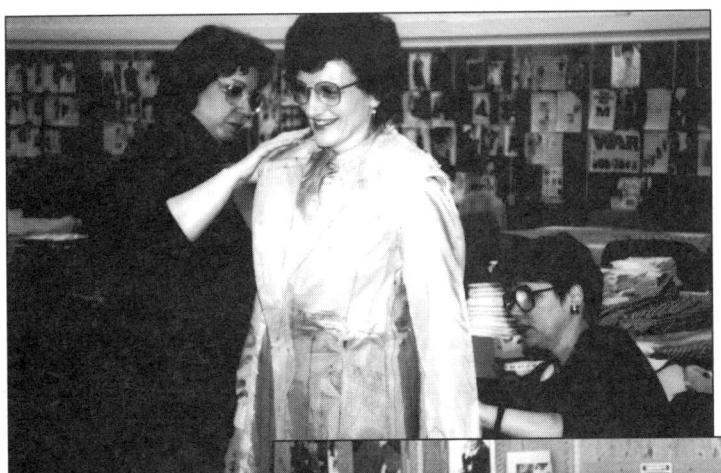

In the overall view of the front of the classroom, above, Lynette Ranney Black introduces the program. At right, a student works at a cutting table.

If you are teaching a crafts class or a make-it-and-take-it session that doesn't require a sewing machine, or a children's hand-sewing class, the setup below works well.

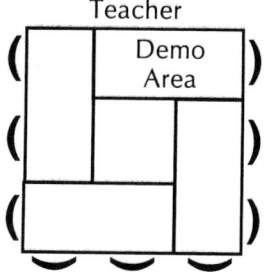

The following setup works well for classes that involve ONLY sewing or serging (no pressing, fitting, pattern prep, etc.).

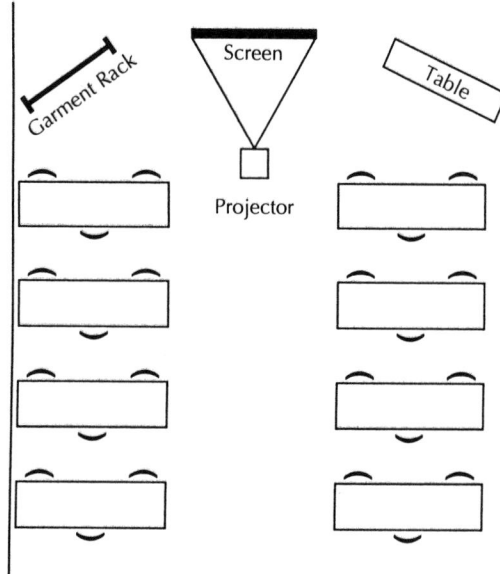

Ideal Work Stations

It is easier for your students to learn and complete their activities if they are physically comfortable. Think about work spaces and tables of various heights for sitting and standing activities. Work spaces for standing activities must be the right height for students of various heights.

Sitting Activities	Standing Activities
Listening and note-taking	Pattern preparation
Pattern preparation	Layout and cutting
Sewing and serging	Marking
Trimming and ripping	Fitting
Hand sewing	Pressing

Cutting Space

If *rotary cutters* are being used, you have better leverage on a lower table. Students may prefer to cut on the same tables on which they will be sewing. If *scissors* are being used, elbow height or slightly lower is preferred. Ideal heights vary between 33" and 42".

Palmer/Pletsch uses the *Sew/Fit* cardboard cutting tables in workshops. They are very sturdy, yet fold flat for easy storage. Printed with a 1" grid, they come in 34" or 40" heights. For rotary cutting, cutting mats are available to fit the tops. The tables, which can be seen on the previous page in the bottom photos, are easily put together, as shown below. See page 108 for the Sew/Fit address.

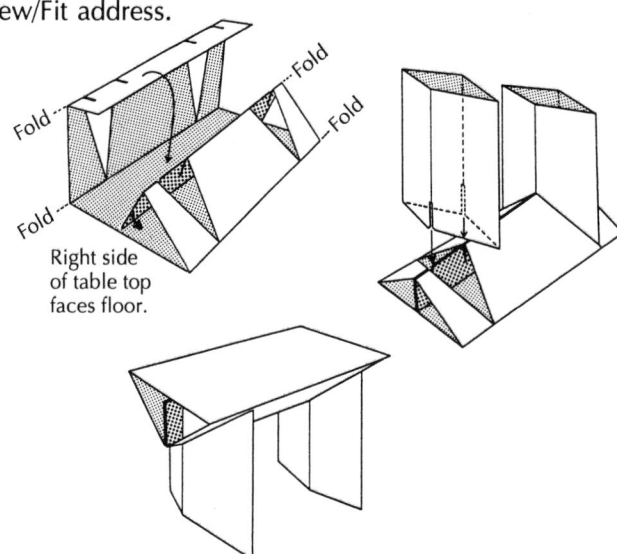

Right side of table top faces floor.

To protect the board when marking tissue patterns with felt-tip pens, place plain newsprint or other paper under the pattern.

Sewing Space

The ideal space to work at a sewing machine is 28" high and 48" wide by 18" deep. These surface dimensions are one quarter of a 3'x8' banquet table. You will note in our hands-on classroom setup on page 68 that we place three people at each banquet table. Because the students face each other and are staggered between tables, this setup has worked well and has saved space. It is fun for the students, too, because they get better acquainted.

ideal classroom sewing space dimensions

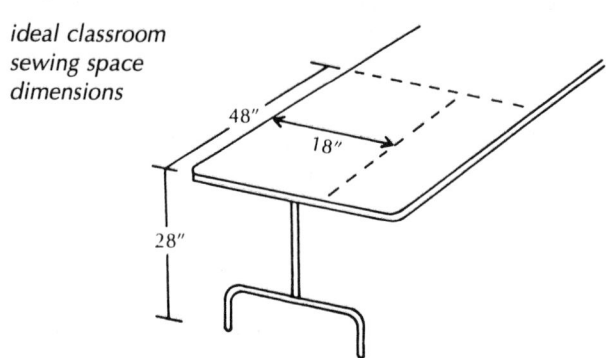

Pressing Space

Pressing surface heights for most people range from 33" to 42", but shorter people can use a surface as low as standard table height of 28"-30" from the floor.

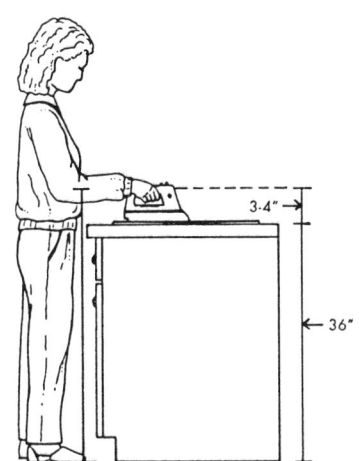

Make Your Own Cut 'n' Press Board

An ironing board is fine for final pressing, but a larger surface is needed for pressing during construction and for fusing. A good way to transform any sturdy table or other surface into a pressing surface is with a cut 'n' press board. A sheet of 5/8" particle board covered with muslin and wool padding makes a perfect pressing and fusing surface as it protects the tabletop from steam and heat.

The cut 'n' press board's generous size (about 32"x48") works well for fusing interfacings or steam-shrinking fabric. You can even use it for cutting out garments. Pin right into the board to secure the pattern pieces to your fabric. For an even larger press board, cover an entire 4'x8' particle board sheet and straddle it over saw horses.

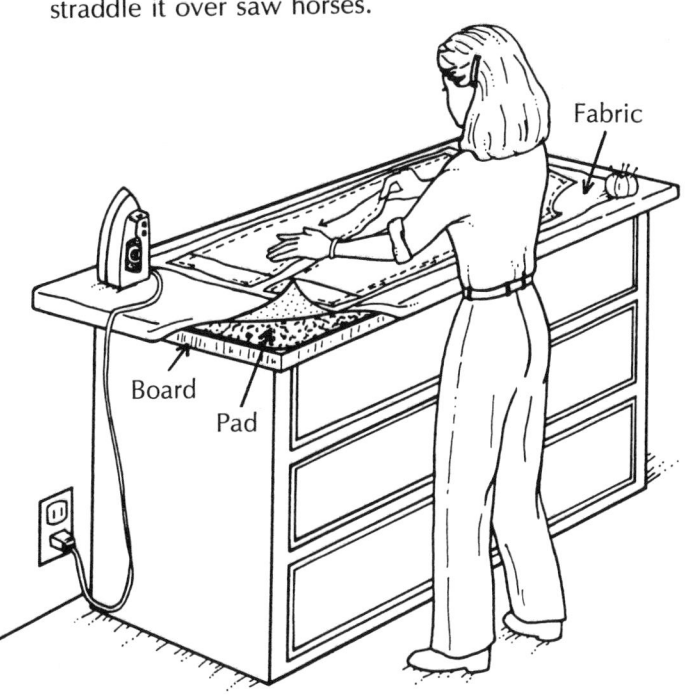

Such a press board can be used on top of a Sew/Fit table or even on your dining room table. It's also sturdy enough to be placed on top of a dresser that has a smaller top; the 5/8"-thick particle board doesn't bend. When not in use, the board can be stored easily under a bed or standing against a wall.

To make your own cut 'n' press board, have the lumber yard cut off 1/3 of a 4'x8' sheet of 5/8"-thick particle board. (Avoid plywood because it can warp if you use lots of steam.) The padding can be a firm wool blanket folded to about 1/2" thick. Or a plain jute rug pad works well if you can find one without a flame retardant rubber coating. Palmer/Pletsch now uses a pad kit from Oregon Tailors' Supply (see Chapter 17, Resources) that consists of cotton waffle cloth and smooth felt. When you order, request the kit they sell to Palmer/Pletsch Workshop students. Provide the dimensions of your board. For the press-board cover, choose muslin or medium-colored, checked gingham.

Follow these instructions from the Palmer/Pletsch pant book:

1. Lay the padding out flat on a large surface.
2. Place the press board on top.

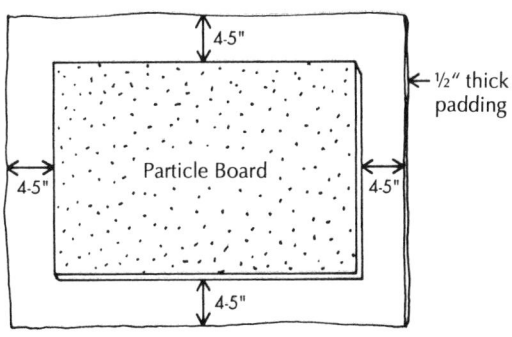

3. Starting in the center of one long side, wrap the padding to the back of the board and staple.
4. Finish one long side, then do the other long side, then the short ends, pulling the padding taut with each staple.
5. To reduce bulk, trim away some of the padding from the corners.

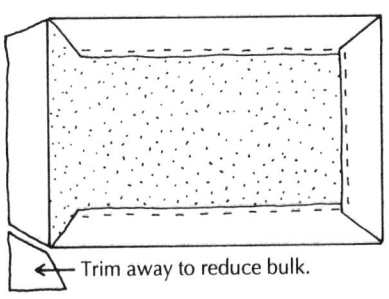

6. Repeat the procedure with the cover fabric. If you are using 1" gingham (we like light blue), and plan to line up your project fabric using the gingham print, double check to make sure the gingham is stretched *evenly*.

7. To reinforce the staples and keep them from scratching you or any surface they rub against, cover them with duct tape.

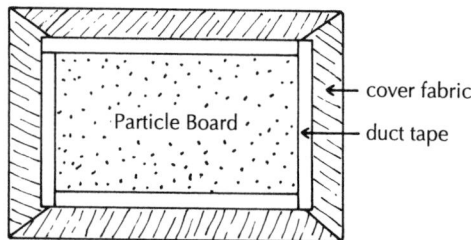

Note: a pre-printed blocking cloth is available from Golden Hands Industries. See Chapter 17, Resources.

When setting up pressing space for hands-on classes, be sure your electrical service will accommodate several irons. Use shot-of-steam type irons and recommend that students purchase their own for home use. We prefer a nonstick coating if students will be fusing interfacings. You might also have a professional iron with a large water tank available for students to use. If distilled water is required, have it available.

Place pressing equipment and press cloths at each pressing station. Take time to show your students how to use all of this equipment including the irons. Be sure to write *"for fusibles, this side down"* on one press cloth with a permanent marker. For safety, write *"NOT for fusibles"* on another.

Other Classroom Setups

Free Demonstration at the Machine

Your purpose in offering free sessions is to promote your paid classes, so do these demonstrations on the sales floor. Try to find a quiet, yet visible space. If you are isolated, you won't draw the crowd you need to get people talking about your classes. Try a location near the front window, yet a distance from the cash register. Because viewing is limited, place a few chairs around the machine and demonstrate to a few people at a time. Keep the demonstrations short so a new group can sit and learn.

Open Sewing Labs

When students are working independently on their own projects, under your supervision, physical requirements are similar to the "ideal" setup on page 68.

Paid Lecture/Demonstrations

An enclosed room is best for paid classes. Check out the room well in advance to decide how it should be set up for best viewing. Always test sound and slides before the first person enters the classroom. If you'll be demonstrating at a sewing machine and the group is not too large, viewing may be best if you're at regular floor level. For large groups, however, speaking from a platform enables both you and your audience to see better. By the way, overhead mirrors don't work well for most sewing demonstrations.

A lecture/demo also can be done in the corner of a store. Then it can help publicize your other classes. Just post a sign indicating the class requires payment so that nonpaying customers don't watch too long. And keep your paying students happy by being sure the area is relatively quiet and free of distractions so you can be heard clearly and easily. A possible setup is illustrated below.

Screened-off areas with sound-reducing dividers can help create a private space in a store. If you are using slides, you must be able to darken the area.

Tables are optional because most people can take notes in their laps. If the lecture is more than three hours and the note-taking more extensive, a table is welcome and provides a leaning post for changing sitting positions.

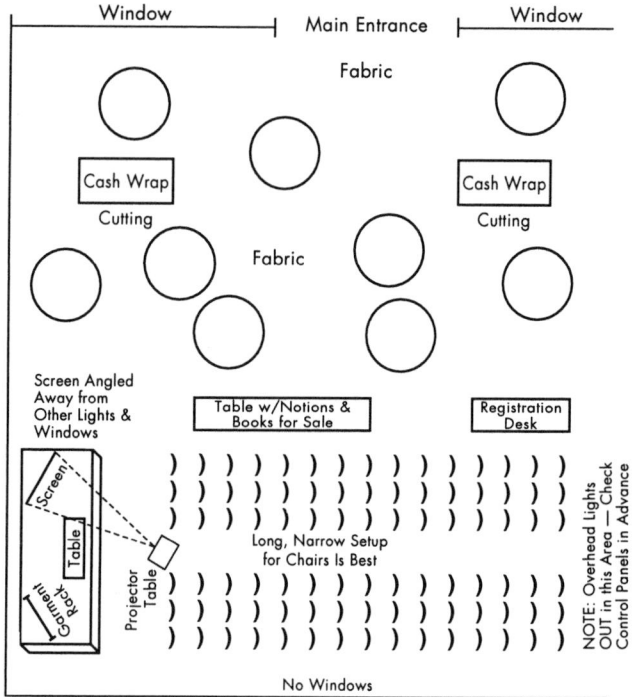

In-store lecture/demonstration

Free Lecture to a Large Audience

To promote your classes to as many people as possible, conduct free lectures near the front of the store at high-traffic times. Have chairs for people to be seated.

When teaching on the sales floor, you'll be competing with other noise. Therefore, speak loudly and clearly, remembering to ask if everyone can hear and see—or use a microphone. Place a table and garment rack near you for your visuals and model garments. If you are showing slides, angle the screen away from any windows and make sure you can dim the lights over the lecture area.

Promote impulse sales for your sponsor by stacking products on a table near the demonstration area.

Make a Checklist of Your Needs

We advised in Chapter 10, Teaching Techniques, to make an instructor's supply list for every class you teach. You might also take photographs of different classroom setups you have used. This will be a valuable instant visual reference.

Who Is Responsible for What?

No matter where you are teaching, discuss the physical setup and arrangements with the store manager and establish responsibilities. Ask a few questions, for example:

- Who is responsible for garment racks, pressing equipment, projectors, screens and mirrors?

- Who will decide the arrangement of tables and chairs, and who will be responsible for their setup? Establish a helping relationship with the staff. Draw a simple layout of the room as you would like it. Don't forget the cleanup and take down.

- Where is the power source? Is there enough power for a sit-and-sew class? Is there enough power for irons?

- How is the lighting? Can lights be dimmed for slides?

Use this handy Arrangements Checklist. (See Chapter 18 for full-size worksheet.)

Instructor's Supply List for Teaching A Pant Fit Course

☐ Have available pant patterns in Misses sizes 6 through 22 (get student measurements ahead to make sure you have correct sizes). You may order the Palmer/Pletsch pant fit pattern, McCall's 4764 at half off the regular retail price of $7.75 in the U.S., $9.60 in Canada, and $9.95 in Australia. In the U.S. call (913) 776-4041, ext. 488; in Canada call (416) 513-9420; and in Australia call 02-550-1044. Just charge to your Mastercard or Visa. Shipping charges will be added. Allow two weeks for delivery. Be careful to order the most commonly used sizes and don't over order as there is no return privilege. You can add great value to your class by including the pattern in the price and make teaching fit easier!

☐ Gingham shells and muslin trousers.

☐ Removable tape in dispensers plus ask students to bring their own.

☐ Soft lead pencils, red and green plastic tip pens, pencil sharpener.

☐ 3 styles pull-on pants

☐ Alteration worksheets

☐ Red pattern alteration tissue plus have students bring their own

☐ Paper trimming scissors, fabric shears, pinking shears for blending ribbon for around your neck.

☐ Cutting and alteration stations with cardboard cutting boards, tape for alterations and demonstration.

☐ Pressing stations with padded boards (recover boards if necessary), pounding blocks, hot iron cleaner.

☐ Precut samples for zippers, darts and waistbands.

☐ Brown paper bags for catching trimmings and wide masking tape.

☐ Dry erase board and markers for fit sign ups.

☐ Model garments

☐ Hanging rack for model garments

☐ Slides and projector, extra bulb, and telescopic pointer.

☐ Visuals/posters

☐ Fashion from "W" for walls

☐ Hand-held and full length mirrors

☐ Basting tape, scotch tape, stay tape, Armoflexxx, tissue, ruler.

©1993 Palmer/Pletsch Inc

ARRANGEMENTS CHECKLIST

Class: _____
Sponsor/Store Name: _____
Contact: _____   Date: _____
Phone: _____   Set Up: _____
                                          Clean Up: _____

Items	Quantity	Provided By
Tables		
Chairs		

Items	Quantity	Provided By

sew easy!
A SEWING SCHOOL FOR GROWN-UPS

TEACHING AGREEMENT

Name of program: Creative Serging

Dates confirmed: Saturday, October 14, 1995   9AM—4PM

Type of class: Hands-on 1-Day Workshop

Fee for class: $75/student   Minimum of 8 students

Payment policy: Payment in full at end of class

I will be providing: Promotional materials - original artwork
Slides, samples
Model garments

You agree to provide: Advertising and flyer distribution
Tables and chairs   Electrical access for machines
Palmer/Pletsch books relating to topic.
Assistant to help with serger problems

Cancellation policy: Up to 1 week prior to program date
I will contact you on October 6

Please read and
sign confirming the

Return this agreement within 5 days, please.
Include a way ref. table for m?

CHAPTER FOURTEEN
Marketing, Promotion and Advertising

"A positive attitude is your best promotional tool."

When you know **what** you want to teach, and **when** and **where** you want to teach it, begin to promote yourself and your classes. Everyone in or out of the trade is a potential student or promoter of your classes, including family members, neighbors and yes, even your doctor, lawyer, hairdresser and dry cleaner.

Getting Sponsors

Before you can promote your classes to potential customers, you must promote yourself to potential sponsors. Sue Hausmann, vice president of education and merchandising for Viking White Sewing Machine Company, offers this valuable advice: "Put together a professional portfolio to assist you as you present yourself, your skills and your classes. Remember, you are the most important part of your portfolio! Dress professionally in a garment you have sewn. Exhibit enthusiasm for and knowledge of the material you will teach. **Maintain a positive attitude at all times!"**

Your Portfolio

- Resume or professional biography (one page—see samples on page 93)
- Black-and-white publicity photo (page 85)
- Biographical paragraph for publicity (page 93)
- Promotional flyers (used for previous classes or mock-up flyers for the classes you want to teach, using guidelines on pages 84-88.)
- Class schedules (if you have taught before)
- Letter(s) of reference
- Class lesson plans (Chapter 9, page 44)
- Finished sample of project
- Handouts, patterns or sample of "kit" if one is to be included
- Sign-up sheet for class registration (page 37)
- Class supply list (page 73)
- Sketch of classroom setup (Chapter 13, page 68)
- Sample agreement form (page 36)
- List of products you will promote (page 55)

Note: If you attend a Palmer/Pletsch Workshop and Teacher Training, you will take home a professional photo of yourself, a camera-ready flyer with registration form, a lesson plan for that workshop topic and many other tools to make your marketing job quick and easy.

Now comes the fun part! Get dressed up in your best "image" outfit, complete with accessories. Gather your date book/calendar, a visual aid or technique sample, and your flyers...and go out and meet the wonderful world of sponsors and customers.

We encourage you to approach prospects you are already familiar with first. Do you have an established relationship with a county extension agent or a fabric or sewing machine store owner or manager? You'll find it easier to get going when the first faces you see are familiar, friendly ones. Calling for an appointment is suggested, but sometimes just stopping by opens doors.

Repetition and consistency are the main ingredients in marketing and promoting yourself. Securing the appointment to return is getting your foot in the door. It is now up to you to make it happen. Be on time, make a good impression and be prepared to answer questions. Be flexible with your program and schedule to meet their needs.

Before this appointment, accumulate some research on their business, products and/or needs. What kinds of customers do they serve? What product lines and brands do they carry? What are their facilities like? A Market Research Form is shown on the next page.

Tell them why you are interested in seeing them. They may have questions you hadn't anticipated or are not prepared to answer. Their questions will help you become better prepared. These friends will also have ideas to add and advice to give. Listen to what they say with an open, positive mind. Use whatever YOU feel is important as sound advice.

As you establish business relationships with new people, be friendly, positive, informed, but more important, businesslike. **Do not waste other people's time in person or on the phone.** A new relationship will develop when mutual respect is established.

Approach a business, such as a fabric shop, by being interested in them and their merchandise. Ask questions that relate to their business and how you might fit in. If you are teaching young children to hand sew, for example, you might ask a fabric store owner or manager if they have many customers with 5- to 9-year-old children. Would these children be interested in a children's class? Would the store be interested in sponsoring children's classes? As a selling point, suggest holding the class on Saturdays so mothers could shop for fabric and patterns while waiting.

Remember to take your date book/calendar. Many of these new acquaintances will want to make a date or an appointment to meet again. They will want to know more at a time when it is convenient for them. Write down these appointments, including names and phone numbers, right on your calendar immediately. If they want a class, schedule it immediately if it fits into your schedule.

A potential "challenge" (nothing is a "problem!") you will face is that many stores with classes will be very loyal to their current teachers. After all, these teachers have been loyal to the store and have contributed to the store's profitability. This is why researching the shops before promoting yourself will help you determine your niche.

At the same time, get to know the other teachers. Introduce yourself to them. If you are aloof, unfriendly or mysterious, they could fear you will replace them. Better yet, take one of their classes and be a good student. See how they teach and see how their students respond. You can tell them that by taking their class, you will be better able to promote their classes.

You are beginning to develop an **"I am interested in helping you"** relationship. The result will benefit your business. Networking to help each other is very important! Establish these relationships with as many other teachers and professionals as you can find.

You know how people like to talk. This is called word-of-mouth advertising—your best and least expensive advertisement. Everything you do—the good and the not-so-good—will be passed on. Keeping this in mind, remember to be professional.

Don't fall into the **unprofessional** role of being a gossip, especially one that speaks negatively or puts down others. Even if someone decides to do that to you, rise above their remarks. You will come out ahead and maybe even eventually turn them around. These people are often jealous or insecure. Most people will take any negative comments they may make about you with a grain of salt. Remember, they are probably damaging themselves more than you.

Even if you are not hired to teach in the store, check to see if the sewing machine dealership or fabric store has an annual **special event**. Why not volunteer to participate in some way? If you are new to the area or to teaching, setting up mini demos will help you gain exposure for and create interest in your classes.

How about short lectures on pattern and fabric selection, or a fashion forecast for the season? Or create a "Knock Off the Designers" lecture with a display of visuals using pictures from fashion magazines with corresponding current patterns. The store may decide to offer your classes, or if they don't have a classroom, let you promote your home-based classes.

Or maybe the store would like their **special event** to be one of your lectures or special-technique demonstrations, for which they would pay you a fee or let you promote your classes. Emphasize to the store owners and their personnel that statistics prove each person attending a class will spend an average of $15 to $20 per visit. Fifty customers at $15 per customer is $750 in sales. Offer to be available for a local newspaper, radio or TV interview to help them promote the event.

Market Research Form

Use this form to record information on each sponsor you meet. See Chapter 18, Camera-Ready Forms, for a full-size form you can copy.

Market Research Form				Date:	
Name of Store or School:			Type of Store or School:		
Address:	City:	State:	Zip:		Phone:
Contact Owner/Manager:			Other VIP:		
Classes		**Fees**	**Type of Merchandise**		**Brands**
Type of Classroom:			Notes:		

In review, use our step-by-step guide for selling yourself to potential sponsors:

A Step-By-Step Guide to Marketing and Promoting Your Classes to Stores

1. **Visit your potential sponsor.**

   a. Act professionally.

   b. Dress professionally.

   c. Carry date book or calendar.

2. **Survey the store for:**

   a. Type of clientele.

   b. Merchandise (kinds and brands).

   c. Physical space and equipment available for a class.

   d. Types of classes.

   e. What is missing.

3. **Fill in your "Market Research Form"** (page 76).

   a. Complete all data.

   b. Determine potential of this sponsor.

   c. Select a sponsor or sponsors.

4. **Ask to speak with the owner/manager.**

   a. Note his or her name.

   b. Introduce yourself and the classes you teach.

   c. Ask for an appointment to discuss classes and promotion.

   d. Leave your card and/or flyer.

   Note: If owner/manager is unavailable, call for an appointment. Ask for the person by name and introduce yourself and class ideas. Then continue the next steps.

5. **Write the appointment on your calendar.**

   a. Call to confirm appointment two or three days before.

6. **Be prepared!**

   a. Assemble your promotional materials.

   b. Bring letters of reference.

   c. Assemble your portfolio, samples, garments, etc.

   d. Plan what to wear.

7. **The appointment:**

   a. Be on time!

   b. Ask for the owner/manager by name.

   c. Introduce yourself and your class.

   d. State what you want, being brief, positive and pleasant.

   e. Schedule a class now if possible or ask if they want to "think" about your proposal.

   f. Discuss arrangements or schedule another appointment to go over them. (Again, be efficient, don't rattle on—these are retailers and retailing is a very time-taking business as is teaching sewing!)

Give Your Sponsors Guidance

Now you have a sponsor. They can help you promote to the public—after all, your customers can be their customers!

Palmer/Pletsch has provided these guidelines to sponsors over the years. More examples are shown on page 100.

Palmer Pletsch SEMINAR PLANNER

Make YOUR Register Ring!
The more people, the more SALES!
Full seminars create shopping fever.

How to Get the Crowds
- **Make the Seminar a Fun Event!!**
- Let **Home Economics Teachers** and **Extension Agents spread the word** for you. Give them a flyer and fact sheet NOW as they could print it in one of their newsletters.

Send out an announcement to calendar sections of newspapers, local TV and radio stations.

Pass Out Our Flyers two months in advance. Mention the program at other store events.

Make a Poster using the enclosed photos of your representative. Place one by the door and one at each register. Post ... in the bathrooms.

... use the flyer as a "bag stuffer." ... then to customers and suggest they ... while you ring up their sale.

... Flyer or Poster in Your Front ...ws.

...age Your Sales People to ...tically promote the program.
... Mouth is your best advertising!

...et Sales

...uying Atmosphere. Place ...es of notions, patterns and ...tsch books on special tables ...hop area.

...% Discount on all ... special items.

...r Salespeople to ...r. It's FREE to them and ...NING to you. Schedule ... can participate.
... seminar if they test-
... sell.

✓ Checklist

Done	Days in Advance	Things to Do
	NOW	Set dates, times and find space.
	NOW	Plan promotion: ads, flyer printing, direct mail, community contacts (extension, teachers, sewing professionals).
	NOW	Put signs in store—everywhere!
	NOW	Print flyers, pass out at prior events, have customers read while you ring up their sale.
	NOW	Tell sales people about workshop.
	45	Order back-up stock of notions and Palmer/Pletsch books.
	21	Call newspaper Fashion or Lifestyle Editor. Explain seminar. Suggest a telephone interview with teacher. Take press kit and flyer.
	14	Send dates to radio, TV and newspaper for their calendars.
	14	Run first ad (mailers go out sooner).
	10	Arrange for screen, garment rack, platform, tables and chairs.
	7	Second reminder ad.
	7	Let the teacher know the number of paid pre-registered customers.
	3	If classes are small discuss with teacher whether or combine or cancel.

FOR MORE INFORMATION CONTACT:

put your name, address and phone number here

Palmer Pletsch ALL-DAY WORKSHOP PLANNER

Make YOUR Register Ring!
The more people, the more SALES!
Full workshops create shopping fever.

How to Get the Crowds
- **Make the Workshop a Fun Event!!** Add a networking lunch. Ideas below.
- Let **Home Economics Teachers** and **Extension Agents spread the word** for you. Give them a flyer and fact sheet NOW as they could print it in one of their newsletters.
- Send out an announcement to calendar sections of local papers, TV and radio stations.
- **Pass Out Our Flyers** two months in advance. Mention program at other store events.
- **Make a Poster** using the enclosed photos of the teacher. Place one at the door and one at each register. Post flyers in the bathrooms.
- Don't use the flyer as a "bag stuffer." Hand it then to customers and suggest they read it while you ring up their sale.
- **Place Flyer or Poster in Front Windows.**
- **Encourage Your Sales People** to enthusiastically promote the program. **Word of Mouth** is your best advertising!
- Tell customers this is a one-day version of the Palmer/Pletsch $550 4-day workshops held in Portland, Oregon.

How to Get Sales
- **Create a Buying Atmosphere.** Place large quantities of notions, patterns and Palmer/Pletsch books on special tables near the workshop area.
- **Serve Food.** A light buffet luncheon, pizza, or, if in a hotel, a sit-down lunch. Often the room is free if lunch is paid for. Add the expense to the workshop fee. If not providing food and no restaurants are within walking distance, suggest students bring a bag lunch.
- **Give a 15-20% Discount** on all merchandise or special items.
- Offer a free workshop or a percentage off if they buy a serger or top-of-the-line sewing machine.
- Offer $5-$15 off the workshop if they test-drive a machine you sell.
- **Encourage Your Salespeople** to attend the workshop. It will make them better sellers. (Only the actual helpers are allowed to attend free. Your representative will tell you how many will be needed, based on attendance.)

✓ Checklist

Done	Days in Advance	Things to Do
	NOW	Set dates, times and find space.
	NOW	Plan promotion: ads, flyer printing, direct mail, community contacts (extension, teachers, sewing professionals).
	NOW	Put signs in store—everywhere!
	NOW	Print flyers, pass out at prior events, have customers read while you ring up their sale.
	NOW	Tell sales people about workshop.
	45	Order back-up stock of notions and Palmer/Pletsch books.
	21	Call newspaper Fashion or Lifestyle Editor. Explain workshop. Suggest a telephone interview with teacher. Take press kit and flyer.
	14	Send dates to radio, TV and newspaper for their calendars.
	14	Run first ad (mailers go out sooner).
	10	Arrange for screen, garment rack, platform, tables and chairs.
	7	Second reminder ad.
	7	Let the teacher know the number of paid pre-registered customers.
	3	If classes are small, discuss with your teacher whether to combine or cancel.

FOR MORE INFORMATION CONTACT:

put your name, address and phone number here

The pages at right go to sponsors at the same time, outlining setup needs. For more about setup guidance, see Chapter 13, Other Classroom Setups, page 72.

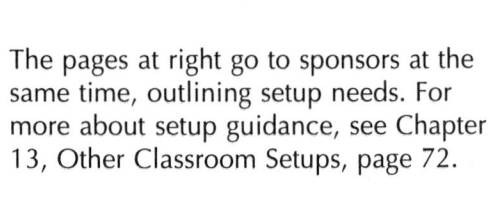

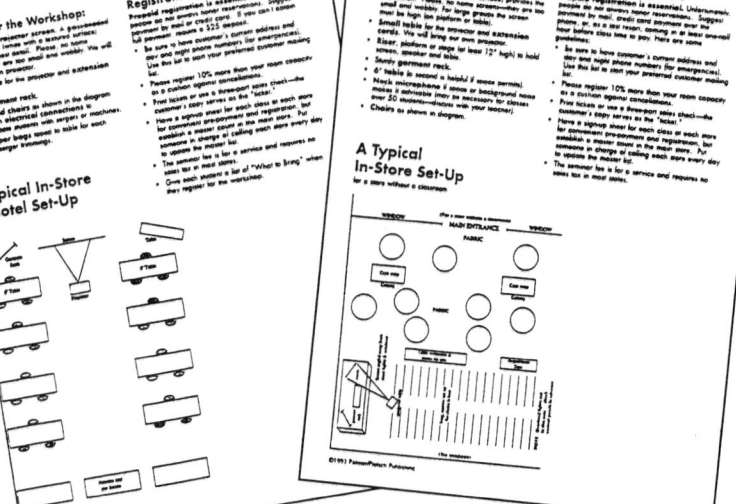

Palmer/Pletsch
Tips to Bring in Customers

Our sew seminar, Creative Serging for the Home, covers a very broad range of
... easier and with better results. People love

Palmer/Pletsch
Tips for Getting Sales

1. Sell tickets — On the 1st 50 people (our minimum) if you charge $25, you get
   $5/person ($250 total to you).
   - On sales over 50 people, you get $7.50/person.
   - **Therefore, if 100 people come - YOU MAKE $625!**

2. Sell fabric — yards and yards, but remember, with home dec they may have to go
   home and plan first so offer a 10-20% discount to get the...

3. Sell notions — Group all the notions...
   display near your ho...
   projects if possible.

4. Have plenty of stock on hand. Our...

and other be...

1. Use our seminar as FREE sales train...
   experience. By encouraging your sa...
   greatest benefit. How do you get the...

   - Romance the seminar...
     attend.
   - Pay them. When they...
     hours salary while they...
     investment!

2. Develop manager awareness. We sug...
   make it their responsibility to know wha...

3. Be a partner with one of the most res...
   known for quality books, videos and th...
   money-back satisfaction guarantee!

Sales Personnel Are Your Best Promoters

Inform store sales personnel about your classes so they can advertise for you. Show each of them your flyer and explain class content. Invite them to attend your classes FREE or at a discount. Create a letter to them describing your classes and giving them ideas of what to say about you and your classes.

SALES PERSONNEL LETTER
Post in bathroom for all to read!

TO: SALES PERSONNEL
FROM: LYNN RAASCH

...wing Seminar

...CESS! Please take the next few minutes to find out what

Your customers are just like you—busy women who work and have families to care for, yet love to sew. Many have minimum sewing skills and lack the knowledge or confidence to do good work the fastest, newest way. In this seminar we will encourage your customer to sew more—and enjoy it!

HOW WILL WE DO IT?

- A 3-hour slide/lecture program will go step-by-step through fast sewing techniques and the use of today's new equipment. Because we use slides, even the smallest sewing tips will be 6 feet tall! Even classes of 100 or more clearly see every step.
- A wardrobe of Spring's best fashions will be used to show your customers how to sew a wardrobe in record time: 2-hour blouses, 3-hour skirts and pants, 8 hour jackets. PLUS...THE dress to sew for Spring—in 30 minutes or less!
- We'll talk about the new SERGERS and show your customers how to use them for fast finishing AND total construction.

WHO CAN BENEFIT FROM THIS SEMINAR?

EVERYONE from beginner to professional will have the chance to update their skills to save time and enjoy sewing more than ever before. Even the more experienced sewer can learn something new about equipment and manufacturer's techniques to make her sewing easier. AND the novice will not be intimidated. She'll learn to sew FAST from the very beginning!

WHAT WILL THEY LEARN?

- How to simplify patterns.
- How to look a size smaller in clothes that really fit.
- Fit-As-You-Sew™ methods for speed and perfection.
- All about time-saving gadgets and speedy sewing techniques, including cutting tips, pressing aids, how to choose and use the fusible interfacings, painless plackets and fast seam finishes.

We will pull fabric from your stock to feature the latest SPRING/SUMMER looks. And since the best results depend on the right tools, we'll also show the latest sewing notions.

Each seminar customer receives the book **Mother Pletsch's Painless Sewing** by Pati Palmer and Susan Pletsch (a $8.95 retail value) as our gift. We guarantee the customer will be satisfied and issue a refund if anyone is not. Remind customers that pre-payment is required, but if they must cancel and do so 24 hours in advance, a full refund is granted. In case of an emergency suggest they treat a friend to their ticket.

We extend an invitation to all of your to attend the seminar... purchase the book for reference during the class, since the complimentary books a...

IT'S A FACT: **YOU** are the best advertising for seminars at... flyer so you know all about it. Your enthusiasm and knowle...

Palmer/Pletsch

GET FREE PUBLICITY

...PAPER

...attendance has tripled when newspaper articles run in advance of the event.
...Most daily newspapers require a 10-day to two-week deadline.
...ur local newspapers and sk for the fashion editor, lifestyles editor, or home living

...they mention your seminar in their calendar of events and SUGGEST AN ARTICLE on
...er/Pletsch representative and seminar. Remember to explain that they will be doing
...ders a service by running an article ahead of time. Be sure to tell the editor the date,
...d location and that pre-registration is necessary. Mention that there is a class fee,
...cludes a free sewing book.

...a telephone interview with the Palmer/Pletsch representative. Give us a phone
...nd convenient time to call the editor, and we will arrange the interview.
...e deadline necessary for submitting a news release and tell the editor you have a
...ou will bring in to them. DELIVER IT YOURSELF. Personal contact brings better

...ditor to attend the seminar free as our guest.

...N AND RADIO

...WS: Our office would like to arrange a TV appearance or radio interview for your
...ch representative when schedules permit. Your help is needed. Please give us
...information 8 weeks in advance: station name, address, phone, and producer's
...call the switchboard and ask!)

...Y CALENDARS: Contact the community affairs department of your local TV and
...and inform them of the seminar. Most stations can broadcast details on any
...pen to the public.

...CE ANNOUNCEMENTS: Call your local stations to inquire about making
...announcements on the seminar and related sewing tips.

...ENSION SERVICE and LOCAL TEACHERS

...ts in your area and surrounding counties of your seminar dates immediately
...y mention the seminar in their newsletter. Call their office NOW, as they only
...ers per year. And don't forget to ask your high school, college, adult educa-

---

Palmer/Pletsch

TO: Sponsors of the Brush Up Sewing Seminar
FROM: Lynn Raasch

I have enclosed your **SEMINAR PLANNER KIT**. It will make your preparation easy and your event run smoothly. Please read through it NOW so you can start your long-range planning and promotion at once. The kit contains:

1. **SEMINAR PLANNER SUMMARY AND CHECKLIST:** Your planning time-line, plus a guide on how to MAKE YOUR REGISTER RING, HOW TO GET THE CROWDS and HOW TO GET SALES. On the back side are a list of items needed for the seminar, a typical in-store set-up diagram, and registration procedures.
2. **SPONSOR RESPONSIBILITY GUIDELINES:** the rules and tips for holding a successful seminar or workshop.
3. **CAMERA-READY FLYERS:** We are sending two copies—one to give to the quick printer to print as flyers/mailers and the other to use for an in-store sign. Be sure to add your name, address, etc.
4. **PHOTOS:** two 8x10 photos are enclosed to use on large in-store posters. Create a poster, using the flyer as a guideline...and get your customers' attention.
5. **ADVERTISING SLICK:** This slick is ready to take to the newspaper. Add your store name, address, hours, etc., or have the newspaper do it. If you need more slicks, let me know.
6. **GET FREE PUBLICITY:** Some helpful ideas to generate news about your seminar or workshop. A press release and 5x7 photo are enclosed.
7. **BOOK ORDER FORM:** To make it easier for you to order your Palmer/Pletsch books for sale at the seminar or workshop. Place your order NO LATER THAN 4 WEEKS BEFORE YOUR CLASSES.
8. **MODEL GARMENT LIST:** This list details the garments I will wear and/or show during the seminar. The list includes Pattern # information, fabric and findings used. You will want to have these patterns and findings on hand to maximize sales.
9. **PRODUCT LIST:** Make sure to have a generous stock of product on hand. I have complied this list of products I will be mentioning in my presentation. I will also review your stock before class and include any other products that relate.
10. **SHOPPING LIST:** To make shopping even easier for students, give you the list at break, beginning of class. They check off what they want to purchase. They appreciate it. YOU make a sale! and you fill their order as they finish their class.
11. **BRING LIST:** Provide this list to students as they register for a class.
12. **SALES PERSONNEL LETTER:** This letter to your sales staff explains the seminar function and content. The more knowledgeable they are about this program, the more effective they will be in taking care of your customers.

I will be contacting you soon to see how you are progressing with your plans. Have any ...questions ready. I'll be glad to help. If you need more materials, or need to contact me for any

---

Palmer/Pletsch

MODEL GARMENTS and Notions

BRUSH-UP SEWING
Seminar

MODEL GARMENT WARDROBE - by Lynn Raasch

McCall's Pattern #	Garment
3533*	Linen suit, lined
3600* / 3478*	Blouse and pleated skirt
3320*	Cotton blend tweed jacket, partially lined
3522	Slim skirt
3522	Top
2934*	Unlined polyester jacket and skirt, silk blouse
3574	Dress in rayon challis
2884	Polyester 2-piece dress
2718*	Polyester shirtdress
2718*	Linen blouse
2987	Cotton knit dress
2914 / 2851*	Linen tweed jacket and sweater knit T
3479	Nubby poly/cotton knit pullover and cotton fleece pant
2913 / 3538	Cotton stripe baseball jacket and woven poly blend pant
2618*	Plaid cotton shirt
3318	Silky 1/2 slip

Products and Notions I use:

Pressing Equipment:
  Pressing hams
  Seam roll   June Tailor board
  Clapper/point presser   Steam irons
  (June Tailor's is my favorite)   (Rowenta or Simac MX 150 are preferred)
Fusible Interfacing:
  Weft Insertion type – Suit Shape, Armoweft, Whisper Weft
  Tricot – Easy Knit, Quick Knit
  Waistband Shaper – ArmoFlexx, Ban Rol
  Waistband Elastic – Non-roll woven knit elastic
Grabbit® and quality pins (not Grabbit refills) such as superfine 1-1/8 glass head pins
Point Turner   Clear elastic – 3/8" or 1/4"
Buttonhole cutter   Chalk wheel marker
Rotary cutter and mat (30" x 36")   Seams Great or Seam Saver
Shoulder pads – 1/2" and 1" raglan styles for a softer shoulder

Flyers

You need a one-page black and white flyer that is simple, explicit and easy-to-read. State and describe the class you teach, the location, dates, times and price.

Designing Your Flyer

A few flyer ideas are shown on these pages. Others can be found throughout the book, including pages 23-27 and page 43. Refer to these examples when making your own. Put your name directly under your photo. If you don't use a photo, your name and business name should be the most prominent words on your flyer next to the class title. Include a brief history of your skills as they pertain to your teaching business and a brief description of your qualifications. Finally, include a phone, address and fax number if you have one. If you take the class reservations, your number is used; if the sponsor handles registration, that number would appear on the flyer.

You can create your own flyer if you have access to a computer and a laser printer. Using the flyer examples in this book, design your flyer with the type (font) styles and sizes available to you. Use no more than two type styles. More can be confusing to read.

Typefaces come in two categories—serif and san serif, i.e., with little crossbars and without:

serif: san serif:

type   **type**

For promotional materials we use Futura Book for content and **Futura Bold** for titles and headings. These have been chosen for their clear, precise letters that combine well and read easily. Another good option is **Helvetica**, which is more commonly found. This paragraph is in **Optima**, a font we find very readable on book pages. Each font, or typeface, comes as a group, or family, which usually includes at least a bold, a regular and an italic version.

If your software does not accommodate large type size, find a copier with an enlarger. Print out from your computer only those lines to be enlarged. On the copier enlarge these lines to the size you need. Cut and paste these lines onto the flyer.

Cut and paste, or "paste-up," is what you have to do when there are separate pieces of art or words that must be combined to create a "camera-ready" flyer that is reproducible on a copier or at your printer. We don't really use paste any more. Glue sticks are an option, as are rubber cement, re-positionable adhesive sprays, and our favorite—wax. A hand-held electric waxer can be purchased at an art supply store. It rolls a thin layer of melted wax on the back of a piece of art or type. The waxed piece can then be positioned

on the page. When it is exactly where you want it, cover with aprotective piece of paper and rub or "burnish" with a blunt object (even the back of your fingernail will do!) to secure it firmly to the surface.

For those who are whizzes at desktop publishing, and can scan or import artwork, paste-up is becoming obsolete.

When laying out your design (deciding what goes where), keep in mind that if you are going to print your flyer, the printer needs a "gripper" or area free of ink along one edge of the piece. Also, if you design a flyer that has artwork or copy "bleeding" off the edge, it may have to be printed on a larger sheet and trimmed down—which increases the cost.

If you are not comfortable designing your own flyer, find a quick printer with computer and laser printing capabilities. Show them our examples. Make a sketch (it can be rough) of what you would like. Give the printer as many ideas or examples as needed to communicate what you are looking for. Also, give them the copy (text) you'd like on the flyer.

If you like this printer and find the cost reasonable, use them regularly. This printing company will become an asset to your new business. By knowing and helping you with each project, the staff becomes more familiar with what you are doing. Eventually, they may even be able to offer YOU new ideas and recommendations.

Use a C-thru ruler to line up your pasted-up items and copy.

your SEW-cial calendar for fall

start with AUGUST

- FREE fashion/fabric seminars . . . learn what's new for fall and how you can create it from our collection of fabrics . . . see latest techniques of working with shaping fabrics, new seams and more. All sessions at our Downtown store, 5th floor:
  Monday, August 6 - 10 a.m. and 7 p.m.
  Tuesday, August 7 - 12 noon
- FREE consultations. Our expert sales staff has just completed a series of training sessions to help you with your fall sewing plans. Plus . . . during the week of August 6, our two home economists will be available to help you in any way they can at our Downtown store.
- FREE scissor sharpening. A craftsman deserves the best tools. If your scissors are dull, bring them into our Downtown Fabric Department Monday, August 6 between 10 and 4 and have them sharpened free. One pair per person (or nominal charge for additional pairs). No pinking shears, please.
- FREE fashion shows. The most dashing looks in town modeled by the men and women who made them. Great opportunity to see popular patterns made up and accessorized. Each show will include fashion and sewing technique tips for fall.
  - Thursday, August 9 - 7:30 p.m. – Lloyd's, Aladdin Room
  - Friday, August 10 - 12 noon – Downtown, Fabric Department
  - Saturday, August 11 - 11 a.m. – Salem, Fabric Department
  - Saturday, August 11 - 2 p.m. – Eugene, Rotunda
  . . . . . and our fall sewing classes start. See schedule below

then comes SEPTEMBER

- VOGUE Fashion Shows: 'The Many Faces of Fall' incorporating all the elegance of Vogue patterns for both men and women as created from Vogue patterns.
  Thursday, Sept. 13 - 12 noon and 1 p.m. in our Downtown Auditorium, 10th floor.
  Thursday, Sept. 13 - 7:30 p.m. – Lloyd's Aladdin Room
  Friday, Sept. 14 - 12 noon – Salem fabric department
  Saturday, Sept. 15 - 12:30 – Eugene Rotunda

fall SEWING CLASSES begin:

- Brush-up Sewing – Monday, August 13* at 6:30 p.m. DT
  Wednesday, August 15* at 10 a.m. DT
  Wednesday, October 24 at 10 a.m. DT
  $15 - 2 hour sessions lasting 8 weeks
  Course covers sewing and fitting of current fashions in both woven and stretch fabrics. For the intermediate and advanced seamstress. Shortcuts, interfacings, underlinings, linings, pressing and more will be covered.
  *free gift to first 100 students
- Custom Tailoring – Thursday, August 16 at 10 a.m. DT
  $15 - 2 hour sessions lasting 6 weeks
  Tailoring basics, adapted from menswear techniques: fitting, hand-pad stitching, selection of fabrics, linings, interlinings, interfacing. Brush-up course is a prerequisite.
- Speed Tailoring – Monday, October 22 at 6:30 p.m. DT
  Thursday, October 25 at 10 a.m. DT
  $15 - 2 hour sessions lasting 6 weeks
  Teaches quality tailoring incorporating hand and machine stitching. Short cuts, new notions and techniques. Brush-up class is a prerequisite.
- Fashion Awareness – Tuesday, August 14 at 7:00 p.m. Lloyd's
  $10 - 2 hour session for 6 weeks
  Thorough grounding in color, lines, designs that are best for you. Survey of the latest accessories, cosmetics as they can be used to enhance your fashion look. Whether you sew or not, you'll enjoy and benefit from this Fashion Awareness class in your wardrobe planning.

check our new SEWING SEMINARS:

- Menswear sewing – Thursday, September 6 - 10 a.m. DT
  Friday, September 7 - 10 a.m. and 6 p.m. DT
  Saturday, September 8 - 11 a.m. DT
  A three-hour session covering all the latest sewing techniques as they relate to pants, jackets, shirts. Learn the speedy way to measure, fit and sew fashions he'll be proud to wear. Cost is $3 for the seminar.
- Pants fitting – Thursday, August 16 - 6 p.m. Salem
  Friday, September 21 - 10 a.m. and 6 p.m. DT
  Saturday, September 22 - 11 a.m. DT
  An intensive three-hour class on fitting and constructing pants for women or men. Please wear slacks to the session. Charge for the seminar is $3.

To register for any of the sewing classes or seminars, please call 227-4411, extension 7133. Registration is suggested as all classes must be limited in size for effective teaching. You may charge your registration fee to your M&F charge account.

just off the press! 'pants for every body'
. . . by Pati Palmer, M&F Home Economist

Her first book! Devoted to perfect fitting pants for you, for him. Covers everything from making a basic pattern in 30 minutes to the last couture finishing touch. 65 pages with dozens of illustrations. Available in our fabric departments for $2.50, order yours today.

This was Pati Palmer's most effective mailer when she ran the educations program at Meier & Frank. She had it printed in plum and red-orange inks on celery-green paper!! The mailing panel is shown above and the inside is at left.

For more flyer ideas see pages 23-27.

A 3-HOUR SEMINAR
Time Saving Sewing

Time...moving too fast and always elusive. Learn how to *find* time to sew by stream-lining the process. Lynn will provide tips and techniques for:

- Our unique continuous sewing
- How to organize a sewing project
- Quick fitting
- Easy interfacing how-tos
- The new notions and sewing tools

Plus special easy ideas for zippers, sleeves, collars, waistbands, buttonholes, pockets, seam finishes and hems.

Time:

Place:

Date:

Price:

Meet Lynn Raasch
Home economist, a Palmer/Pletsch sewing professional and co-star of the Palmer/Pletsch video, Sewing Today the Time Saving Way. Lynn's seminars are a combination of teaching, inspiration and entertainment.

A FREE SEMINAR
Tools FOR Easy Sewing

The right sewing tools and notions can make the difference between a professional-looking garment and one that looks "homemade." They can also make your life easier! Come see the newest and best... and how to use them.

date:

time:

place:

price:

Meet Marta Alto
Palmer/Pletsch Corporate Educator and sewing expert.

Offer a FREE seminar. You'll be surprised at how many who attend will sign up for your other classes

Using Photographs

If a photo is used on a flyer, it needs to be "screened" to turn it into dots of different sizes. A screened photo is called a *halftone* image. This allows a printing press with only black ink to re-create all the gray tones you see in a photograph. A fine line screen of over 100 dots per square inch is best. Newspapers used to handle only 80 lines or the photo would get muddy because of the quality of their paper. That has changed. Talk to your printer about how fine a screen they suggest. Your printer may also have a scanner. Ask to see the quality of their scanned photo.

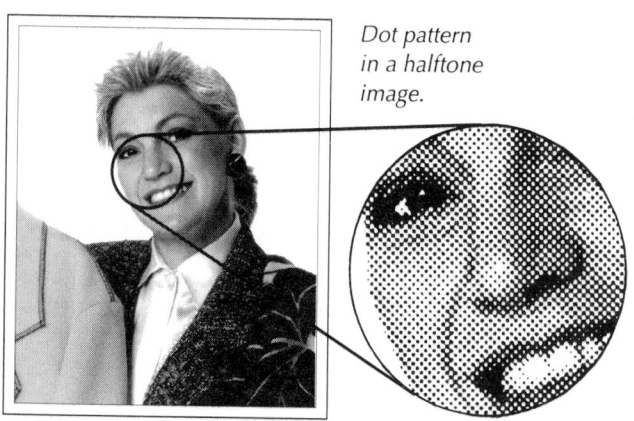

Dot pattern in a halftone image.

If the flyer has a photo, always see a "proof" before printing, or be there when the printer runs the flyer. Some printers do an excellent job; others allow a photo to become too dark or too light. Do not accept poor quality.

Using Line Art

If you are on a tight budget, use line art rather than a photo, and your own typewriter or computer printout combined with attractive handwritten script for a title. Cut and paste the parts onto a flyer and photocopy (see page 80). After one copy, use correction fluid to remove any paste-up lines from the photocopy. Some copiers have a blue-erase button that you can push before making a copy. It often eliminates paste-up lines. Now you have your "original" from which to make more copies. Photos will not turn out professionally on a copier, though that could change!

Teachers who use Palmer/Pletsch books as class textbooks may use, without special permission, line art from the books on flyers. Any of the books' **fashion line art** may be just what you need to add a touch of professionalism to a flyer. A photo or picture of some sort will make your flyer noticed MUCH MORE QUICKLY than one with copy only.

from *My First Embroidery Book*

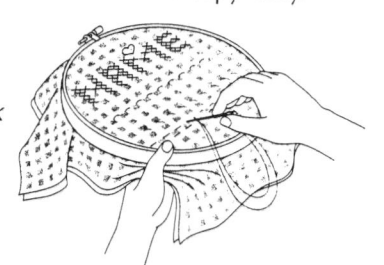

Ultrasuede Accessories

Sew A Beautiful Wedding

Fabulous *Ultrasuede*

Easy, Easier, Easiest Tailoring

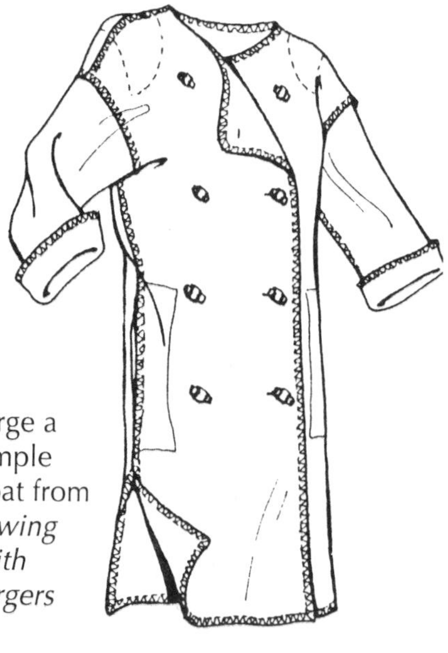

Serge a Simple Coat from *Sewing With Sergers*

Examples of Illustrations from Palmer/Pletsch Books

Buttonholes from *Couture- the Art of Fine Sewing*

Fit-As-You-Sew™ from *Pants For Any Body*

Terrific Trousers from *Pants For Any Body*

narrow rolled hem on curtain

wall quilt with decorative serged edge finish

narrow serged seams in unlined lampshade

serged piecing seams

serged blinsdtitched hem

gathered ruffle

rolled or narrow unrolled hem

from Sewing with Sergers

My First Doll Book

My First Sewing Book

from *Sewing with Sergers*

Decorative Serging

Professional Finishing WITH A SERGER

Personal Style from *Clothes Sense*

83

Printing Your Flyer

Your sponsor may be willing to print your flyer for you. After all, getting customers into the store is certainly to their benefit.

If you're offering children a class at school or for after-school enrichment, 30-50 flyers for lunch boxes may be adequate. If flyers are passed out in a store, you may need 1,000. If so, you might be better off making an attractive sign with your photo or a display with a sample of the class project with a class registration form nearby.

To handle the printing yourself, quick printers are the fastest, most economical sources for flyers. Compare their prices and quality with those of office-supply warehouse outlets that offer printing. Often the two sources vary little, so location may be the determining factor. Accessibility is worth what it saves you in time.

Nowadays, many copy centers also are able to print out your computer disc, and to print in larger type sizes.

Be aware that different printers have different types of printing presses. If you ask a quick printer who has a small press and uses paper printing plates to print a flyer for you that has heavy ink coverage or photographs, you may not be happy with the results. The job might require metal plates and a different press—and will, of course, cost more to print.

Ask to see samples of their work to help you, and the printer, to decide what will give you the results you want.

Professional Photos

Your photo adds a personal touch and makes any flyer or poster more eye-catching. You will want your photo to be the best one ever taken. It will be part of your identity; your image.

We recommend a closeup and an **"action"** shot of you doing something related to the class you'll be teaching. Explain to the photographer that you need this photo for the purpose of promoting your classes. The photo should be friendly as well as business-oriented.

If your area has a "glamour" photo studio which does makeup and hairstyling, sign up! This "makeover" service is showing up in malls everywhere. Tell them you want a publicity photo, not a glamour photo, but that you certainly want to look great. This may affect the way they do your hair and makeup and your pose.

Take two businesslike outfits and props (garments or technique samples) for your action shot. Medium tone colors are better than either very dark or very light. Larger earrings with a little shine show up better and make a fashion statement. Stand up straight and don't slouch. Relax your face after each shot and put on a new smile for the next one. A light (but not white) background reprints better on flyers and in a newspapaer. Make sure your hair and clothing do not blend into the background. Hair may need to be smoothed so whisps don't stand out against the background. The edge of a hand next to a face is

This price list is for reference only. Call Producers & Quantity Photos Inc. (Resource page 109) for current prices and shipping information.

Producers & Quantity Photo Inc.
Price List

Effective February 20, 1995
All prices subject to change without notice.

Black & White

Machine Run Contacts
(swg = Single Weight Glossy; swm = Single Weight Matte)
Priced per single print, from each negative

Print Size	Copy Neg	1-4		5-24		25-49		50-99		100-499		500-999		1,000 and Up	
		swg	swm	swg	swm	swg	swm	swg	swm	swg	swm	swg	swm	swg	swm
4x5	6.50	1.10	1.20	.85	.95	.60	.70	.45	.55	.34	.44	.30	.40	.28	.38
5x7	7.50	1.20	1.30	.90	1.00	.65	.75	.50	.60	.39	.49	.36	.46	.34	.44
8x10	**8.00**	**1.60**	**1.70**	**1.50**	**1.60**	**.80**	**.90**	**.65**	**.75**	**.42**	**.52**	**.39**	**.49**	**.37**	**.47**
8x10 Bleed	14.00	2.30	2.40	1.80	1.90	1.00	1.10	.85	.95	.62	.72	.59	.69	.57	.67
Full bleeds are charged at next larger size															

daintier than the entire hand facing the camera. (Shake your hands over your head to temporarily diminish veins.) A thorough photographer will shoot a Polaroid to check the picture before the film is shot.

Buy at least one print and have a camera shop make a black and white glossy print from it to send to Quantity Photos. On this page are examples of action shots taken during a Palmer/Pletsch workshop. Any of these can be cropped so you will have only what you want in the photo. You might want to show these to the photographer.

A Source for Quantity Prints

Send your print to Producers & Quantity Photos. A sample of their order form is on the previous page. Order SWG (single-weight, glossy) paper and your choice of size and quantity. The cost for 50 or more is approximately 60 cents each—a bargain. (Prices subject to change.) They also will charge you for an "inter-negative." The company can even crop an action photo to a "head" shot if you "frame" the area you want with sticky notes or a grease pencil on an acetate overlay, using a 5" x 7" or 8" x 10" proportion.

Crop photo for "head" shot.

Promote Using Direct-Mail

Your flyer/brochure is your major mode of communication. Mail flyers to local youth and women's groups as an announcement. Keep copies with you all the time. The opportunities are endless for distributing them to those who may be interested.

Ask the retailer to send flyers to their mailing lists. If you are handling the mailing, ask for their mailing list. If your class is held outside the store, they're more likely to provide you with it if you promise to refer business to them.

If they think the postage is too high to help you promote your classes, maybe they at least can provide preprinted, adhesive address labels of their mailing list, from which you can do your own mailings. However, asking for their mailing list is a sensitive issue. They own it and may not be willing to share it. Be understanding.

One of the best direct-mail pieces Pati Palmer ever did was when she was a buyer/instructor for a department store. It was carried around for months. Why? It had many components: fall fabric sale information; a three-month calendar with class dates as well as FREE events; and a sewing technique with art and instructions. Not only that, it was printed in bright orange and green ink with black lettering. You couldn't lose it!

Here are examples of more recent direct-mail pieces:

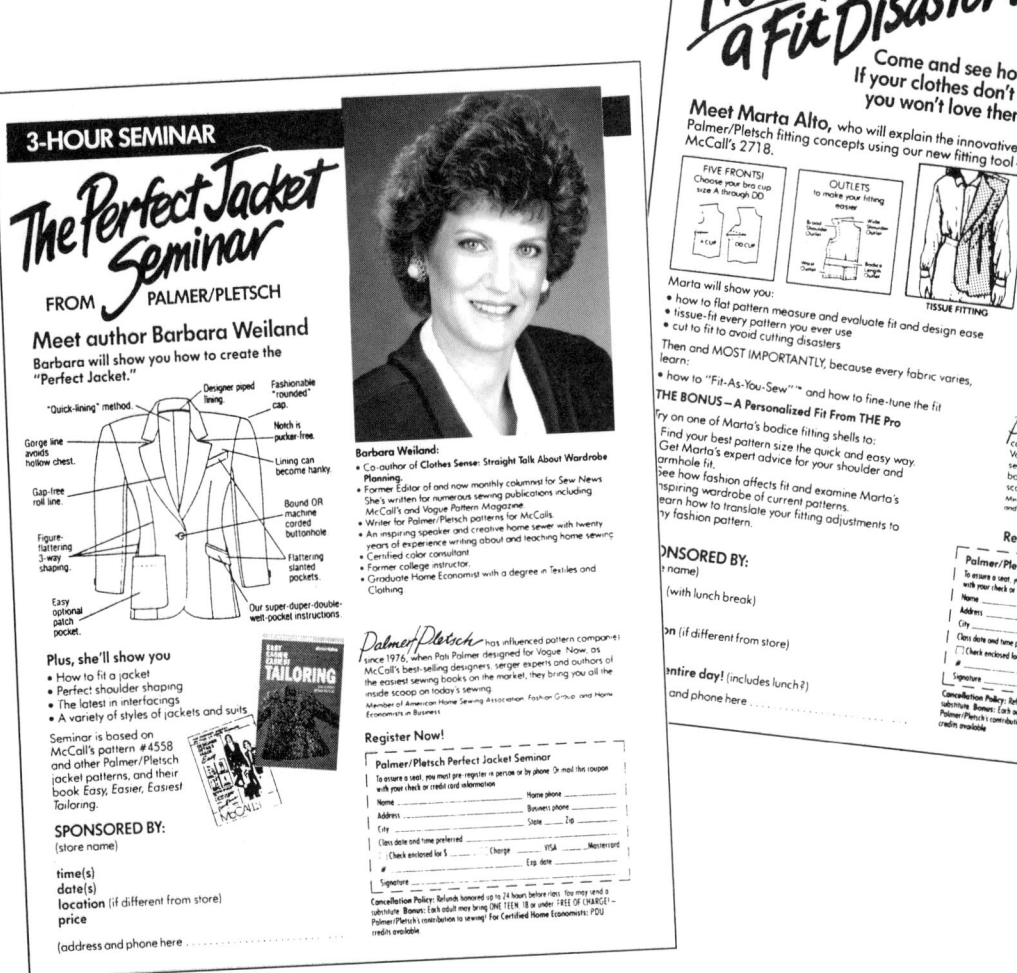

In-Store Posters

Mounting your flyer to a poster gives your marketing campaign consistency. One or two large posters about your new class should be placed near the store entrances or checkout counters or both. You will probably need to provide the posters and a way to display them. For more information on visuals, see Chapter Eleven, Teaching Tools.

One option for a poster is to have your flyer enlarged at a copy center. You can also create posters on a computer and enlarge at a copy center. If you make a poster without the benefit of a computer, and you are not comfortable with your own hand lettering, use rub-off letters of varying sizes and styles from office or stationery stores. They are easy, inexpensive and neat.

This poster needs to be neat and professional and uncomplicated. Simply mount a copy of your flyer and print the date and time of the class on the poster. You may want to add registration forms to the poster or have additional flyers with a registration form on them. Other items that may be attractively mounted to this poster are the following:

Pattern envelopes
Fashion photos
Notions
Samples of techniques
A book cover

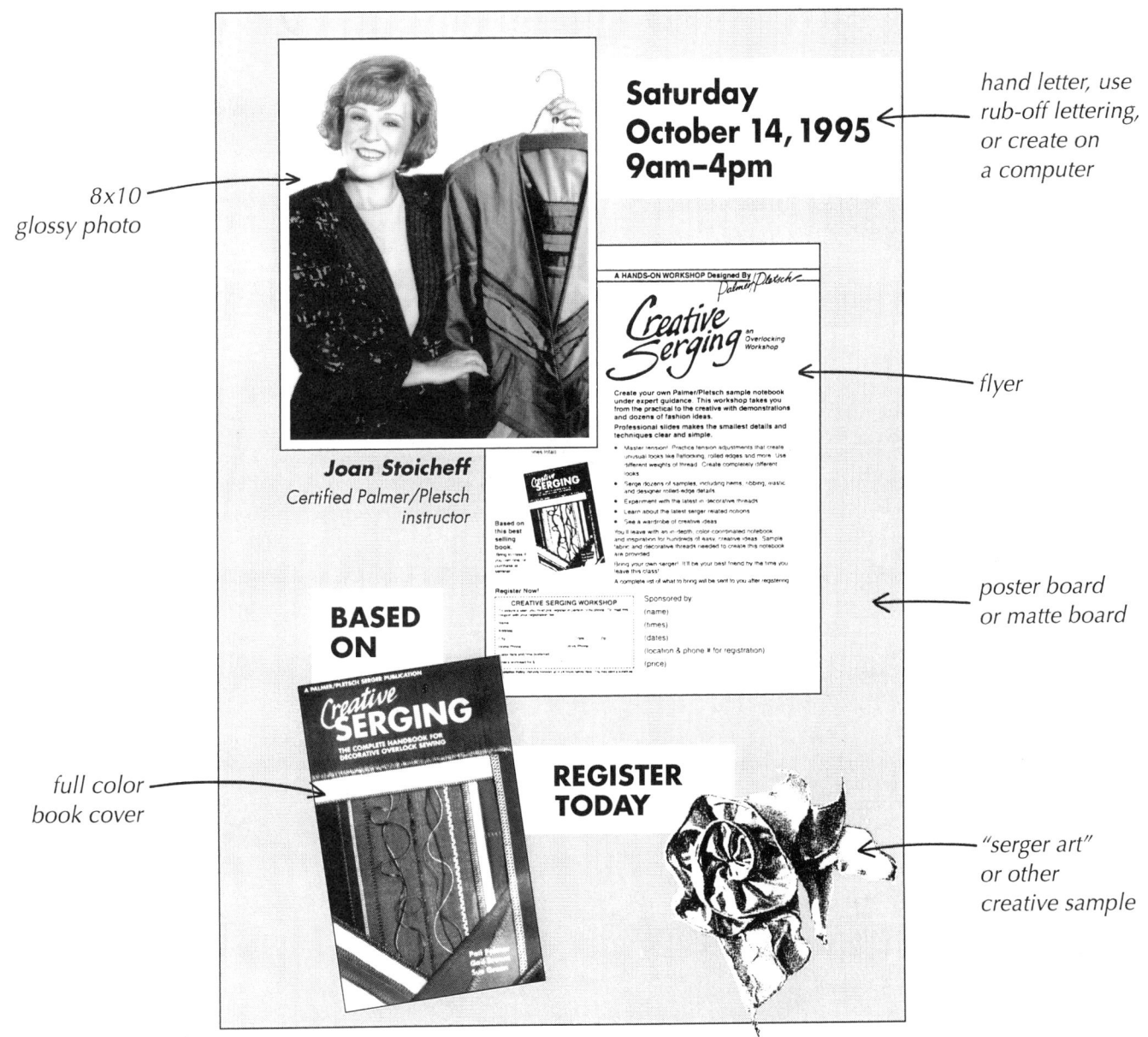

8x10 glossy photo

hand letter, use rub-off lettering, or create on a computer

Saturday October 14, 1995 9am–4pm

flyer

Joan Stoicheff
Certified Palmer/Pletsch instructor

poster board or matte board

full color book cover

BASED ON

REGISTER TODAY

"serger art" or other creative sample

Additional In-Store Promotion

Model Garments

An eye-catching way to promote your classes in a fabric store or sewing machine dealership is to lend them your model garments with your label for display. Your garments should be current fashions and well-made. Attach an attractively printed card with your name explaining that this type of garment will be made in your class. Have the store hang the garment high and securely so it won't be damaged or stolen.

Free "Teaser" Demonstration

Offer to do brief demos during peak traffic periods. Set up near your model garment display or near a poster promoting your other classes. Page 72 in Chapter 13, Classroom Setup, discusses how to set up.

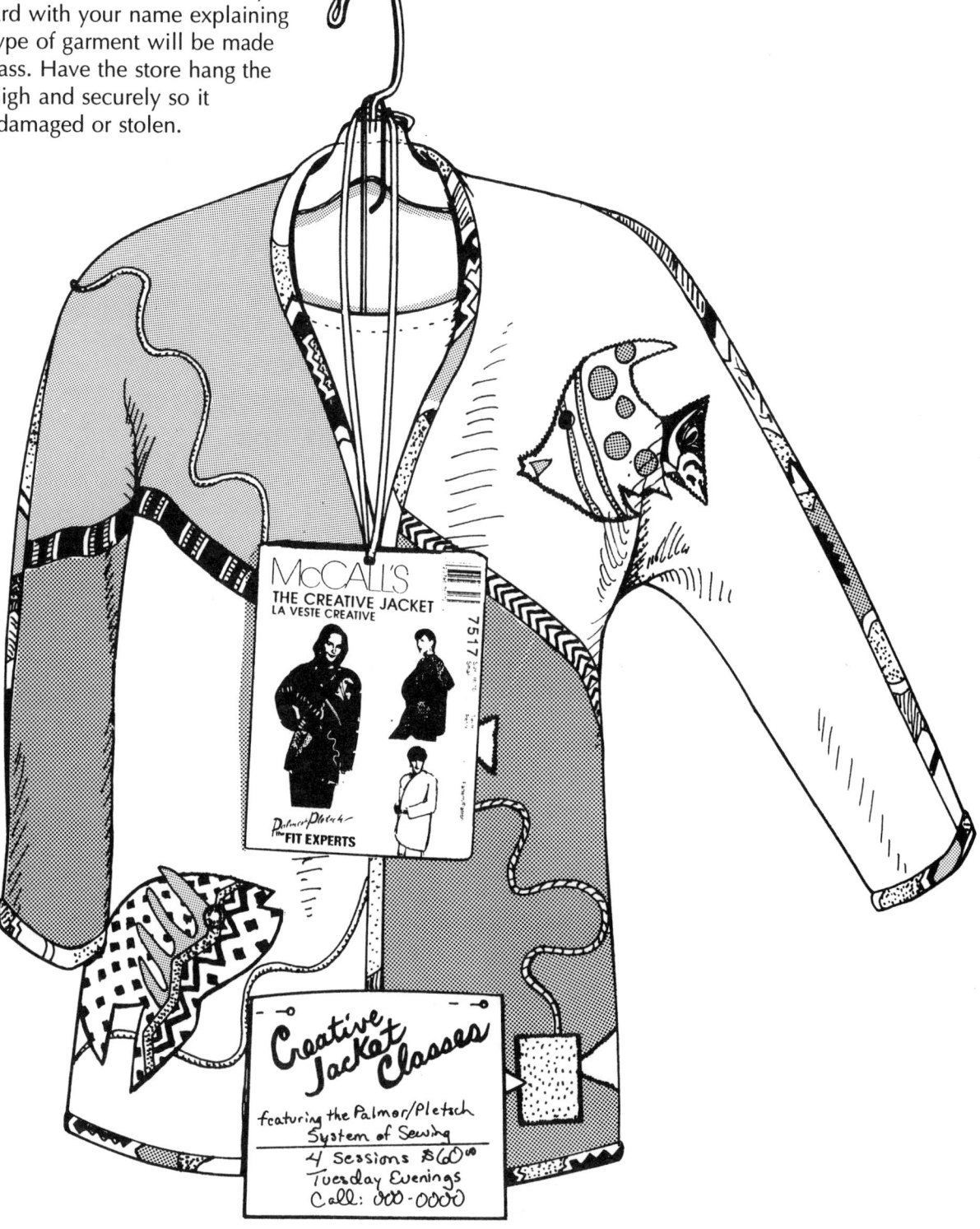

Promoting Classes Not Sponsored by a Store

How you promote your teaching business will depend on your topic and the kind of class. List likely prospects for your class, then likely places to reach them, for example:

children	day-care centers, schools
teens	schools, youth groups
adults	church, stores, county extension offices
working people	work facilities, lunch rooms
retired people	senior citizen centers retirement communities
beginners	home, work, church
young mothers	home, work, community centers

Join your local chapter of the American Sewing Guild (ASG) or other guilds, such as the quilt or embroidery guild, if you are not already a member. This is possibly your best resource of ideas and word-of-mouth advertising.

These organizations are always looking for speakers and teachers with refreshing new ideas and expertise. Volunteer to do a presentation. This will develop interest in your classes. The ASG publishes a newsletter with timely articles and reasonable advertising rates. Take advantage of it! The exposure you get from being a member of this group is invaluable. The cost of this exposure is the membership fee. The American Sewing Guild is a bargain. If there is no chapter in your area, start one!

A good way to reach groups of adults is through professional or hobby group newsletters. Are there any other organizations that would write about you and your classes?

If you want to offer an after-school class for children, you will need to have it approved by the principal or head of the school.

To publicize these classes, use the lunch box. It is one of the best ways to get information to parents about opportunities for their children. All moms and pops know to check the lunch box or back pack for communiques because this is how teachers often send information home. Provide a flyer with registration form stating the necessary information.

Consult with parent leaders of school about presenting your children's class idea at one of their meetings. This is a perfect opportunity to measure the level of interest and commitment. The parents could help you convince the school, day-care center or church group that your class would be good for their children. You also could ask for permission to put a flyer on the bulletin board near the main entrance or the principal's office.

For help in marketing classes through schools, see Winky Cherry's teaching manual. It also includes a packet of camera-ready flyers. See page 127 for ordering information.

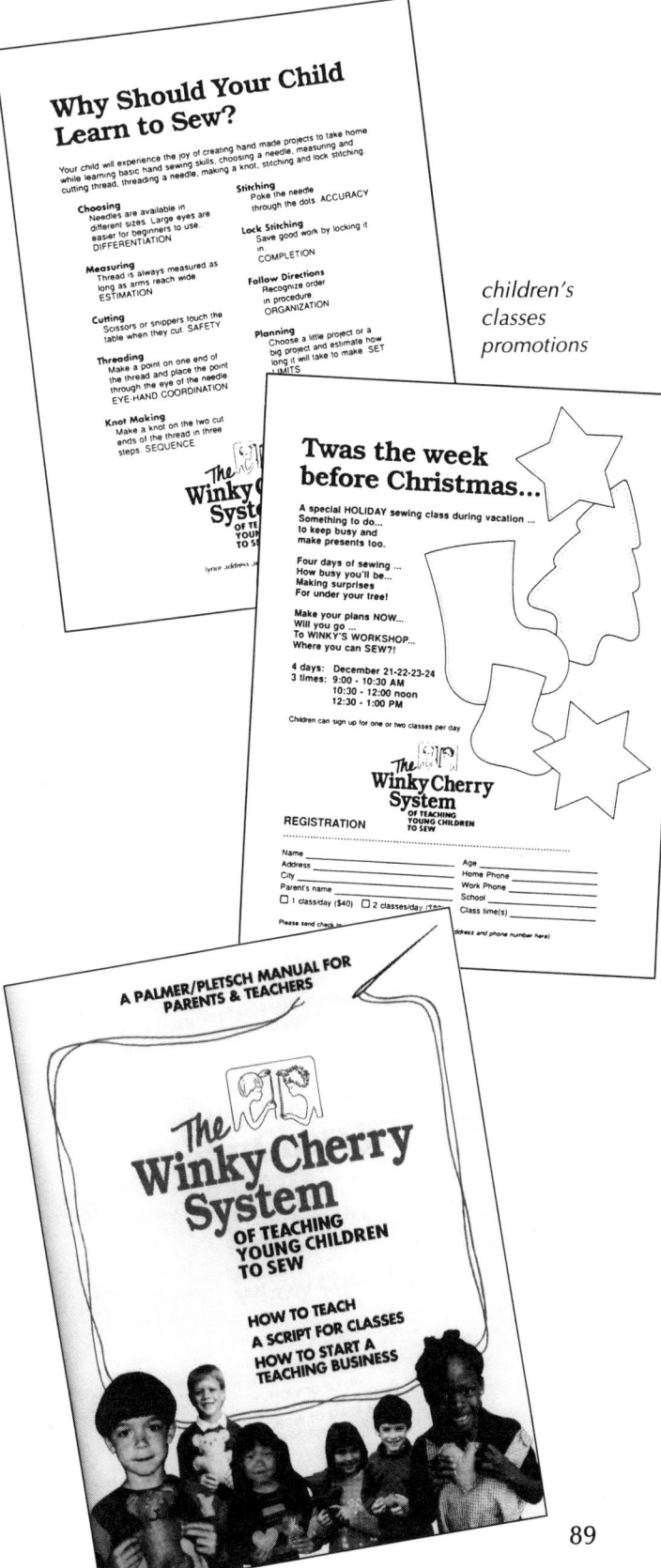

children's classes promotions

89

Newspaper Publicity

Your local newspaper probably has a living, home, women's or business section that may be interested in stories about instructors and classes available in the area. Almost every newspaper has a calendar listing of classes available to the public. Keep your local newspaper up-to-date about your activities. Calendar items need to be at the newspaper well in advance. Ask for the deadlines.

A good press release, one that a newspaper will print and one that will be read, must have an **angle** of interest. What makes an article regarding you and your classes newsworthy and interesting enough for the public to read?

In general, a story is newsworthy when it contains one or more of the following characteristics:

It is new.
It is unusual.
It directly affects large numbers of their readers.
It involves conflict or competition.
It is humorous.
It is secret.
It has to do with the future.
It is romantic.

Interesting **angles related to sewing** are:

- money- and time-saving
- current fashion
- personal and human interest
- value
- a trend in sewing
- an event that's free or for a charity

Tips for Writing a Press Release

1. Use "inverted pyramid" style. The most important information goes in the first one or two paragraphs. The point is that if the story were cut, the essentials would still be there.

2. The first or second paragraph should answer the questions who, what, where, when, why, and how.

3. Use the following paragraphs to fill in important details.

4. The last paragraph can include standard information about how to register or exact times.

5. Keep press releases to one page if possible.

6. Write in the present tense using active voice.

Hiring a publicist to write releases for you may be worth the investment unless you have writing experience. Publicists put life into words describing you and your classes. This helps the public develop an interest in you to help create a response. Cost will be the key.

Ideas for Other Angles

TIME SAVING:
Tips for Time-Saving Sewing
Fast Fashion
Sewing Machine's Fast Footwork
Home Dec in a Sec
    (based on a McCall Pattern Company series)

CURRENT AND TIMELY:
Heirloom Touches for Dainty Dresses
Costumes and Creatures for Halloween
Mardi-Gras and Make Believe
Summer Sizzlers and Coolers, Sundresses,
    Hot Swimsuits, Cool Clothes
Christmas in July Giftmaking Ideas

HUMAN INTEREST:
Faux Fur, Environmentally Correct
Wearable Art, Sewing as an Art Form
Fund-Raising Fashions, fashion shows for
    charities sponsored by local sewing guild

PERSONAL:
Local personalities who sew for their family,
    home and themselves
Over Forty and Fit for Fashion, fashion and
    the maturing figure
Invite a local celebrity to learn to sew and
    have them report in the local news
Tell your story of sewing, attending workshops,
    number of students you have taught, why you
    sew, who you sew for, how you began
Humorous sewing anecdotes

VALUE:
Children who learn to sew develop valuable skills
Sewing as a Business
Sewing for a College Education
Teaching Sewing, a Creative, Rewarding Business

Press Release Format

1. Use your letterhead unless you are being sponsored by a guild. Then use theirs.

2. Type double-spaced on 8½" x 11" paper with wide margins on both sides to give editors room to make notes.

3. It used to be recommended we use only one side of a page. Today's **ecological trend** is to print on both sides to save paper.

4. In the upper right-hand corner, type CONTACT: then list your name, address and phone number. This gives editors a name to call with questions.

5. In the upper left-hand corner, mark FOR IMMEDIATE RELEASE or give a date after which the material can be printed.

6. Write a catchy headline.

7. If your release runs more than one page, type –MORE– at the bottom of the page and indicate to turn the page over. Never separate a paragraph from one page to the next. Put "Page 2" at the top of the second page with the headline in case the pages get separated.

8. Staple all the pages together.

9. Type ### at the end of the release.

10. Proof your release CAREFULLY to make sure there are no grammatical or spelling errors. If you are interested, we can direct you to a professional proofreader whose fee is reasonable.

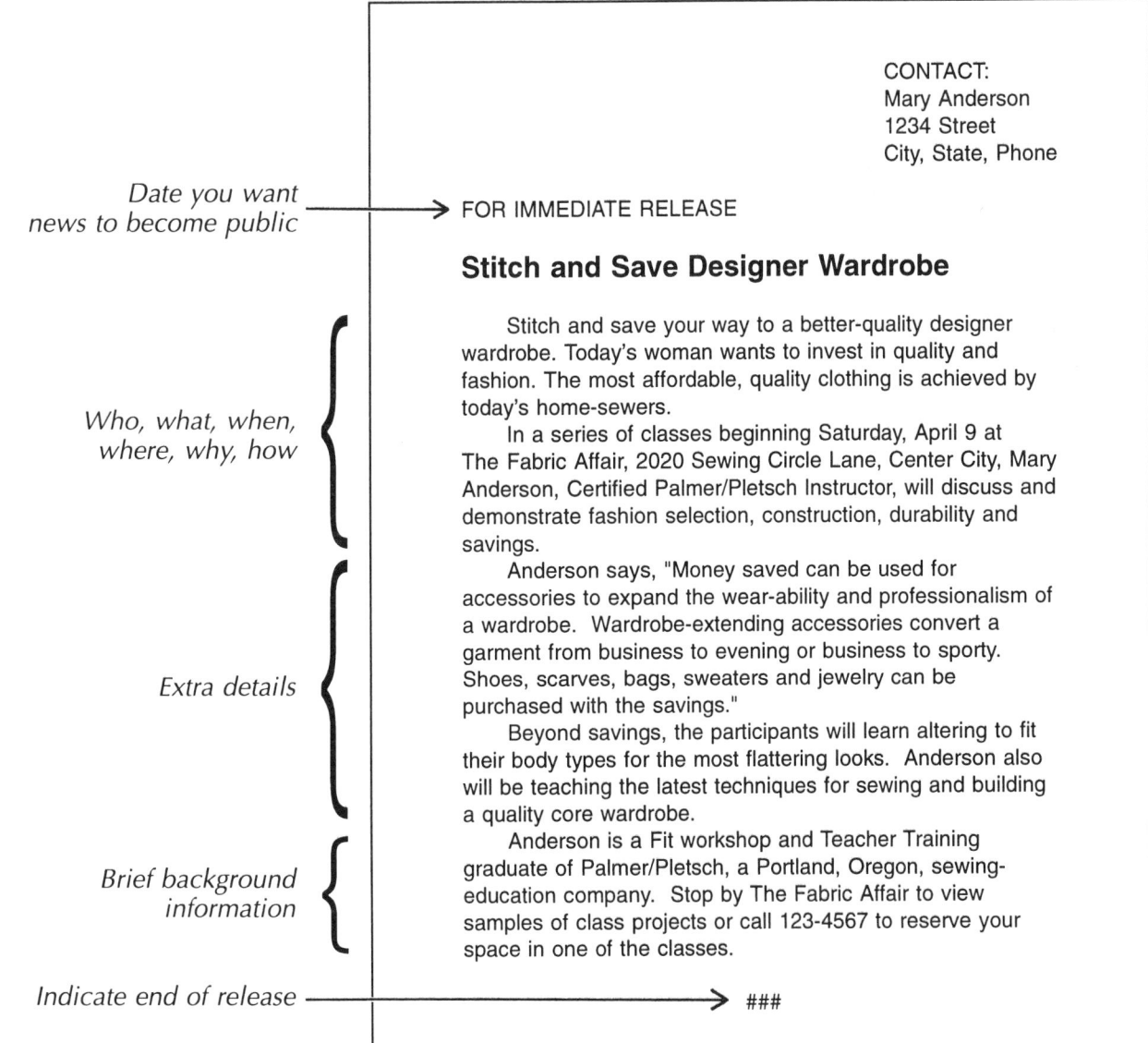

CONTACT:
Mary Anderson
1234 Street
City, State, Phone

Date you want news to become public → FOR IMMEDIATE RELEASE

Stitch and Save Designer Wardrobe

Who, what, when, where, why, how {

Stitch and save your way to a better-quality designer wardrobe. Today's woman wants to invest in quality and fashion. The most affordable, quality clothing is achieved by today's home-sewers.

In a series of classes beginning Saturday, April 9 at The Fabric Affair, 2020 Sewing Circle Lane, Center City, Mary Anderson, Certified Palmer/Pletsch Instructor, will discuss and demonstrate fashion selection, construction, durability and savings.

Extra details {

Anderson says, "Money saved can be used for accessories to expand the wear-ability and professionalism of a wardrobe. Wardrobe-extending accessories convert a garment from business to evening or business to sporty. Shoes, scarves, bags, sweaters and jewelry can be purchased with the savings."

Beyond savings, the participants will learn altering to fit their body types for the most flattering looks. Anderson also will be teaching the latest techniques for sewing and building a quality core wardrobe.

Brief background information {

Anderson is a Fit workshop and Teacher Training graduate of Palmer/Pletsch, a Portland, Oregon, sewing-education company. Stop by The Fabric Affair to view samples of class projects or call 123-4567 to reserve your space in one of the classes.

Indicate end of release → ###

Calendar Release

This is a short release listing only the pertinent facts. Check calendars of publications to which you plan to send your release to see how items are presented. For example, some allow listing of prices for paid events, while others may not.

CONTACT:
Lynette Ranney Black
(503) 123-4567

FOR IMMEDIATE RELEASE

Free Time-Saving Sewing Seminar

7:00 pm, Thursday, September 10, 1977, Lynette Ranney Black will offer a free one-hour seminar at The Fabric Depot, 700 SE 122nd Ave., Portland, OR. For more information call 123-4567.

Feature Story

Wouldn't it be fun if an editor decided to do a feature on you? This is a longer, more loosely written story than a news release and it often contains a photograph. One of the Palmer/Pletsch graduates was "featured" in her local paper as shown below:

Journal Review Photo by Christine LaVigne

Dolores Epperson (left) and Connie Hamilton check out sewing machine

Variety key for new sewing shop

Dolores Epperson and Connie Hamilton are partners in The Sewing Connection, a sewing machine sales and repair service that opened Monday in Liberty Square on U.S. 231 south of Crawfordsville.

The store will offer a variety of sewing classes and will have accessories and hard-to-find notions for sale. Sewing machine brand names available are New Home and Viking.

Epperson has 18 years experience with sewing machines including 15 years at The Knick-Knack Shop, a former Crawford-sville store; and one year at the Plainfield Sewing Center. She is a sewing consultant for the Montgomery County Extension Office and has taught classes to adults and 4-H members.

Hamilton is a certified teacher of Palmer/Pletsch Pant Fitting and has conducted Kids Can Sew classes at Sugar Creek Elementary School for several years. She also has designed and constructed costumes for theater and helped sew flags and outfits for high school flag corps.

The women will offer sewing classes once a classroom in the back of the shop can be completed.

Hours are from 9 a.m. to 5 p.m. Monday through Saturday and a grand opening is scheduled for Nov. 20 and 21. The telephone number is 362-3040.

Photographs to Go with Press Releases

Photos on glossy paper will reproduce more clearly than photos on matte paper. Most newspapers will reduce your photo, so sending a 5"x7" is adequate and will lose less quality in reduction. Print your name, address, and phone number on a small sheet of paper. Add a caption describing the photograph. Tape the caption wrong sides together to the bottom back of the photograph. Then fold it up and over the picture so the copy is visible from the front.

Marcy Miller,
Certi... Palmer/Pletsch
sewi...

Press Kits

A press kit is a compilation of press releases, your bio, photos with captions, and a cover letter stating why this press kit has been sent. It is usually sent in an attractive folder or in a colored envelope.

Biographical Information

Biographical information is an important element of a press kit. Below are some examples.

Biographical paragraph as it appeared in the A-1 Vacuum & Sewing Center Newsletter.

Biography — Sam Gauthier

Sam Gauthier is a successful entrepreneur in the sewing and image industry. She started developing her career at age eleven under her mother's watchful eye in their family den. Today, her business, *Sam* specializes in image, color, design, custom clothing, and teaching. She is a Beauty For All Seasons® Color Consultant, trained style and figure specialist for Flatter your Figure® and a Certified Palmer/Pletsch Instructor. Sam is also a chartered member of the Professional Association of Custom Clothiers, New Orleans Chapter.

A-1 VACUUM & SEWING CENTER
3715 Westbank Blvd
Harvey, LA 70058
(504) 347-8423
1597 Gause Blvd.
Slidell, LA 70458
(504) 641-4107
4439 Veterans Blvd.
Metairie, LA 70006
(504) 455-

Marcia M. Miller
See Strasse 130
8700 Kusnacht
Switzerland
41 1 810 1511

CAREER OBJECTIVE: To inspire as many sewers as possible, beginning or advanced, to sew more often, to sew better, to have fun sewing, to be confident and to prove to be proud of their talent and themselves.

EXPERIENCE:

1994 Relocating to Switzerland. Developing sewing classes.
MARCY MILLER, SEWING TEACHER, DESIGNER AND AUTHOR.

1992 - 1993 Building a new house and a new sewing client base.
MARCY MILLER, SEWING TEACHER, DESIGNER AND AUTHOR, Arlington, TX.

1990 - 1992 **DESIGNING AND DRESSMAKING** for private clients.
TEACHING private sewing classes in my studio.
AUTHORING "The Busine$$ of Teaching Sewing" for Palmer/Pletsch.
MARCY MILLER, SEWING TEACHER, DESIGNER AND AUTHOR, Seal Beach, CA.

1989 - 1991 **DESIGNER** of kitchens, bathrooms and sewing rooms.
Alexander Cabinet Company, Los Angeles, CA

1981 - 1989 **OWNER/DESIGNER** of kitchen design and remodeling contracting firm.
Kitchen's Kitchens, Beaverton, OR

1977 - 1981 **DESIGNER** of kitchens and bathrooms.
Portland Builder's Supply, Portland, OR

1974 - 1977 **FREE LANCE HOME ECONOMIST** authoring "Microwave Meals In A Minute."
TEACHING microwave classes for consumer groups and local colleges.

1969 - 1974 **HOME ECONOMIST** coordinating and teaching for the community, programs on the use, safety and conservation of electrical energy. Emphasis on community, county extension agencies, 4-H, church and school groups.
Clark County Public Utility District, Vancouver, WA

1960 - 1965 **HOME ECONOMICS TEACHER.**
Weatherwax High School, Aberdeen, WA

EDUCATION: WASHINGTON STATE UNIVERSITY, B.S.
Major: Home Economics Education

PERSONAL: Excellent Health, Married, Own Home

REFERENCES: AVAILABLE UPON REQUEST

Palmer/Pletsch Associates
1728 SW PROSPECT
PORTLAND, OR 97201
(503) 294-0696

BACKGROUNDER

INTRODUCING LYNETTE RANNEY BLACK

Lynette Ranney Black describes herself as a craft-person rather than a fashion sewer. Her expertise lies in the home decorating field. She has recently co-authored, with Linda Wisner, a fabulous new Palmer/Pletsch book, *Creative Serging for the Home and Other Quick Decorating Ideas.*

Pati Palmer, Palmer/Pletsch CEO, hired Lynette to be her administrative assistant and to coordinate the firm's promotional activities. One of Lynette's responsibilities is to organize and supervise the 4-day sewing workshop programs that Palmer/Pletsch holds in Portland 8–10 times each year as well as 400 seminars held throughout the U.S., Canada, and Australia.

Lynette is a home economist with a Clothing & Textiles/Education degree from Montana State University with a minor in Business. She began her career working with the Northwest distributors of Elna and White sewing machines, selling and teaching consumers and dealers.

In the spring of 1982, she stepped out of the home sewing market and into the home decorating business as a kitchen designer/sales representative. Lynette earned a professional credential as a Certified Kitchen Designer, studying and passing stringent certification requirements set up by the National Kitchen and Bath Association. During her six year design career, she served as Chairperson for the regional chapter of NKBA.

Black re-entered the home sewing industry in 1987 when she joined Palmer/Pletsch, after designing custom sewing studios for several of the Palmer/Pletsch personnel. She authored Palmer/Pletsch's first "Trends Bulletin," entitled, *The Newest in Sewing Room Design and Organization,* drawing from her design background.

The success of the Palmer/Pletsch series of serging books and videos triggered the creation of the home decorating book. Lynette admits that writing is not one of her passions, but that creating the new looks for her daughters' rooms, her living room and her kitchen, stretched her imagination and inventiveness. When it comes to home sewing/home decorating, she says, "I enjoyed solving the special and construction problems that we encountered on the 25 rooms we photographed for the book."

As a volunteer, Lynette plays an active part in her local chapter of Home Economists in Business. She has served as Chairman of the chapter and for the past three years served as Exhibit Chairman for the successful HEIB Sewing Fair.

When asked about her goals, Lynette speaks of her two daughters: Jessica, 8 months old and Kelsey, 3. "I bring my daughters to my workplace for childcare...so I am a working mother who has learned to live one day at a time. I'd love to set long-range goals, but I am happiest doing what is in front of me, considering my busy life that combines business and babies. I'm a modern mother with old-fashioned values. I like to do things myself, so I invent problem-solving methods that save time and money, and I love sharing my knowledge with others."

Types of Editors and Their Functions

You might send your press releases to all possible editors at the same time. If you are sure only one would be interested, save yourself time and money.

City Editor—Writes stories pertaining to events in your community or metropolitan area.

Features Editor—Covers stories other than hard news or timely features. An example would be a story on food trends. Sewing as an emerging popular trend would be another topic. The Fashion Sewing Council of the American Home Sewing and Craft Association sends press releases to these editors.

Lifestyle Editor—Writes more about issues dealing with the family and home.

Fashion Editor—Covers all aspects of the industry from ready-to-wear to home sewing. This person also covers beauty-related stories. In some cities, this title was dropped and became the Lifestyle Editor. However, now that newspapers are re-evaluating the interest in fashion, we feel the trend is reversing itself in the '90s.

Home Furnishings or Decorating Editor—Covers stories relating to re-decorating, decorating trends, re-modeling, and sometimes gardening.

Timing

If a guild is planning a big fashion-show event, the press release should go out one to two months in advance, because the paper may want to do a feature and needs to plan for a photographer.

For classes you plan to teach, three weeks to a month may be enough lead time. Follow up with a phone call 10 days to two weeks before the event to make sure the release was received and to offer to answer any questions. Be very enthusiastic, hoping your enthusiasm will catch on.

After an event, follow up with photos and a release on its success. This will help you spread the word about sewing.

When Your Story Isn't Published

Editors are swamped with press releases and phone requests. They get so many press releases that sometimes the best they can do is to file them into categories for future reference when they are ready to write a story that involves that subject. Other reasons your article may not make the newspaper are the following:

1. The news angle of your release was misunderstood. (A phone call may have corrected this.)

2. Other news on the same day is more important than yours.

3. The right person didn't get your story.

4. Your story is good, but not well-written or presented.

Collect Clips

Part of your "history" and portfolio is the publicity you have received. The following are samples of articles generated by Palmer/Pletsch on their classes over the years. They might give you some ideas.

Even use glue

Lightning won't strike you if take shortcuts, says sewing expert

BY KAREN KANE
Chronicle Staff

YOU PROBABLY LEARNED to sew in seventh grade. But a young woman with a degree in home economics education encourages you to forget the hallowed rules you learned long ago and take as many shortcuts as possible in sewing.

Sewing, even tailoring, doesn't have to be slow torture. There are contem-

is comparable to the one you would have purchased. Our methods are designed to give satisfactory results for a minimum investment of time and money.

Home sewing techniques have been simplified by a number of new products. One time saver in blazers is the use of fusible interfacing.

It used to take eight

frequent wear. Still, there are ways to cut corners.

She advises women to use bound buttonholes in blazers. Ah, the thought of bound buttonholes! But the Palmer-Pletsch method employs a fusible web to keep the "lips" of the buttonhole in place while you stitch.

"You know the notches that you cut around that are supposed to be used to line up the pieces. I cut

---

Sewing workshop planned

By MARY FARRELL THOMAS
Daily Journal

Whenever there's a slump in the economy, one thing's for sure — interest increases in home sewing.

That's one of the reasons Kathy Pizza, owner of Heirlooms Forever in Tupelo, is bringing in a certified instructor with Palmer- help instruct

For Your Info

Knight-Ridder News
What: Sewing Workshop
When: 6-9 p.m. Feb. 21; 10 a.m. to Feb. 22 rlooms Forever.

842-4275; res-b. 19

85, the Sewing creased

trim and speed of Although the con-tag is a great ewing

in use to ng, e

Teacher starts kids sewing

By BARBARA PESCHIERA
Special to The Oregonian

Winky Cherry knew from the time she was teaching sewing at age 12 that she wanted to be a sewing teacher when she grew up.

She didn't know until she was about 30 that she wanted to teach kids to sew.

Now Cherry has 20 years of professional experience behind her, having taught thousands of children to sew. She will talk about her teaching method during the Sept. 25th and 26th Sewing Fair at Memorial Coliseum.

Her seminar will planned during th sponsored by the of Home Economis a fund-raiser for it gram.

Cherry has been dubbed "the Dr. Seuss of home sewing" by Pati Palmer, publisher of a series of books Cherry has written that teach aching as well as sew-

The books explain Cherry's structured method of teaching children, beginning with hand-sewing and graduating to machine sewing.

"My main focus is getting people primed to teach; that's the hard

Winky Cherry watches one of her students try out newly learned sewing.

Marta Alto, left, will show the upcoming class members the proper way to fit a pattern with new, innovative tools.

Serge ahead

Speedy sewing machines allow you to do impressive feats

By REBECCA DUMLAO
Special writer, The Oregonian

Want to sew something special, but can't find the time? Serger sewing machines may change your mind.

Consider these speedy serger feats:
● A simple top can be serged in one hour.
● A set of six placemats and napkins can be finished in half an hour.
● Elastic-waist slacks can be completed in 45

● Stitch professiona quarter the cost of ready-
● Finish table linens w rolled edge.

How do you do it? Some entirely with a serger, b serger and a conventional

Did you throw out yo your microwave? Of cou when you need both. Sim ventional machines work you have lots of new sewi ways to speed up your se offer a quick way to u potential. If you're like once you've tried a serger

What is a serger anyw is a special sewing mac food processor. Sergers overcast edges in one s ed of a conventional m

Sergers use a knittir bobbins on a serger

'Easy, Easier, Easiest,' the book written by Pati Palmer, was the basis for a seminar on sewing a blazer or jacket in eight hours. Here, Palmer, a well-known sewing expert, shows Quad-Citians her book and some of the patterns she recommends for the blazer.

Here's just a portion of the women in attendance at one of three Quad-City seminars on sewing, presented by Pati Palmer. Palmer and her associate, Susan Pletsch, are pattern designers and sewing instructors who travel the United States giving seminars.

Sewing pro likes Ultrasuede for suits, coats

(Continued From Page 27)

cutting out the pattern. (Ultrasuede sells for about $45 a yard in the Quad-Cities.)

Returning to the point she made about shoes, she added, "Speaking of shoes — I figure I saved enough by making this coat that I'm entitled to buy $800 worth of shoes. That's what I call sewer's logic," she laughed.

PALMER SAID she enjoys sewing items like the elegant coat, but she is equally proficient with sport-swear patterns.

Palmer and her associate have just designed a pattern called "Jeans That Fit" that will include sewing instructions to fit every member of the family.
The pattern will

"People seem to be really tuned-in to sewing now."

"I THINK it is easier to sew for yourself than for others. The directions in patterns are getting easier to follow. And it's just not that hard if you put some logic behind it."

She said she thinks more women are returning to their sewing machines for economical reasons, and for the personal satisfaction of creating a garment that is unique.

"Indications are that people are interested in tailor-ing and making suits," Pal

"We have seen more women wearing skirts and dresses lately, but I feel the fashion will be reversing to pants again." Many people are requesting seminars on the "how-to" of making pants, she said.

She pointed out that although pants have been narrow-legged recently, the trend will be returning to wider legs again.

Palmer cited purple, navy and grey as ors for fall and

therapy for me," she said.

Besides traveling to teach seminars, Palmer and Pletsch will be turning out more patterns. They have established their own publishing company and have co-authored four books on sewing. One of their books, "Easy, Easier, Easiest Tailoring," is now in the sixth printing. Inquiries about their book

95

Radio and Television

Spreading the word is the job of television and radio. Check programming for the type of audience you feel would be interested in "how-to." Local home and talk shows will have audiences for you.

Radio has many talk shows on AM and FM. These vast networks of news carriers are looking for information of interest to their audiences. Producers are the filters through which this information is delivered to their specific audience. Your goal as a communicator is to get your story to the producer persuasively and positively. Start with an introductory phone conversation. Ask: "Is this a good time, or could I call you back at a more convenient time?"

You will not be able to talk to the host. The producer decides on show content. The best time to contact a producer is one hour after their show or after lunch, four to six weeks in advance of being scheduled on their program.

Be enthusiastic on the phone so they will feel you might be "entertaining" as a guest. Be original and offer new insights. Be informative, educational and timely. Offer an exclusive.

Most stations will want an "exclusive." Proper etiquette is to offer an idea, then politely wait a week or two until you have been definitely turned down. Then you can offer the same idea to a competing program.

After the first contact, send a letter plus a news release. Include a 5"x7" photo of yourself. You might include possible interview questions or a synopsis of one or two short demonstrations you have to offer.

Convince the producer and host that this interview will be informative to their audience!

Sample questions for them to ask you in an interview might include:

- How many people sew today?
- Do people sew to save money?
- What are people sewing today?
- Is sewing difficult?
- How is sewing different from when my grandmother sewed?
- How young can you start sewing?
- Are people sewing to earn money today?
- Are there any networking organizations for these people?
- Can you show me some ways people are saving time sewing today?
- Can you show me designer fashions one could sew and save hundreds of dollars?

A Short Demonstration Might Include:

- Christmas gift ideas you can sew
- Back-to-school clothes
- New products
- New equipment and what it can do
- Wearable art
- How to wash silk
- How to look 10 pounds thinner in clothes that fit

Usually, four calls directly to an editor or producer are necessary to get an interview scheduled. Ask again, "Is this a good time, can I call you back at a more convenient time? Did you get the information I sent?" Most of the time they did although they may say no. You may need to send it again.

Practice for the Interview

Before you begin an interview, PRACTICE answering the questions you may be asked. Write down the answers and rehearse. Your answers need to be structured toward your objectives.

This is a selling situation for you to persuade this audience, though you need to be very subtle. Your objective is to convince the listeners or watchers to sign up for your classes. Structure your answers and comments to this objective. Use examples, facts, your experience or that of the audience to create a relationship between yourself and them. This friendly approach is more inviting and results in more students wanting to be a part of your classes.

Rehearse wearing what you plan to wear on television. Know how your clothing will behave in potentially awkward situations, i.e., getting out of a low, deep, overstuffed chair or couch, or perching on a stool that doesn't allow your feet to touch the floor.

Also rehearse using the visuals you plan to show.

Use, and wear, medium-shade colors on television. Red should be avoided in large quantities because it causes flare on film. Small checks and narrow stripes can do the same. Avoid "noisy" jewelry also. Have someone videotape a mock interview to see how you look and how your visuals or garments show up.

The Interview

The host will want to see you about one hour before airtime to meet you and become familiar with the major points of your topic. Be careful you don't say anything negative because the host may throw it back to you during the interview. Be sure you give the host a phone number where the audience can get class information.

You will wait in the "green room" with other guests. This can be exciting. Pati remembers waiting with the Osmonds and Julia Child. Sometimes, you can wait on the set, but you must remain very quiet.

Most interviews are less than five minutes. Do not talk too much. Talk quickly (not too quickly!) and clearly. Remember to breathe. Avoid "ummms" and "uhhhs." Look at the camera or at the host. Hold visuals so the camera can "see" them. Be relaxed and smile so your natural warmth will come through to the audience.

Don't let the interviewer interrupt. Often they are outgoing people who like the stage. Raise your voice slightly and finish your sentence. Watch the time to allow time for your classes to be mentioned. If the host doesn't bring them up, you might subtly state that you will be showing this in your class at Josephine's Fabrics this weekend.

If you make a mistake or say the words wrong, don't apologize, just make the correction and keep going. If the station invites "call ins" and a caller decides to disagree with you, don't argue. Gracefully restate the points you came to express.

At the end of the interview, don't move or say, "Phew, I'm glad that is over." Wait for a cue that the cameras have stopped rolling. You can continue chatting with the host about your topic even though you are being faded out or credits are rolling over you.

A good interview has some of the following elements:

- Humor
- Imagination
- Visuals or visual language
- Concrete examples
- Easy-to-follow steps
- Persuasiveness
- Audible voice
- Relaxed manner
- Animated face
- Good posture
- Varied pace
- Good gestures
- Clarity
- Calm recovery from mistakes

A weak interview has the following elements:

- Too much formality
- Colorless words
- Slang
- Mispronunciation
- Nervousness
- Mumbling
- Monotony or monotone voice
- Lack of variety
- Toying with props
- Tenseness
- Shuffling and shifting
- Listless, apathetic expression

The News Director or News Assignment Editor

These persons plan television or radio news stories, delegating story assignments to reporters. A station may have both a weekday and a weekend assignment editor. Reach the weekday editor early in the morning and the weekend editor on Friday. Always ask for the station's weekend phone number so you will be able to reach this person.

Sometimes a sewing event can be news. A major sewing fair with celebrity speakers and local retailer exhibits may catch their attention. Send your short release to the newsroom the week before the event.

Cable Access and Public Television

Contact your public-television station or cable company for cable-access information. Visit them to find out the possibilities. If you do a show on cable access, they do not pay you and they have the right to show it many times. This can be good publicity.

Paid Advertising

Naturally, free publicity is the best method of promoting your classes. However, paid advertising is guaranteed. Research publications to determine which are read by the people you want to reach and request their advertising rates. Athletic clubs that publish monthly magazines, for example, may be more affordable than a newspaper.

Saturday rates are less than Sunday rates in a newspaper because the circulation is less. Some stores tell us they think people have more time to read a Saturday paper and it is smaller than Sunday's so there is less to wade through to find your ad. When they've advertised classes in the Saturday paper, they fill classes that take place that same day.

A good exercise in making sure a class sounds interesting is to WRITE THE AD even before you design the final class. Ask yourself if it sounds interesting. Then make the class content match the promises you made in the ad.

The ads on the next page have been used for Palmer/Pletsch classes.

Advertising Examples

The New Palmer & Pletsch
CREATIVE SERGING
All-Day Workshop!

Bring your serger and sew with the pros. Join Palmer/Pletsch at their intimate, hands-on all-day WORKSHOP, complete with:

- demonstrations • fashion ideas • sewing tips, and . . .
- time to master tension adjustments by creating a notebook of stitch samples you serge yourself using the latest decorative threads.

McCall's 3369

Featuring Lynn Raasch,
sewing pro and Certified Palmer/Pletsch Instructor.

(Times, days and dates of seminar, store logo, address and phone here)

Palmer/Pletsch All-Day Creative Serging Workshop

To ensure a seat, you must pre-register in person or by phone. Or ... with your check or credit card information.

Home phone _____

_____ Mastercard
_____ ate _____
_____ re class. You may

Tailoring How-to's

Palmer & Pletsch Seminar on 8 Hour Blazer. Don't miss it!

TAILORING SEMINAR

Pucker Free Notch

Speedy Machine Lining

The Right Interfacing

Quick to Tailor Fabrics

Crisp Collar Point

Smooth Set In Sleeves

Good Fit

Perfect Pockets

Make a blazer in just 8 hours! Create a quality jacket for a fraction of its ready-made price. Sew coats and learn tips on tailoring luxury suedes like Ultrasuede® and men's tailored jackets. Meet Pati Palmer, a nationally known sewing expert, and plan to attend our 2-3 hour lecture/slide show for only **$22.00**. Bonus book included: "Easy, Easier, Easiest Tailoring" by Pati Palmer and Susan Pletsch. Please preregister in person or call the preregistration number below. Use your Woodward's account.
Monday, September 14th, 10:00 a.m.–1:00 p.m. and 6:30 p.m.–9:30 p.m.
Public Library, 810 - 5th Ave. South
Preregistration Phone: 329-3131   FASHION FABRICS

Woodward's
The Store That Has It All!

Do you know the new tailoring shortcuts?

Tailoring can be fun, fast and easy. Learn timesaving tricks in our 3-hour seminar.

Easiest Tailoring
for today's jackets and coats.

**Meet
Lynn Raasch**
Home economist and Palmer-Pletsch sewing professional. Lynn's seminars are a combination of teaching, inspiration and entertainment.

Palmer/Pletsch Associates

Dates & Times of Seminar.
Store Logo, Address, Phone

Easiest Tailoring
3 hours for only $20— Free Book Included!

To assure a seat you must pre-register in person or by phone. Or you may mail this coupon with your check or credit card information. Each adult may bring one teen 16 or under **free**. (No book included.)

NAME _____
ADDRESS _____
CITY _____
HOME PHONE _____
STATE _____ ZIP _____
CHECK ENCLOSED FOR _____ BUSINESS PHONE _____
CARD # _____ I PREFER TO CHARGE ☐ VISA ☐ MASTERCARD
CLASS DATE AND TIME PREFERRED _____ EXPIRATION DATE _____
CANCELLATION POLICY: Refunds honored up to 24 hours before class. May send substitute.

98

CHAPTER FIFTEEN

Traveling and Teaching

"If you love to travel and it fits into your lifestyle, take your show on the road."

When you teach more than 50 miles from home, you may need to stay overnight. These "traveling classes" require more administrative and organizational time because of additional phone calls, copying costs and postage, to say nothing of travel expenses.

You must consider all of these costs plus the additional time involved when you calculate fees. To make traveling classes profitable to you and your sponsor, you may have to schedule two or more classes in one location with a minimum total attendance.

Estimating Expenses

Preplanning helps you anticipate costs before you set your fees. Calculate the total cost of driving your car to and from the class using the per-mile expense allowance set by the IRS. (Call the IRS or your tax professional for the current figure.)

When air travel is required, take advantage of special airfares and advance ticketing (seven to 30 days) to keep expenses down. The best airfares are for flights over a Saturday night with tickets that are nonrefundable or nonchangeable. Before purchasing such a ticket, be sure you know the class will not be cancelled. Accumulate air-travel miles in the airlines' frequent-flyer programs and you can use your awards for upgraded or free travel on a future business or pleasure trip.

If you must fly, consider the additional transportation expenses you may encounter, such as a rental car, taxis or shuttle buses. And don't forget all those incidentals, such as tips to skycaps and bellmen.

Determine an affordable range for your lodging. There are many modestly priced, clean motels and hotels. If you are unable to find one through a national reservation service, such as Budgetel, Super 8 or Hampton Inns, ask your sponsor for a suggestion. Ask for a place that is convenient, comfortable, safe and within your price range. The sponsor might offer to make the reservation for you, but handling it yourself helps ensure you get the details straight. If the motel has no elevator, you may want to request a "down and out" room (ground floor near an exit) to make it easier to carry your bags and equipment back and forth from the car.

Setting Your Fees

You may charge for your services in one of two ways: a fee per student or a flat fee. Either way, be sure you at least cover your expenses and the cost of your time.

Fee-Per-Student Program

If you agree to be paid a set amount for each attendee, you have the chance to make more money than with a flat-fee arrangement. Unless you set a minimum attendance figure, however, you also run the risk that your class will not attract enough students to cover your costs.

For example, if your airfare is $500, lodging and meals $300, and you want to earn $600 from conducting the class, you must generate $1400 in revenue. Schedule an all-day hands-on workshop at $50/student, and you must register a minimum of 28 students to generate that revenue. But 28 students may be too large a class to teach effectively. Could you still sell the class if you raised the fee to $75/student? Then you'd need only 18 students to meet your needs. If more students were to sign up, the additional revenue would be pure profit!

For a three-hour slide/lecture seminar, you might be able to handle as many as 100 students in a class. If you scheduled a day and evening presentation at the same location and charged only $20/student, you would generate $2,000—more than enough to cover your minimum needs.

Flat-Fee Programs

When you negotiate a flat fee, the sponsor guarantees to pay you that figure, which covers your income plus expenses. Thus, the sponsor must take more responsibility to generate attendance. If the agreed-upon minimum attendance is not reached by a specified date before the class, the class is canceled.

If your sponsor is inexperienced in promoting special events, out-of-town experts or sewing celebrities, you'll need to help them to ensure their and your success. (See Chapter 14, Marketing, Promotion and Advertising.) You know what works. In the end, you'll secure a happy new client.

Scheduling

We recommend scheduling your classes at least six months in advance to give you and the sponsor time to promote and advertise your event. Many of the "famous" expert teachers schedule their appearances one to two years in advance.

When presenting two- or three-hour seminars in more than one store in a region, schedule an evening session first and the second one the next morning. When that seminar is over, you can start driving to the next town and arrive before rush-hour traffic. You'll be able to check into a new hotel room and freshen up before setting up for the evening seminar in the new location. You'll again teach a second session the next morning.

Another advantage of evening-then-morning seminars: You can leave your garments and samples set up and locked in the store overnight. This not only saves you time, but keeps your materials more secure.

Guiding Your Sponsor

Teaching out of town requires at least as much planning as teaching in your own locale. And because you're unable to meet your sponsor in person at the time of scheduling, you need more guidelines to be in writing.

You can use several formats, such as those shown below, previously used by Palmer/Pletsch. Note the headlines and subheads for the kinds of guidelines to give your sponsors. For more information on sponsor agreement forms, see page 38 in Chapter Seven, Money.

Communicating early and often with your sponsor from the time of scheduling to the time of presentation directly affects the number of students registering for your classes. We recommend a minimum of four contacts, as follows:

1. **Three months before the class:** to verify information on your sponsor agreement form or class confirmation, to check that the planning information has arrived, to answer questions, and to establish future contact times.

2. **One month before class:** to check on registration progress and to answer questions.

3. **Two weeks before class:** to discuss attendance and possible cancellation if necessary. (Make this call before purchasing an airline ticket.)

4. **One week before class:** to confirm attendance figures and last-minute details.

Assuming the trip is a "go," also confirm all your travel plans before you leave home.

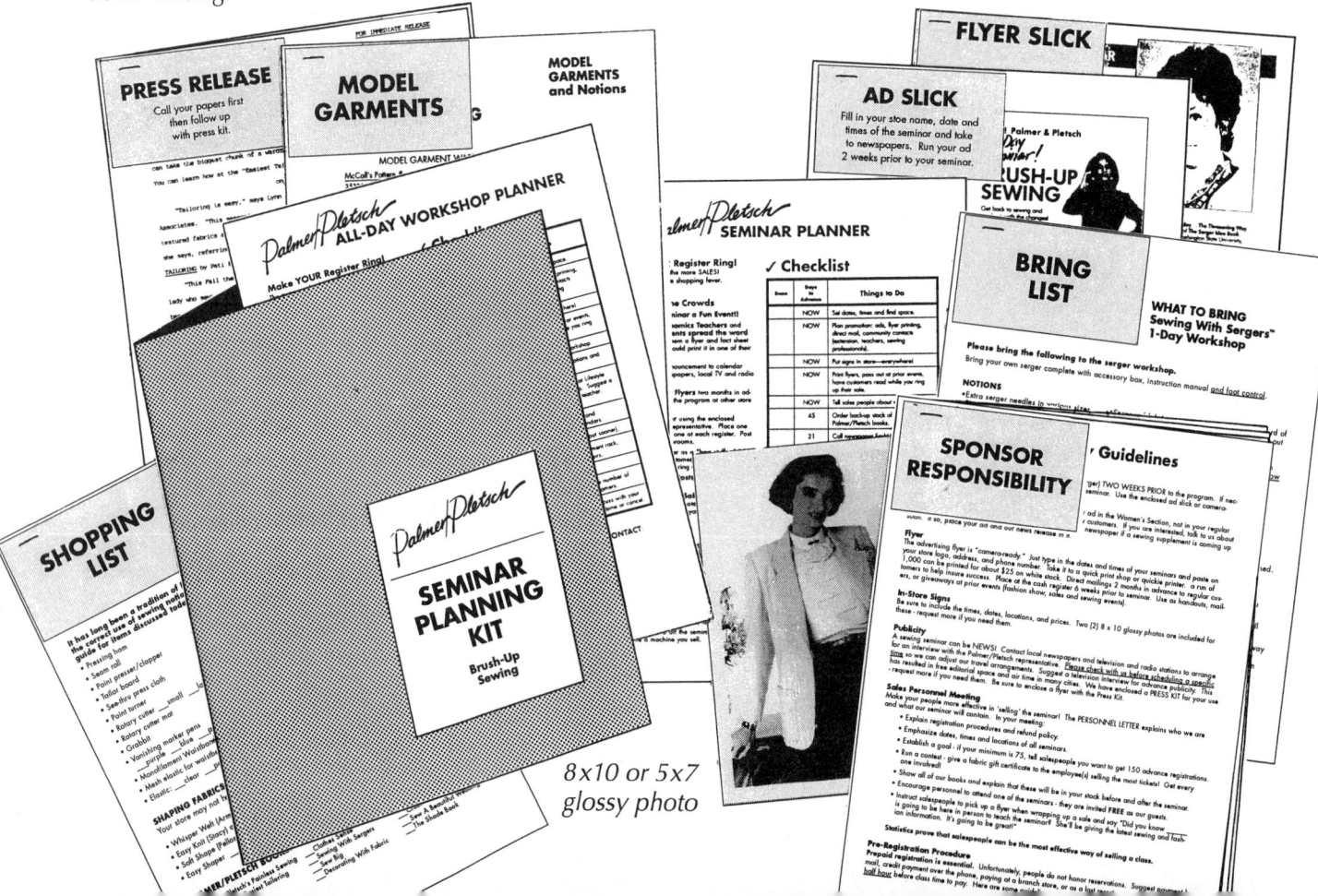

8x10 or 5x7 glossy photo

Canceling and Rescheduling

Be sure to spell out your cancellation policy on the sponsor agreement form. You shouldn't cancel a class except for financial reasons, such as minimum registration not met. Because such circumstances are discussed two weeks ahead of class, there are only four reasons to cancel a class at the last minute:

1. Severe illness.
2. Severe illness or death in your family.
3. Airline cancels flight at the last minute and there is no other way to arrive on time.
4. Your death—in which case you should have a substitute in mind!

If your class must be rescheduled for one of the above reasons, we recommend the following procedure to maintain a good relationship with the sponsor:

1. Call the sponsor and explain the situation. Discuss postponing, sending a substitute, or, as a last resort, canceling. Arrive at a mutually agreeable option.
2. If the store manager is not the owner or officer in charge, call that person and explain the changes and why they were made.
3. Follow up with a written summary of your discussions.

FOR THE ABOVE REASONS, you must always ask for the home phone number of the people in charge and recommend the sponsor get the home and work phone numbers of each registrant.

Arriving for Your Class

How you arrive for your class affects your image. Be fresh, be organized, be early and begin your setup with as little disruption to the sponsor's business as possible. No one appreciates a "prima donna" showing up at the last minute (unless it was absolutely unavoidable; then everyone will just be glad you made it!). Thus, when scheduling classes in two or more stores within the same area, take into account travel time when you set your starting times.

When traveling by air, allow three to four hours between the flight arrival and your first class. Obviously, flights can be delayed, to begin with. Claiming baggage often takes at least 20-30 minutes; locating transportation at least 30 minutes; travel from airport to class 30-60 minutes; traffic delays add even more time; and setup time can take an hour, especially if people want to talk to you before class.

Keeping Track

Keep a record of each class and each sponsor. Not all your teaching will be in stores or will have sponsors in the retail business. You may do seminars for sewing guilds, county extension agents, home economics associations, sewing machine clubs, 4-H groups, Camp Fire, Girl Scouts, other youth organizations or colleges. From this list of diversified sponsors, you must record a diversity of circumstances for future reference. After all, each class will have a different location, accommodations, physical setup, attendance numbers and other circumstances—and all these are impossible to remember.

These records will simplify keeping in touch with your sponsors and checking your progress on your goals. During slow times, call one of your favorite sponsors and set up a seminar or two. The following form includes most of the information you need to keep in your files. A camera-ready version can be found on pg. 118.

SPONSOR/CLASS INFORMATION

Class: _____ ❑ Hands On   Date: _____
_____ ❑ Seminar
_____ ❑ _____

Sponsor/Store Name: _____   Phone: _____
Address: _____   Store Hours: _____
_____   Best Time To Call: _____
Contact: _____   Position: _____
_____   Home # _____

Media Contacts: _____   Phone: _____
_____   Phone: _____
Media Activity: _____

Physical Set Up: _____   Total Attending: _____
_____   ❑ AM ❑ PM ❑ SAT ❑ All Day
_____   Transportation to Store: _____
_____
Comments: _____
_____   Airport: _____
_____
_____   Hotel/Rates: _____

Thank-yous

After any seminar, workshop or presentation, write a note of thanks to your sponsor for their efforts on your behalf. This small gesture provides more benefit to you, long term, than the money itself, by promoting a continuing profitable relationship. A small gift of appreciation or a bouquet of flowers also leaves a lasting impression.

Add words of praise to others who helped make your event a success. Whenever you had store personnel help you in any way, such as setup or pack-up, be sure to reward them with praise to their supervisor.

Doing Better Next Time

If your class wasn't as successful as hoped, ask your sponsor what they think went wrong and what they would suggest doing differently. Assure your sponsor that next time you'll make changes to correct any problems that took place. In future conversations focus on the positive points of your experience. Separating the good points from the bad makes it easier to resolve the difficult parts.

Tips From Past & Present PALMER/PLETSCH Travelers

Suitcases

- Get one that locks so you can tuck away a camera or jewelry while out of your room.
- Built-in wheels are great. Try pulling your suitcase to see how easily it pulls without toppling over. Suitcases sold in airline magazines are travel tested.

Packing

- To minimize wrinkling, pack garments on hangers and cover with plastic cleaner bags. (The only time this doesn't work is in extremely hot and humid weather.) When you arrive at a hotel, hang up your garments immediately. Hang them in the bathroom when taking a shower to help steam out wrinkles.
- To pack pants, leave the legs hanging over the side of the suitcase while packing other clothes on top, then fold over on top when the suitcase is full. Do the same with dresses, packing skirt portion and allowing bodice to hang over the edge. Alternate the direction of necklines and bottom edges as you layer blouses and jackets.
- Pack shoes in large Zip-Loc® bags or shoe bags.
- Put all liquids like shampoo or contact lens solutions into sealed Zip-Loc bags.
- Pack heavy items near the hinges in suitcase.
- Electric travel pots are available for heating water in your room for tea.
- Take a travel iron or use one hotel provides. Iron on the white sheets on the bed.
- If you travel frequently, purchase a second set of all your toiletries and cosmetics so you always have a **packed bag!**
- Put your business card inside your suitcase in case it gets lost and the outer tags are missing. Use only your business address. Don't alert a burglar to your home address.
- Make a "trip list" and keep it in your suitcase. If you have forgotten an item, add it to the list. Keep a separate list for pleasure travel. Keep a copy of both. It comes in handy for insurance claims if you ever have lost or stolen luggage.

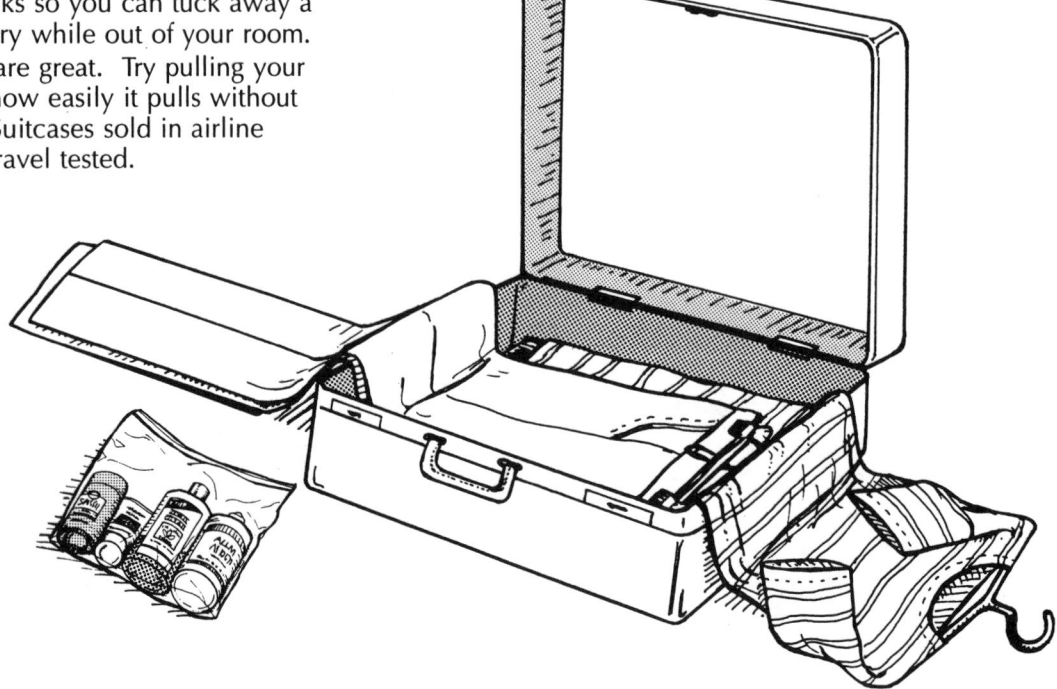

Airline Travel

- CONFIRM your reservation 24 hours before departure for international travel. (Check with your travel agent.)
- If a lower airfare is offered after you bought your ticket, you are entitled to a refund of the difference in most cases. A good travel agent will do this for you automatically.
- Order a special meal 24 hours before flight time if you want something different from standard, or need to accomodate a special diet or food allergies.
- Use sturdy wheels for carry-on luggage or sewing machines and projector.
- Arrive one hour before departure.
- Sign up for frequent-flyer programs.
- Use hotel/motel transportation to and from airport when possible.
- Check shuttle rates at your airport and compare to parking rates or cab costs.
- Consider the door-to-door service offered by the airport shuttle companies.
- Aisle seats are easiest for restroom access. Window seats are easiest for sleeping.
- Wear clothes you could teach in and carry on makeup and medications in case luggage is delayed. If you teach with slides, NEVER check them in your baggage. By carrying them onto the plane, you will always be able to teach your class.
- Wear layered clothing to allow you to adjust for varying temperatures while flying.

Car Travel

- Keep auto in tip-top condition.
- Never let gas tank go below half-full.
- Practice changing a tire or join AAA–or both!
- Periodically check tires during long trips.
- NEVER leave keys in car.
- NEVER LEAVE CAR UNLOCKED.
- Try to drive against traffic—avoid rush hour.
- Park in well-lighted areas.
- Never leave samples or garments in car overnight, even in a trunk.
- Carry a cellular phone if possible.

Rental Cars

- Use frequent-flyer coupons for better or free rates if available.
- Make sure the trunk or back seat is big enough for your luggage.
- Be sure you can lift the luggage in and out of the trunk.
- 4-door sedans are easier to load and unload from the back seat than 2-door cars.
- Will you have other passengers and will there be room for them and luggage?
- Check out the operational parts of the car immediately:

  Lights
  Heater
  Air conditioner control
  Windshield wipers
  Radio controls
  Gas tank location
  LOCKS

- Though we don't recommend leaving anything in a car overnight, you may need to during lunch or travel time. Thus, a car with trunk is better than a hatchback.
- Fill the gas tank BEFORE returning the car. Car agencies charge high gas prices.

Hotel-Motel Room

- Park in well-lighted area of lot or garage, as close to entrance or elevator as possible.
- At check-in ask that your room number NOT be announced to a bellman.
- Consider valet parking if available.
- ALWAYS have room key in hand and ready to unlock door.
- Ask for a nonsmoking room. Your model garments need fresh air.
- Second floor is safer if room door leads to exterior, but if no elevator, harder to carry everything to room. Sturdy wheels can help you get your bags to first-floor room or upper room where there is an elevator.
- Check door to make sure you removed key from outside.
- Do not sign your room number to a meal check and leave it on the table in the restaurant. Take it to the cashier.

CHAPTER SIXTEEN

Continuing Education

"You can never know enough."

Keeping current on sewing and fashion or home decorating trends will help you be a better teacher and a more valued resource to your students. Network with other professionals, attend trade and consumer shows, take workshops and classes, and read and watch for the latest news and information that relates to your subject matter. We recommend you consider the following opportunities (see Chapter 17, Resources for addresses and phone numbers).

Professional Associations

• **The American Home Sewing and Craft Association (AHSCA)** is dedicated to expanding the industry by promoting sewing as an easy, fun and fashionable hobby. The trade group brings together manufacturers, wholesalers, retailers and publishers with educators and consumers. Through its public-relations arm, The Sewing Fashion Council, it publicizes sewing to the consumer through educational booklets, press coverage and television campaigns.

Through AHSCA representation in Washington, D.C., September was named National Sewing Month. During the month, special promotions and in-store events are publicized with promotional material provided free to all member retailers. This major nationwide campaign involves sweepstakes and contests which consumers find exciting and fun. Entry forms are available at participating retailers.

Consumer education is another main focus. AHSCA has a video for beginners, "Sew Easy, Sew Beautiful." The association has also given major grant money to 4-H through the National 4-H Council. It is meant to encourage sewing education by having 4-H leaders or county 4-H agents apply for money needed to get a program off the ground. Many 4-H clubs use the money for community volunteer sewing projects, like sewing clothes for premature babies.

At the AHSCA annual trade show, manufacturers display and market their products to retail stores. This is where the new products are first introduced. It is a big event, well attended and lots of fun. All those involved in the home-sewing and craft industry, be it manufacturer, publisher or consumer, enjoy meeting with each other at this conference/trade show.

There are three membership categories for AHSCA: manufacturer, retailer and educator. The dues are quite high to manufacturers because this is the only apparel fabric association that puts money back into promoting home sewing. However, the educator membership category is a bargain at $25. It's worth the fee just to get the quarterly newsletter to be informed about what is going on in the industry.

• **The American Sewing Guild (ASG)** is a nonprofit sewing organization with membership open to the public. It was started by AHSCA in the '70s. The first organization for home-sewers of all skill levels, the Guild provides information, education and programs in more than 70 chapters in more than 30 states. Consumers and retailers are united by national and regional newsletters, seminars and classes. The annual convention, held during the AHSCA trade show, includes special events and speakers offering many seminars. ASG members are allowed to visit the exhibits at the trade show and see the fashion show of next season's pattern designs and fabrications.

• **Professional Association of Custom Clothiers (PACC)** is an association uniting designers, custom dressmakers, contract sewers, tailors, artists, authors, pattern makers, alteration specialists, and image and color consultants. The organization provides the opportunity for professionals in many related fields to improve themselves and their businesses through networking.

The prototype of this organization was started in the '70s in Portland, Oregon, and was called the Custom Clothing Guild. There were similar groups throughout the United States, but with no knowledge of each other or the ability to network. Now there is a national newsletter that goes to every member. It profiles successful members to give all members growth ideas.

• **American Association of Family & Consumer Science (AAFCS)** is a national organization promoting professional growth among graduate home economists. Many state and local chapters unite home economics educators with other home economists through conferences and special programs.

AAFCS is the new name for what was know as the American Home Economics Association (AHEA). In 1993, home economists representing many different professional associations met to select the new name for the profession. At the same time the structure was revised into nine new divisions of educational and professional focus:

1. Apparel and Textiles
2. Art and Design
3. Communication
4. Education and Technology
5. Family Economics and Resource Management
6. Family Relations and Human Development
7. Housing and Environment
8. International
9. Nutrition, Health and Food Management

Through AAFCS, those with college degrees in any of these areas can network. The Business Section (formerly HEIB—Home Economists in Business) is bringing business and industry liaisons to the academic and research side. There is an annual meeting in June.

Palmer/Pletsch Workshops

Palmer/Pletsch workshops are in-depth, hands-on "learning and doing" experiences held in Portland, Oregon. They combine all the best knowledge gained from years of experience conducting seminars for sewing enthusiasts nationwide.

Home-sewers of all skill levels have attended these friendly, informative workshops. They leave feeling inspired with what they have learned and enthusiastic about having advanced their skill levels. Because of the camaraderie they feel with other sewing enthusiasts and their exposure to Portland's fabric market and scenic landscape, they graduate feeling they have had an enjoyable *vacation*. Workshops are offered in these skill areas:

**Tailoring • Fit
Pant Fitting and Sewing
Couture Pant • Ultrasuede
Creative Serging
The Best of Palmer/Pletsch**

For information on
Palmer/Pletsch Workshops,
call (503) 631-7443,
fax (503) 631-8224
or write
P.O. Box 12046
Portland, OR 97212-0046.

Palmer/Pletsch Teacher Training

Separate teacher-training sessions are offered for each workshop (except Ultrasuede and Couture Pant). They include up to 300 slides, script, practice demonstrations, a makeup/hair session, camera-ready handouts, promotional materials, and a graduation certificate. The fit and pant fit workshops include all the patterns and fabric for making the try-on fitting shells.

Teacher Certification

Once you have completed a workshop, you can apply for certification through Palmer/Pletsch. Certification promotes continuing education. There are two levels, one for the topic in which you were trained and one for a higher level attained, after completing fit, pant fit, and tailoring. After learning these three areas, you could teach anything. Certification renewal is every two years. The certificates can be framed and hung in your studio, giving you added credibility. If you are Certified in Family and Consumer Science (formerly C.H.E.), these workshops have been approved for PDU credit. Graduates become part of a teaching network complete with a **VIP Newsletter**.

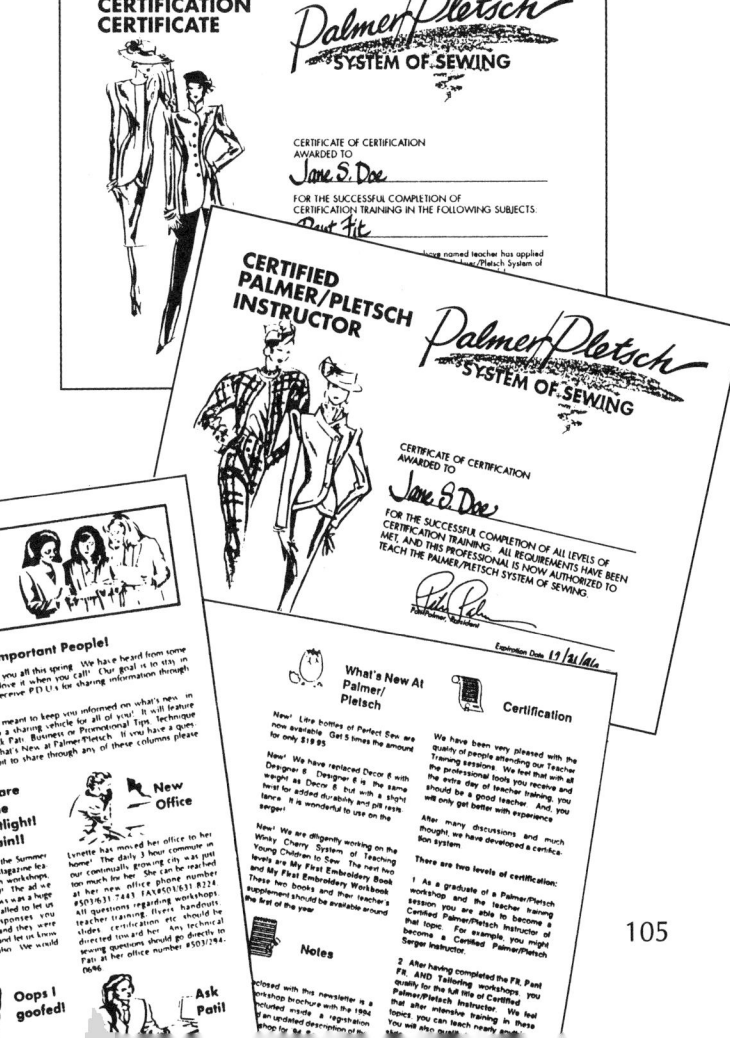

105

Additional Educational Opportunities

There are many workshops, classes, seminars, consumer shows, tours and other enticing, enriching and enhancing opportunities for learning something new. Be sure to get all the information you need before making arrangements that might be nonrefundable. You may want an add-on tour. If you are not familiar with the program, ask for referrals.

• **Roberta Carr Sew Weeks** are week-long retreats in Roberta Carr's design studio and home in San Jose, California. Each week-long retreat features a different subject: designer details, decorative touches, pattern drafting and design, and wearable art or art-to-wear. Classes are lecture/demonstration in the mornings with supervised hands-on sewing in the afternoon. The classes are limited to five each session and they fill fast. Contact Roberta at the Fabric Carr, Box 32120, San Jose, CA 95152, telephone (408) 929-1651.

• **Linda McGehee** specializes in artistic embellishments. The results are wearable art pieces...embellished hand-bags, garments and accessories. Her 4½-day workshops are scheduled four times a year. The remainder of Linda's time is spent "on the road" with her classes. Contact Ghee's, 2620 Centenary Blvd., Bldg. 3, Suite 205, Shreveport, LA 71104, telephone (318) 226-2701.

• **MacPhee Workshops** by designer and owner Linda MacPhee are one- and two-day classes scheduled throughout the year. For vacationers, a group of classes is usually offered in August. Contact MacPhee Workshops, R.R. 8, Edmonton, AB T5L 4H8, Canada, telephone (403) 973-3616.

• **Martha Pullen School of Art Fashion** offers 4- to 6-day sessions emphasizing heirloom sewing (French sewing by machine and hand). Held in February and August at the Hilton Hotel in Huntsville, Ala., classes offered are American Girl Doll Dressing, Beginning, Hand Sewing, Master's, Martha's Attic, Bernina, Elna, Pfaff and Viking. The sewing machine companies furnish machines for the brand-specific classes, but you may bring any brand machine to the others. Free brochure available by contacting Margaret Taylor, Martha Pullen Co., 518 Madison St., Huntsville, AL 35801, telephone 1-800-547-4176.

• **The Sewing Workshops** in the "City by the Bay" enable you to learn about sewing while visiting one of America's most enchanting cities. For the best use of your travel time, schedule a summer vacation around the Sewing Workshop's schedules. Contact The Sewing Workshops, 2010 Balboa St., San Francisco, CA 94121, telephone (415) 221-7397.

• **Shirley Smith's Art of Sewing® Seminars** offer a week-long experience for both the novice and the expert. The novice will enjoy Dressmaker Techniques & Class Act for Slacks. The expert will enjoy Couture Techniques and Tailoring. Classes are limited to six and are lecture/demonstration in the morning with hands-on sewing in the afternoon. Seminars are held in Shirley's fully equipped studio. Lunch is served every day except the shopping day. Contact Sewing Arts, Inc., Box 61418, Denver, CO 80206, telephone (303) 321-8037.

• **Nancy Zieman's Sewing Weekend Expo™** is held annually at Nancy's Notions headquarters. Nancy invites other nationally known sewing experts to teach two-hour classes on various topics through the weekend. You can shop their warehouse, too! For more information, contact Nancy's Notions, Box 683, Beaver Dam, WI 53916-0683, telephone 1-800-833-0690.

• **Islander School of Fashion Arts** offers week-long seminars with evening workshops (limit 20) in Pattern Drafting, Japanese Tailoring, Fabric Design (bleach and dye), Couture Techniques, Advanced Pattern Drafting and Pattern Alterations (commercial patterns). Contact Margaret Islander, Box 66, Grants Pass, OR 97526, telephone (503) 479-3906 or 1-800-994-0213.

Note: Ann Hyde is no longer offering the **Ann Hyde Institute of Design Summer Workshops**. She thanks people for their interest and support during the 18 years her school operated.

Workshops and Schools Sponsored by Sewing Machine Manufacturers

• Bernina University
Bernina of America Consumer University
3500 Thayer Court, Aurora, IL 60504-6182
Telephone (708) 978-2500

• Sewing in The Mountains with Elna
130 Elizabeth Chapel
Waynesville, NC 28786

• Pfaff School of Creative Sewing
610 Winters Ave., Box 566
Paramus, NJ 07653
Telephone 1-800-526-0273

• Art of Sewing By Viking Sewing Machine Co.
11760 Berea Road
Cleveland, OH 44111
Telephone (216) 252-2452

CHAPTER SEVENTEEN

Resources

Home-Based Business Resources

SEW TO SUCCESS
(book and video)
Kathleen Spike, Author
Palmer/Pletsch, Publisher
P.O. Box 12046
Portland, Oregon 97212
A complete list of home-based business resources is included at the back of the book.

SEWING AS A BUSINESS
(pamphlet)
AAFCS or
the Mississippi Cooperative Extension Service
publication 1667
See professional associations for contact information.

U.S. Small Business Administration and SCORE agencies. See your local listings under U.S. government.

Cooperative Extension Service See your local listing under county government. Ask to speak with the Clothing Specialist about sewing as a home business.

BUSINESS GUIDE TO FEDERAL TRADE COMMISSION
Mail Order Rule Book
Superintendent of Documents
U.S. Government Printing Office
Washington DC 20402

Professional Associations

The American Sewing Guild (ASG)
P.O. Box 8476
Medford, OR 97504-0476
(503) 772-4059
Fax (503) 720-7041

The American Home Sewing and Craft Association (AHSCA)
1375 Broadway
New York, New York 10018
(212) 302-2150
Fax (212) 391-3009
Educator membership $25/yr
Many publications available
for $1-$2: *Signature Styling, Home Styling, Wedding Belles, Member Directory, Sewing As A Business* and more.

The American Association of Family & Consumer Sciences (AAFCS) (formerly AHEA)
1555 King Street
Alexandria, VA 22314
1-800-424-8080
Fax (707) 706-4663

Professional Association of Custom Clothiers (PACC)
P.O. Box 8071
Medford, OR 97504

The Fashion Group International Inc.
597 Fifth Avenue
New York, NY 10017
(212) 593-1715

The National Needlework Association
650 Danbury Road
Ridgefield, CT 06877
(203) 431-8226

Costume Society of America
55 Edgewater Drive
P.O. Box 73
Earleville, MD 21919
(410) 275-2329

Embroiderer's Guild of America
Suite 100
335 W. Broadway
Louisville, KY 40202
(502) 589-6956

Smocking Arts Guild of America
4350 DiPaolo Center
Dearlove Road
Glenview, IL 60025-5212
(318) 741-3084

Consumer Publications

Sew News
Sewing Decor
Update Newsletters
P.O. Box 1790
Peoria, IL 61656
(309) 682-6626

McCall's Pattern Magazine
11 Penn Plaza
New York, NY 10001
(212) 465-6800

Threads
Taunton Press, Inc.
630 S. Main Street
Newton, CT 06470
(203) 426-8171

The Creative Machine
P.O. Box 2634-NL
Menlo Park, CA 94026-2634
(415) 366-4440

"W"
Subscription Service Department
P.O. Box 2603
Boulder, CO 80321

Crafts Plus
Camar Publications Ltd.
130 Spy Court
Markham, ON L3R 5H6
Canada
(905) 475-8440

Sew Up a Storm Newsletter
SewStorm Publishing
944 Sutton Rd.
Cincinnati, OH 45230-3581

Trade Publications

Craftrends
3761 Ventura Drive, Suite 140
Duluth, GA 30136

Round Bobbin
P.O. Box 338
Hilliard, OH 43026

Craft and Needlework Age
225 Gordons Corner Plaza
P.O. Box 420
Englishtown, NJ 07726-9982

Craft Supply Magazine
Box 420
Englishtown, NJ 07726
(908) 446-4900

Draperies & Window Coverings
450 Skokie Blvd., Suite 507
Northbrook, NJ 60062
(708) 498-9880

PCM
P.O. Box 1790
Peoria, IL 61656
(309) 682-6626

Children's Class Sources

THE WINKY CHERRY SYSTEM OF
TEACHING YOUNG CHILDREN
TO SEW (see Palmer/Pletsch
products on page 127)

KIDS CAN SEW
P.O. Box 1710
St. George, UT 84771-1710
(801) 393-3286

PRIMARY PATTERNS BY
KIDSEW, INC.
P.O. Box 19429
Detroit, MI 48219-0429
(313) 538-4201

SEWING KIDS STUFF
PJS Products
P.O. Box 337
Mt. Morris, IL 61054
1-800-435-0715

Sewing Notions and Supplies

Clotilde
2800 Hoover Road
P.O. Box 8031
Stevens Point, WI 54481-8031
1-800-772-2891
*Great video on notions and
mail-order catalog of notions.*

Fairgate Rule Co.
22 Adams
Cold Spring, NY 10516
1-800-431-2180 Or
(914) 265-3677
*Metal yardsticks, T-squares,
L-squares and French curves.
Catalog and price lists available.*

Golden Hands Industries, Inc.
P.O. Box 720279
Atlanta, GA 30358
(404) 998-1323
*Printed blocking cloth for the
Palmer/Pletsch cut 'n' press
board (page 71).*

June Tailor, Inc.
P.O. Box 208
Richfield, WI 53076-0208
(414) 644-5288
Fax (414) 644-5061
*Pressing, quilting and other
sewing equipment.*

Nancy's Notions
P.O. Box 683
Beaver Dam, WI 53916-0683
1-800-833-0690
*Extensive mail-order catalog of
notions, books and videos.*

Oregon Tailors Supply Co.
4123 S.E. Division St.
Portland, OR 97242
(503) 232-6191
*Supplies for the professional
dressmaker industry,
Palmer/Pletsch cut 'n' press board
kit (pg. 71).*

Sew/Fit Company
P.O. Box 293
Bedford Park, IL 60499
1-800-547-ISEW
*Cardboard cutting tables (pg. 70),
mats and other cutting aides.*

Sewing Center Supply
Catalog Division
9631 NE Colfax
Portland, OR 97220
1-800-542-4727

Business and Other Products

J. E. Foss
P.O. Box 357
Bethel Park, PA 15102-0357
1-800-245-6240
Fax (412) 831-3792
*Discount audio-visual products,
catalogs and buyers guide (pg.64).*

Image Street
Moore Business Products
P.O. Box 5000
Vernon Hills, IL 60061
1-800-462-4378
*Business image products including
software, pre-printed papers,
graphic and printing services.*

NEBS, Inc.
500 Main Street
Groton, MA 01471
1-800-225-6380
Fax 1-800-234-4342
*Inexpensive standard & custom
printed forms, checks and
supplies.*

G. Neil
720 International Parkway
P.O. Box 450939
Sunrise, FL 33345-0939
1-800-999-9111
Fax (305) 846-0777
*Discount catalog of business forms
certificates, motivational and
training materials.*

Northwest Tag and Label
111-A Foothills Road
Lake Oswego, OR 97034
Inexpensive fabric labels for your garments

Papers Direct
P.O. Box 677
205 Chubb Ave.
Lyndhurst, NJ 07071-0677
1-800-A-PAPERS
(201) 507-0817
Mail order, economically priced, very professional business papers with a wide variety of color and kinds of paper. They offer printing and personalizing your stationery, cards and brochures.

Producers and Quantity Photo Inc.
6660 Santa Monica Blvd.
Hollywood, CA 90038
(213) 462-1334
Fax (213) 466-0939
Inexpensive 5X7 or 8X10 black and white prints. Order SW (single weight) paper.

Your Town Press
2773 Cherry Ave. N.E.
Salem, OR 97303
(503) 364-2122
Inexpensive quality color flyer printing.

Consumer Shows

THE ORIGINAL SEWING FAIR
Portland HEIB
P.O. Box 2009
Portland, OR 97208
(503) 222-6573

SEWING AND STITCHERY EXPO
Washington State University
Cooperative Extension
P.O. Box 112072
Tacoma, WA 98411-2072
(206) 840-4575

THE CREATIVE $EWING &
NEEDLEART EXPOSITIONS
American Sewing Guild
P.O. Box 369
Monroeville, PA 15146
(412) 325-1878

THE ORIGINAL
SEWING & CRAFT EXPO
26612 Center Ridge Rd.
Westlake, OH 44145
(216) 899-4712

PROSHOW, INC.
Creative Inspiration
P.O. Box 369
Monroeville, PA 15146
1-800-249-3154

CANADIAN SEWING &
NEEDLECRAFT EXPOS
The Canadian Sewing &
Needlecraft Association
224 Mentor Street, Suite 204
Toronto, ON M4S 1A1
(416) 482-7724

CREATIVE SEWING &
NEEDLEWORK FESTIVAL
International Showcase
Association, Inc.
2900 John Street, Suite 200
Markham, ON L3R 5G3
(905) 470-7057

IN STITCHES
Carol Dodge
936 Peace Portal Drive
P.O. Box 8014 - #42
Blaine, WA 98231-8014
1-800-468-6739
Canada: 13718 28th Avenue
Surrey, BC V4P 1T3
(604) 538-7477

AMERICAN STITCHES Fashion
Sewing, Quilting and Needle Arts
Expo, Janet Pray
1385 Clyde Road
Highland, MI 48357
(810) 889-3111

INTERNATIONAL
QUILT MARKET
14520 Memorial Drive, Suite 54
Houton, TX 77079
(713) 496-6864

VANCOUVER ISLAND
SEWING SHOW
3575 Douglas St.
P.O. Box 48033
Victoria, BC V8Z 7H5
(604) 479-7373

Pattern Company Hot Lines

Burda Patterns	1-800-241-6887
Butterick/Vogue	1-800-221-2670
Kwik Sew	(612) 521-7651
McCall's	(212) 880-2624
New Look	(212) 576-0500
Simplicity	(212) 576-0668
Style	(212) 576-0500

CHAPTER EIGHTEEN

Camera-Ready Forms

This set of camera-ready artwork is provided to save you the time and expense of creating your own promotional and support materials. Add your name, logo (if you have one), address and phone number to these materials before you reproduce them for your own use.

Some Tips for Use

1. If you decide to use these materials exactly as they are, you need only add your name, address and phone number where indicated before printing or copying. We suggest you match the same typeface we have used. Headlines are in Futura Bold. All the rest of the words are in Futura Book, Bold or Oblique (italic). All are available as Adobe Postscript fonts. If Futura is unavailable, please use Helvetica, Helios or Swiss. If you do not have access to a computer with these fonts, your local typographer, printer or copy shop should be able to help you.

2. To add your address or additional information you will be creating a "paste-up." Use glue-stick or re-positionable spray mount. Make sure the type you add is "square" on the page...that is, it should be lined up straight. Crooked type looks unprofessional. And YOU are professional.

3. If you decide to re-arrange or change these materials, we suggest you make crisp black copies to cut up, keeping the originals intact.

4. Remember to opaque out or cover up the page numbers!

5. Decide how many copies you need of each piece. If you require more than 100, quick printing may be less expensive than reproducing on a copy machine. Ask for a cost estimate from your printer. Be creative with paper colors!

6. You WILL want to use your printer to print and cut stiff card stock, cover weight or bristol. Most copiers do not handle these heavier papers very well. Save paper by combining cards (pg. 118) to print two-up on an 8½x11 sheet of paper.

7. Whether you copy or print these pieces, please use recycled paper whenever possible!!

For additional guidance on creating materials to be printed see pages 13-16 and 80-85.

A C-Thru ruler helps you line up type you are adding to a flyer or form.

Market Research Form

Date:

Name of Store or School:

Type of Store or School:

Address: City: State: Zip: Phone:

Contact Owner/Manager: Other VIP:

Classes	Fees	Type of Merchandise	Brands

Type of Classroom: Notes:

Sewing Experience Checklist

1. I have _____ years of sewing experience.

2. I am proudest of my ability to _____
   _____
   _____

3. My family and friends are proud of my ability to _____
   _____
   _____

4. My sewing specialties are _____
   _____
   _____

5. I have other sewing experience: _____
   _____
   _____

6. I own _____ sewing machines and _____ sergers.

   Other equipment: _____
   _____

7. My sewing education experience is _____
   _____
   _____
   _____

8. I have managed myself, home and family for _____ years.

9. I have _____ (months or years) business experience as _____
   _____
   _____

10. I have taught _____ people. (Teaching a neighbor to sew on a button, children to tie their shoes, etc. counts.)

11. If I could only teach one thing, I would teach _____,
    because I'm most skilled in this area and therefor have confidence and could sell myself.

MY BUSINESS PLAN

I Business Description

_____

_____

II Marketing

Item   Date planned for completion

_____   _____

_____   _____

_____   _____

_____   _____

_____   _____

_____   _____

III Promotion

Who   What   When

_____   _____   _____

_____   _____   _____

_____   _____   _____

_____   _____   _____

_____   _____   _____

_____   _____   _____

IV Time Schedule

6-Month Teaching Goals

_____

_____

_____

_____

1-Year Teaching Goals

_____

_____

_____

_____

3-Year Teaching Goals

_____

_____

_____

_____

V **Equipment** owned

Item $ Value

_____   _____

_____   _____

_____   _____

_____   _____

_____   _____

_____   _____

VI **Equipment** to purchase

Item $ Cost

_____   _____

_____   _____

_____   _____

_____   _____

_____   _____

_____   _____

_____   _____

VII **Additional Training Needed**

What   When   Where

_____   _____   _____

_____   _____   _____

_____   _____   _____

_____   _____   _____

_____   _____   _____

_____   _____   _____

VIII **Personal Goals**

What   When

_____   _____

_____   _____

_____   _____

_____   _____

_____   _____

_____   _____

INDUSTRY CONTACTS WORKSHEET

Include potential class sponsors, as well as VIP's you should get acquainted with.

Name	Phone #	Name	Phone #
Chairman of local American Sewing Guild:		Other sewing instructors:	
Neighborhood group leaders for ASG:		Craft guilds:	
All nearby county extension agents:		Middle school and high school home economics teachers:	
4-H clothing leaders:		Women's organizations:	
Sewing machine dealers:		Sewing and dressmaking friends:	
Fabric store managers:			

Other important contacts (newspaper fashion editor etc.)

Name: _____

Title: _____ Phone: _____

_____ _____

_____ _____

_____ _____

Getting Started Countdown

Name of Class _____

# of Days in Advance	Date Done	Things to Do	Target Date

TEACHING AGREEMENT

Name of program: _____

Dates confirmed: _____

Type of class: _____

Fee for class: _____

Payment policy: _____

I will be providing: _____

_____

_____

You agree
to provide: _____

_____

_____

_____

Cancellation policy: _____

_____

_____

_____

Please read and
sign, confirming the
acceptance of
this agreement: _____

Signature: _____ Date: _____

Name: _____

Store/Organization: _____

Address: _____

City, State, Zip: _____

Thank You: _____ Date: _____

Note: These two forms could be back to back on an index card or printed together as seen on this page.

SPONSOR/CLASS INFORMATION

Class: _____ ❑ Hands On   Date: _____
_____ ❑ Seminar
_____ ❑ _____

Sponsor/Store Name: _____   Phone: _____
Address: _____   Store Hours: _____
_____   Best Time To Call: _____
Contact: _____   Position: _____
_____   Home # _____

Media Contacts: _____   Phone: _____
_____   Phone: _____
Media Activity: _____
_____

Physical Set Up: _____   Total Attending: _____
_____   ❑ AM   ❑ PM   ❑ SAT   ❑ All Day
_____   Transportation to Store: _____
Comments: _____   _____
_____   Airport: _____
_____   _____
_____   Hotel/Rates: _____
_____   _____

ARRANGEMENTS CHECKLIST

Class: _____   Date: _____
Sponsor/Store Name: _____   Set Up: _____
Contact: _____   Clean Up: _____
Phone: _____   _____
_____

Items	Quantity	Provided By	Items	Quantity	Provided By	Ordered
Tables	____	_____	Books	____	_____	____
Chairs	____	_____		____	_____	____
Electricity	____	_____		____	_____	____
Lights	____	_____		____	_____	____
Projector	____	_____		____	_____	____
Screen	____	_____		____	_____	____
Machines	____	_____		____	_____	____
Pressing			Notions			
Equipment	____	_____		____	_____	____
Fitting Mirror	____	_____		____	_____	____
Other Products	____	_____		____	_____	____
	____	_____		____	_____	____
	____	_____	Patterns			
Notes _____				____	_____	____
_____				____	_____	____
_____				____	_____	____

Put your class titles here

CLASS SIGN-UP SHEET

Please let me know if you are interested in…

1. **Beginning Sewing**   3. **Children's Sewing Classes**

2. **Fit for You**   4. **Sewing for Brides**

Class #	Name	Address	Area Code & Phone #

STUDENT QUESTIONNAIRE

Dear Successful Sewing Student:
We would like to help you as much as possible, so please tell us more about you by answering these questions:

What is your occupation?_____

Where do you live? _____

How many are in your family?_____

What specific activities do you participate in?_____

_____

_____

_____

What is your most demanding clothing need?_____

_____

_____

Why did you sign up for this class?_____

_____

_____

What would you like to learn or see?_____

_____

_____

How much sewing do you do?_____

_____

_____

What sewing experience do you have?_____

_____

_____

_____

Name: _____ Class attended: _____

STUDENT'S EVALUATION OF CLASS & TEACHER

Class Title: _____ Date: _____

Location: _____

Rating Scale
Rating Scale
5 = excellent
4 = very good
3 = average
2 = fair
1 = needs improvement

Please rate the following:

___Quality of instruction   ___Value for your dollar

___Overall class content   ___Physical classroom arrangements

___Amount of information   ___Other _____

Comments: _____

_____

What was the most useful thing you learned in this class? _____

_____

_____

What was the least important thing you learned? _____

_____

_____

Would you attend another of my classes?_____
If yes, what would you like to learn more about?

_____

_____

_____

_____

_____

_____

_____

_____

_____

Please rate me on the following:

	Poor	Good	Average	Excellent
Level of knowledge				
Appearance				
Cleanliness				
Patience				
Clarity of presentation				
Quality of model garments				
Quality of visuals				
Enthusiasm				
Interaction with students				
Professionalism				

Name (optional): _____

TEACHER'S EVALUATION OF STUDENT

Student name: _____ Class: _____

Address: _____

Phone:_____ Date:_____

Rating Scale
5 = excellent
4 = very good
3 = average
2 = fair
1 = needs improvement

Rating the following:

___Collars

___Facings

___Pressing   ___Topstitching

___Fitting   ___Hems

___Neatness   ___Waistbands

___Sleeves   ___Buttons

___Other _____

_____

___Buttonholes

___Lining

___Interfacing

___Pockets

___Special details

___Completing work

Comments: _____

_____

_____

_____

_____

_____

_____

_____

_____

_____

_____

_____

Teacher: _____

SPONSOR EVALUATION OF CLASS

I am very interested in your opinion and comments regarding the following class:

Class Title:_____ Date: _____ Time: _____

Instructor: _____

Please take a few minutes to answer questions that will help me
improve the quality of the class and be of maximum benefit to you.

Did the class meet your expectations? _____
_____
_____

Was the attendance what you expected? _____

If no, how could we improve attendance? _____
_____

Was the preparation and promotion what you expected?_____
_____

What should be changed or added? _____
_____
_____

Did you sell product? _____

Are you interested in more classes? If so, when?

_____

_____

_____

_____

What topics are you interested in? _____

_____

_____

_____

_____

Please rate me on the following:				
	Poor	Good	Average	Excellent
Level of knowledge				
Appearance				
Cleanliness				
Patience				
Clarity of presentation				
Quality of model garments				
Quality of visuals				
Enthusiasm				
Interaction with students				
Professionalism				

Name: _____ Phone: _____

Store or organization name:_____

Address:_____

SELF-EVALUATION

Class Title: _____ # Attending: _____

Date: _____ and Time: _____ Average age: _____

Name of store or other class location: _____

Contact person: _____

Phone number: _____

Address: _____

Directions: _____

The successes: _____

_____

_____

_____

_____

The difficulties: _____

_____

_____

_____

_____

Physical setup comments:

_____

_____

_____

_____

_____

Student names to remember:

_____

_____

_____

_____

_____

Notes: _____

_____

_____

_____

_____

Index

Palmer/Pletsch
PRODUCTS

These ready-to-use, information-filled sewing how-to books, manuals and videos can be found in local fabric stores or ordered through Palmer/Pletsch Publishing (see address on last page).

8½ x 11 BOOKS

☐ **Looking Good**
by Nancy Nix-Rice, 160 pages, $19.95
This book provides everything women need to look their personal best—not by following fashion trends, but by spotlighting their best features to create the most flattering, effective look possible.

☐ **The BUSINE$$ of Teaching Sewing,** *by Marcy Miller and Pati Palmer, 128 pages, $29.95* If you want to be in the BUSINESS of teaching sewing, read this book which compiles 20 years of experience of Palmer/Pletsch, plus Miller's innovative ideas. Chapters include: Appearance and Image; Getting Started; The Lesson Plan; Class Formats; Location; Marketing, Promotion & Advertising; Pricing; Teaching Techniques; and Continuing Education—Where To Find It.

☐ **Dream Sewing Spaces—Design and Organization for Spaces Large and Small,** *by Lynette Ranney Black, 128 pages, $19.95* Make your dream a reality. Analyze your needs and your space, then learn to plan and put it together. Lots of color photos!

☐ **Couture—The Art of Fine Sewing**, *by Roberta C. Carr, 208 pages, softcover, $29.95* How-to's of couture techniques and secrets, brought to life with illustrations and dozens of garments photographed in full color.

Books are also available spiral bound— additional $3.00 for large books, $2.00 for small.

☐ **The Serger Idea Book—A Collection of Inspiring Ideas from Palmer/Pletsch,** *160 pgs., $19.95* Color photos and how-to's on inspiring and fashionable ideas from the Extraordinary to the Practical.

☐ **Creative Serging for the Home— And Other Quick Decorating Ideas,** *by Lynette Ranney Black and Linda Wisner, 160 pgs., $18.95* Color photos and how-to's to help you transform your home into the place YOU want it to be.

☐ **Sewing Ultrasuede® Brand Fabrics— Ultrasuede®, Ultrasuede Light™, Caress™, Ultraleather™,** *by Marta Alto, Pati Palmer and Barbara Weiland, 128 pages, $16.95* Color photo section, plus the newest techniques to master these luxurious fabrics.

Coming in late 1996:
☐ **Fit for Real People**
by Marta Alto & Pati Palmer. The authors write from 25 years of hands-on experience fitting thousands of people. Their practical approach is explained in their simple, logical style. Learn to finally buy the right size, then tissue fit to determine alterations. Special sections include fitting young teen girls, history of sizing, and fitting REAL people. Write or call for publication date and more information.

Not available with spiral binding.